A Class-Book of Chemistry

Edward Livingston Youmans

BIBLIOLIFE

A CLASS-BOOK

OF

CHEMISTRY,

IN WHICH

THE PRINCIPLES OF THE SCIENCE ARE FAMILIARLY EXPLAINED
AND APPLIED TO THE ARTS, AGRICULTURE, PHYSIOLOGY,
DIETETICS, VENTILATION, AND THE MOST IMPOR-
TANT PHENOMENA OF NATURE.

DESIGNED FOR THE USE OF ACADEMIES AND SCHOOLS,
AND FOR POPULAR READING.

BY EDWARD L. YOUMANS,

AUTHOR OF "A NEW CHART OF CHEMISTRY."

—— To know
That which before us lies in daily life
Is the prime wisdom.   MILTON.

NEW-YORK:
D. APPLETON & COMPANY,
846 & 848 BROADWAY.
M.DCCC.LVII.

PREFACE.

The present volume is designed as a popular introduction to the study of Chemistry. It aims to present the subject in such a manner as to win the attention and engage the interest of beginners, and is especially adapted to the wants of that large class, both in and out of school, who would like to know something of this interesting science, but have neither leisure nor opportunity to pursue it in a detailed and experimental way. As such will necessarily be more concerned to know what facts, principles, and results have been arrived at by chemical research, than to trace the routes by which they were reached, or the operations by which they may be confirmed, the following pages will be found chiefly occupied with the explanation of established principles, and their application to the most practical and familiar affairs of common life.

The department of Physics, which considers light, heat, electricity, and magnetism, has been left to Natural Philosophy, where it properly belongs and is always treated. Its introduction into Chemistry involves a repetition of topics in the two branches of study; and, in a volume of moderate size, it crowds out much useful matter which ought, on no account, to be spared. A knowledge of these agents is of course important to the chemical student, but so is that of mechanics and mathematics. In leaving each to its appropriate teacher, the example of some of our latest and best authorities has been followed Descriptions of those chemical substances which are not frequently met with, as the rarer metals, are entirely omitted, and directions for making experiments have been much condensed. Experimental demonstrations, if not resorted to merely to captivate the senses by their alluring brilliancy, are highly useful; but they are always accompanied by the oral instructor, and should therefore, to a great extent, speak for themselves. It is entirely impossible

1*

in the present advanced state of the science, to embrace in a popular school-book both that information which learners generally require and also directions for a course of experiments sufficiently minute to be valuable. In order, for example, to unfold with any thing
like clearness the august part which oxygen gas plays in the scheme
of nature, it has been necessary to abridge the account of the various
processes by which it may be prepared. Where experiments are
given, the lecturer will supply this branch of instruction; where they
are not to be had, it is superfluous.

Space has been thus afforded to consider the practical and useful ap-
plications of the science, in which all are interested, with greater fulness
than is customary in text-books for schools. Organic Chemistry, both
vegetable and animal, embracing much of agriculture, domestic processes, dietetics, the physiology of digestion and respiration, ventilation, the effects of alcohol upon the human system, and the relations
of the vegetable and animal world to each other, and to the atmosphere, has been brought forward into that prominence which its obvious importance demands. If there should even be found repetition
upon some of these points, the excuse must be a desire to impress
certain great principles deeply upon the mind, rather than to encum-
ber it with a mass of details, which, in most cases, are forgotten as
quickly as they are acquired. By treating of familiar things, and
presenting facts and truths alike valuable and entertaining, in a style
free, as far as possible, from technicalities on the one hand and puer-
ilities on the other, the author has endeavored to adapt the work to
fireside reading as well as class-room study.

There is an idea prevalent that Chemistry is one of those dry and
difficult subjects which belong exclusively to professors and lecture-
rooms, and which cannot be invested with popular interest, or successfully taught as a branch of common education. How a science
which gives law to nearly all the processes of human industry, con-
nects its operations with our daily experience, involves the conditions
of life and death, and throws light upon the sublime plan by which
the Creator manages the world, can be regarded as lacking the elements of universal interest, it is not easy to imagine. That it is generally looked upon as difficult, may be readily accounted for. The
science is so recent in its development, and chemists have been so
much occupied in the field of original research, that but little has
been done to popularize it. Books adapted to elaborate courses of

experimental instruction, with expensive apparatus, and showing how all the facts of the science may be confirmed, have been put into the hands of those who have neither time nor means for experimenting with about the same propriety that the higher mathematics might be introduced into common schools to *verify* the truths of astronomy. That it should be considered "hard" is, therefore, quite natural. But to suppose there is any thing in the nature of the subject peculiarly difficult, is an error. The fundamental laws of Chemistry are as definite, as clear and simple, and as capable of being understood by juvenile minds, as those of numbers, which are taught in every primary school. The general notion that it is, pre-eminently a science of hard words and intricate principles, has arisen from the want of those facilities for rendering the subject lucid and attractive which have been employed with such effect in other branches of study.

In order to supply this want, and place Chemistry upon the same favorable basis, in regard to simplification, with Geography and Astronomy, the Author has prepared a Chart by which the great principles of chemical combination, which constitute the groundwork of the science, are accurately and beautifully represented to the eye by means of colored diagrams. The numerical laws of quantity, by which all chemical combination is governed, are eminently adapted to the diagramatic method of illustration, and it seems equally natural that a diversity of elements in compound substances should be indicated by variety of colors. In proportion as the objects of our inquiry are removed beyond direct observation, or, from their nature, do not admit of inspection, there arises a necessity for the use of representatives and symbols. Such, in a marked degree, is the fact with Chemistry. It deals constantly with atoms, their laws, properties, and relations, but these atoms are beyond the sphere of the senses, and it is as impossible to convey a distinct idea of their habitudes without some form of visual representation, as it would the geographical situation of countries, or the distribution of the planets. The laws of combination must be learned at the threshold of the subject; and no progress can be made unless these are perfectly understood. By the use of the Chart the acquisition of this formidable portion of the science is changed from tedious task-learning to agreeable pastime. The success of this method of simplifying the subject has not only been attested by the most distinguished chemists and educators of the country, but practically demonstrated by numerous teachers and lecturers. It may not be improper to state that the Chart was devised while the Author was in a condition of blindness, during which, for a long period, he was cut off from the use of diagrams and figures as aids to study. The necessity and value of these means of illustration were thus brought forcibly to his attention, and it became apparent that those who have the perfect use of vision lose much by not employing them more extensively. Although adapted to the Chart, the present work may be used without it with the same advantage as any other class-book. No pains have been spared to give the latest authentic facts and views of the science, and the most standard authorities have been consulted in its preparation. In the department of Physiological Chemistry the Author would acknowledge especial indebtedness to the labors of Professor Draper and Dr. Carpenter. He would also express his obligations to Dr. S. M. Elliott and J. R. Burdsall, Esq., for valuable assistance in the preparation of the present work. If his efforts shall have the effect, in any degree, of promoting a popular interest in Chemistry by presenting the subject in a more attractive aspect, the Author's highest object will have been attained.

New York, Sept. 1851.

CONTENTS.

10 CONTENTS.

INTRODUCTION.

The importance of a knowledge of Chemistry to each person, its value to various classes of society, and the necessity of making it a fundamental branch of popular education, will be apparent from the following considerations.

The physical system of every human being may be looked upon as a *chemical laboratory*, in which exactly the same kind of changes are carried on as are produced by the working chemist in his shop, and by means of similar instruments; the main difference being, that here, as elsewhere, the operations of art are coarse and bungling compared with the matchless perfection of nature. The chemist finds it necessary to dissolve all solid substances; that is, to bring them into the condition of fluids, in order to separate the various elements of which they may be composed. For a like reason, in order to separate the nutritious from the innutritious portions of food, it must first be dissolved or digested in certain cavities or vessels of the body, provided exclusively for the purpose. The chemist in his laboratory makes use of knives, rasps, and mortars, to cut, pulverize, and grind down the substances which he wishes to dissolve. The teeth in man perform a similar work; the incisors (front teeth) cut, the molars (double teeth) crush the food which is to be digested within the system. The principal substances which the chemist uses to bring solids into the state of solution are acids, such as vinegar and oil of vitriol; and alkalies, such as potash or soda. Precisely the same agents are employed by nature in the living laboratory. The juice of the stomach is acid, while that poured into the intestines is alkaline; and the class of foods which is not acted upon ·by one is dissolved by the other: in both cases that which is capable of forming blood is separated from that which is not. To aid and hasten chemical action, the operator stirs and agitates the mixtures in his vessels. For a similar purpose, to facilitate digestion, the food in the stomach is kept constantly in motion by a peculiar action of that organ.

This parallel may be much further extended by those who are acquainted with Chemistry and Physiology; showing that the animal system has for one of its great objects, to effect just the same kind of changes in matter which the chemist produces by artificial means.

Nor are the chemical operations of the living body carried on upon an insignificant scale; their *extent* is even more remarkable than the nice adaptations of the mechanism by which they are conducted. A man of average size, in the course of a single year, introduces into his system from eight to nine hundred pounds of solid food, above eight hundred pounds of oxygen gas, and three-fourths of a ton of water; making altogether upwards of three thousand pounds of matter. The solid and liquid elements contained in the blood are carried through the lungs by means of the great circulation at the rate of very nearly ten pounds per minute, which is equal to the enormous quantity of twenty-five hundred tons in the course of a year. The chief object of this perpetual circulation of the blood is to bring it into contact with atmospheric oxygen, by which it undergoes a very important chemical change. To effect this, no less a quantity than twelve thousand hogsheads of air are introduced into the lungs annually. Incredible as these statements may appear to those not familiar with the subject, they nevertheless rest upon numerous and accurate experiments, and are among the established facts of chemical physiology.

As man is thus, from necessity and by nature, a chemist, his bodily system being a chemical apparatus, and each act of eating, drinking, breathing, and digestion, a chemical experiment; and as this chemical action goes on at a rapid rate, involving the conditions of health and disease, and never ceasing for an instant from birth to death, it is certainly proper that he should understand something of a science of which he is himself so complete and wonderful an illustration. Few subjects can compare, either in interest or importance, with that which informs us of what our physical being is composed, the character and object of those remarkable changes which incessantly take place within us, and the nature of our relations to the surrounding world. Physiology, which teaches the structure and uses of the various parts of the human body, is pursued as a regular branch of study in a great number of schools; it should be in all. But physiology is in a large measure dependent upon chemistry for the explanation of its principles; and the discoveries of every succeeding year tend to make that dependence more and more complete.

Chemistry possesses also great interest from its application to the arts of daily life. It is the object of industry in acting upon the outward world to produce two classes of changes in the materials which it employs. The first are mechanical changes, which influence only the *forms* of matter, as in the operations of cabinet-making and cotton-spinning: the second are *chemical* changes, wrought in the *nature* of the substances used, and altering their properties, as in glass-making and tanning. In both these cases the changes which take place are governed by certain fixed principles or laws, to which the workman must conform if he would operate successfully.

The principles of mechanics, taught by natural philosophy, are quite generally understood; indeed, as this science considers only the relations of *masses of matter* which readily strike the senses, it was very naturally investigated earlier, and has always been a more popular study than Chemistry which inquires only concerning the relations of *invisible atoms*. Yet the laws which control chemical action are as unchangeable as those which hold the planets in their places ; every kind of matter is subject to them, and no vocation in which they are concerned can be pursued to the best advantage unless they are clearly understood.   The farmer, the miner, the metalurgist, the paper-maker, the bleacher, the dyer, the druggist, the soap-manufacturer, the painter, and innumerable other craftsmen, are constantly acting upon chemical substances—constantly dealing with chemical laws—and hence, it is clear, require to know what they are.   The greatest economy of process and perfection of product can only be obtained where the *principles* of a manufacture are distinctly comprehended.   In such case the skilful operator is enabled to work *with* the natural laws, and not *against*, or regardless of them.   It is said that in civil affairs it is always best to keep the law on our side, but in dealing with nature this is vastly more important ; because when *natural laws* are violated there is no such thing as escaping the penalties.

A most instructive illustration of the effect of neglecting chemical principles, while those of mechanics are thoroughly understood and applied, is afforded by the present condition of the United States Capitol at Washington.   The architectural beauty and mechanical excellence of that edifice are well known ; but the freestone (sandstone) of which it is constructed was selected without due attention to its chemical and physical properties, and is totally unfit for its purpose, being rapidly acted upon and crumbled to dust by the common

atmospheric agents. This destructive process has been partially arrested by the free use of paint; but the Secretary of
the Interior has informed Congress that this expedient is
ineffectual, and that unless scientific men come to the rescue,
and invent some new preparation, which, by being applied to
the stone, shall completely protect it from the action of the
air, the whole structure will be reduced to a mound of sand
in *one-fifth* the time that it would last if built of common
marble.* It is thus seen that chemical principles are involved
even in avocations most purely mechanical, so that the best
reasons exist for making them objects of universal study.

Among the various occupations which require a knowledge
of this science to be successfully carried on, that most noble,
useful, and universal of all human pursuits, agriculture,
stands prominent. The farm is a great laboratory, and all
those changes in matter which it is the farmer's chief business
to produce are of a chemical nature. He breaks up and
pulverizes his soil with plough, harrow, and hoe, for the
same reason that the practical chemist powders his minerals
with pestle and mortar; namely, to expose the materials
more perfectly to the action of chemical agents. The field
can only be looked upon as a chemical manufactory; the air,
soil, and manures are the farmer's raw materials, and the
various forms of vegetation are the products of manufacture.
The farmer who raises a bushel of wheat, or a hundred weight
of flax, does not fabricate them out of nothing; he performs
no miraculous work of creation, but it is by taking a certain
definite portion of his raw material and converting it into new
substances through the action of natural agents; just as those
substances are again manufactured in the one case into
bread, and in the other into cloth. When a crop is removed

* The United States Patent Office and Treasury Building are constructed of the
same material.

from the field, certain substances are taken away from the
ground which differ with different kinds of plants; and if the
farmer would know exactly what and how much his field
loses by each harvest, and how in the cheapest manner that
loss may be restored, Chemistry alone is capable of giving
him the desired information. To determine the nature and
properties of his soil, its adaptation to various plants, and
the best methods of improving it; to economize his natural
sources of fertility; to test the purity and value of commercial
manures, and of beds of marl and muck; to mingle composts
and adapt them to special crops; to improve the quality of
grains and fruits; to rear and feed stock, and conduct the
dairy in the best manner, farmers require a knowledge of this
science. Nor can they, as a class, much longer afford to be
without it; for it has always been found that the application
of scientific principles to any branch of industry puts power
into the hands of the intelligent to drive ignorance from the
field of competition; so that as discoveries multiply, and
information is diffused, those farmers who decline to inquire
into the principles which govern their vocation, or who prefer
the study of politics to that of agriculture, will have occasion
to groan more deeply than ever over the unprofitableness of
their business.

As agriculture in this country has no established system
of collegiate education, such as is possessed by the other pro-
fessions, the rudiments of those sciences upon which it
depends should be communicated to the young in common
schools and academies throughout the land. It is not
expected that Chemistry can be taught in a full and complete manner in ordinary schools; but very much of its
general principles may and should be inculcated there, so that
if higher advantages are not subsequently afforded to the
pupil, he will be enabled to pursue the subject privately, in

whatever application of it his business may chance to require.

There are also potent reasons why Chemistry should be embraced in a liberal system of mercantile education. The extent to which a vast variety of commercial articles are adulterated, for fraudulent purposes, and thus greatly depreciated in value, is little suspected by those unacquainted with the facts. These gross impositions upon the public cannot be arrested by penal enactments; the only effectual way of preventing them, or of sheltering the community from their effects, is for the merchant to possess himself of the necessary knowledge to determine between spurious and genuine articles.

It is eminently proper also that Chemistry should be taught to girls. In the present arrangements of society, domestic duties, either by supervision or direct performance, devolve chiefly upon females; and household operations, such as the cooking and preparation of food for the table, the preservation of fruits and meats, and the various processes of cleansing, can only be best performed when the principles of Chemistry are well understood. It is also worthy of consideration, whether substantial information upon this subject might not be beneficially substituted for much of that trivial knowledge which is imparted in fashionable female education.

But besides those more palpable benefits which spring from the application of Chemistry to daily business, there are others connected with the mind itself, which deserve to be noticed in this place. The superiority of the natural sciences over all other objects of study, to engage the attention, and awaken the interest of pupils, is conceded as a fact of experience by the ablest teachers. This cannot be otherwise; for the infinite wisdom of the Creator is nowhere so perfectly displayed, as in the wonderful adaptation which exists between the young unperverted mind, and the natural world with which it is encompassed.

On one hand there is the realm of nature, endless in the variety of its objects, indescribable in its beauty, immutable in its order, boundless in its beneficence, and ever admirable in the simplicity and harmony of its laws; on the other, there is the young intellect, whose earliest trait is curiosity, which asks numberless questions, pries into the reason of things, and seeks to find out their causes as if by the spontaneous promptings of instinct. The study of nature is therefore the most congenial employment of the opening mind, and one of its purest sources of pleasure. Every fact that is learned becomes a key to others; every progressive step discloses wonders previously unimagined. The more we acquire, the greater is our desire to learn, while each advance multiplies the sources of delight instead of exhausting them.

But the advantages of studying the natural sciences are by no means confined to the interest or enthusiasm which they are capable of exciting. They are also eminently fitted to train the mind to habits of careful observation; to teach it discrimination in deciding upon evidence, caution in forming opinions, method in study; to discipline it to patient and persevering effort, and store it with valuable knowledge. And yet, in our current systems of instruction, how frequently is the mind cut off from the glorious works of Almighty power, and directed to the crude and imperfect performances of man! how often does the bright volume of Creation, "written," to use the impressive words of Lord Bacon, "in the only language which hath gone forth to the ends of the world unaffected by the confusions of Babel," remain a sealed book, while the youthful mind is inflated with fictitious learning, or occupied in acquiring the least valuable kinds of information! It is not to be forgotten, that so long as men neglected the study of nature, despised experiment, resorted to fanciful theories for the explanation of all natural occurrences, and wasted their energies in aimless and sterile speculations, society remained in a condition of barbarism, and learning was only an empty boast, a something of which the great mass of mankind knew absolutely nothing, and which was of little service to those who possessed it. But when at length men became the students of nature, when they began to appreciate the significance of her facts, and to search for them with earnestness, then came the knowledge which put stagnant society in motion, which conferred power upon the masses to elevate and improve their condition. Then came the discovery of the New World, of the art of printing, of the telescope, the microscope, the steam-engine, the chronometer, the power-loom, the steamboat, the locomotive, the electric telegraph, the daguerreotype, and ten thousand other inventions in all the departments of human activity; and which constitute but the beginning of what yet remains to be done. The benign results which thus flow from the study of natural science, are in an eminent degree characteristic of Chemistry. Its principles are of universal import, of the utmost breadth of practical application, and are involved in all the vicissitudes of being which we daily contemplate around us. And in acquainting ourselves with them, we may not only gain a deeper and clearer insight into the wonders of existence, but we shall likewise obtain the most striking proofs of the wisdom of the Great Maker of the Universe.

PART I.

INORGANIC CHEMISTRY.

NATURE OF THE SCIENCE.

1. THE creation by which we are surrounded can only be understood in all its parts by that Omniscient Being who is its author. The mind of man is capable of learning a great deal about it, but it cannot comprehend the whole; because its powers are limited, while the works of God are infinite. It has been found necessary, in exploring the domain of nature, to cut it up, or parcel it out into sections; in order that each mind, by being confined to a field within the range of its capacities, may observe and study to the best advantage.

2. The vast realm of natural knowledge thus becomes marked out into divisions, which are known as the departments or branches of natural science. Our knowledge upon the subject of light, for example, forms the science of *Optics;* the science of *Geology* treats of rocks; *Botany*, of plants; *Anatomy*, of the structure of the body, and *Pathology* of its diseases; *Astronomy*, of the stars; *Meteorology*, of the weather; and *Zoology*, of animals. These distinctions, it is to be remembered, do not exist in nature, for there all is linked and blended into one great system. They are entirely artificial, and created only for convenience of study.

In studying the natural world, why is it necessary to divide it into parts or sections?

What are these divisions called? Are they natural or artificial?

3. If now you ask the geologist whether all forms of rocks are made up of the same kind of substance, or why limestone grows lighter in tne fire, while soapstone remains un‑ changed, and coal disappears; or if you seek to know of the zoologist why the various parts of a young animal cannot be formed out of water as well as milk; or if you inquire of the botanist of what materials plants are formed, and why they will not all grow equally well upon the same soil; or if you demand of the pathologist why pure air is healthful, while impure air produces disease—they will all tell you that they cannot answer these questions without calling in the aid of another science, upon which each depends; and that science is CHEMISTRY.

4. It is the province of Chemistry to investigate the prop‑ erties and relations of the atoms or particles of which all matter is composed. It teaches us of what the various sub‑ stances in nature, the earth, the ocean, the air, the trees and plants, our own bodies, and those of all animals, are made. It shows us the nature of the changes which these substan‑ ces are constantly undergoing, the number and properties of their elements, and the laws which govern their union and separation : in a word, it embraces the study of all kinds of matter in natuie which are accessible to man.

5. *Chemical Elements.*—The globe upon which we live is made up in its various parts of several distinct kinds of mat‑ ter, very unlike each other in properties, and called simple bodies or chemical elements. If the earth were composed of but one kind of substance, as iron or sulphur, there would

How are the different sciences related to Chemistry?
What is the province of Chemistry? What kind of information do we get from Chemistry?
If the earth were composed of but one kind of matter, why could thero be no such thing as Chemistry?

be no such thing as Chemistry ; for this science grows out of
the relations of different sorts of matter to each other.

6. *Chemical Action.*—These elements are subject to the
operation of chemical forces, by which their atoms are made
to change places, and enter into new conditions. Every person is familiar with many of these changes. Thus, polished
iron in damp air becomes covered with rust; sugar turns to
spirits, and spirits to vinegar; flesh putrefies and becomes
unfit for food ; wood decays, or is burned and converted into
invisible gas; air, by being breathed, becomes poisonous;
rocks are gnawed down by the action of the atmosphere, and
crumbled into soil ; living plants are built up apparently out
of the dead earth ; and our own bodies, nourished for a time
on the products of vegetable growth, at length perish and fall
to dust. These are examples of what is called chemical
action.

7. *Simple and Compound Bodies.*—The chemist divides all
bodies into two classes, *simple* and *compound.* Compound
bodies are such as can be taken to pieces, or separated into
parts having different properties. Simple bodies or elements
cannot be thus separated. A compound body being made
up of simple substances or elements, may be decomposed,
or divided into its elementary or component parts. Thus
brass is a compound body, and may be shown to consist of
copper and zinc; but neither copper nor zinc can be further
separated . they may be ground, crushed, melted, dissolved,
dissipated a thousand times, but the copper can be made to
yield only copper, and the zinc, zinc.

8. *The true Idea of Simple Bodies.*—It is not meant that
all bodies now ranked as elements are certainly so, but only

Mention some familiar examples of chemical action.
What is the difference between simple and compound bodies ?
What is the true idea of an elementary or simple body ?

that hitherto, in our hands, and exposed to all the various agencies which we can bring to bear on them, each element has yielded only one kind of matter, and no more. Future researches may show that bodies now regarded as simple are really compound. Potash was for a long time thought a simple element, but Davy decomposed it into potassium and ·xygen, a metal and a gas.

9. *Analysis and Synthesis.*—Analysis consists in taking to pieces a compound body, to find of what elements it is composed. Synthesis is putting them together again to form a compound. *Qualitative* analysis ascertains the qualities or nature of the elements forming a compound. *Quantitativ·* analysis determines the quantities of these elements.

10. *Number of the Elements.*—In glancing at the vast diversity of natural objects, we might at first conclude that the elements which compose them are infinite in number; but this is not so. Chemists have as yet discovered but sixty-five; of these about twelve are reckoned as non-metallic bodies, and the remainder are classed as metals. Of the metals not more than one-third are in common use; the remaining two-thirds being so rare as to be seldom met with. The following table contains a list of all the elementary bodies at present known. Several of them have been but recently announced. The letters or symbols opposite each name stand for the substance in the new chemical language (51)* ; and the numbers show what quantity of each element is taken when it enters into union with another (17).

* These numbers refer to sections.

What is analysis? What is synthesis? What are qualitative and quantitative analysis? Are the elements innumerable? How many are there? How many are not metals? Of the metals, how many are in common use?

TABLE OF ELEMENTARY SUBSTANCES.*

(Those in *italics* are rare.)

NAMES OF THE ELEMENTS	Symbols	Atomic numbers Hydrogen=1.
*Aluminum	Al.	13·69
Antimony (stibium)	Sb.	129 03
Aridium	Ar.	?
Arsenic	As.	75·
Barium	Ba.	68·64
Bismuth	Bi.	70·95
Boron...	B.	10·90
Bromine	Br.	78·26
Cadmium	Cd.	55 74
*Calcium	Ca.	20·
*Carbon...	C.	6·
Cerium...	Ce.	46·
*Chlorine	Cl.	35·50
Chromium	Cr.	28·15
Cobalt...	Co.	29·52
Copper (cuprum)	Cu.	?
Didymium...	D.	31·66
Donarium	Do.	?
Erbium	E.	?
*Fluorine"	F.	18 70
Glucinum	Gl.	26·50
Gold (aurum)	Au.	98 33
*Hydrogen	H.	1·
Ilmenium	Il.	?
Iodine	I.	126 36
Iridium	Ir.	98·68
*Iron (ferrum)...	Fe.	28·
Lanthanium	La.	48·
Lead (plumbum)	Pb.	103·56
Lithium	Li.	6·43
*Magnesium	Mg.	12·67
*Manganese	Mn.	27 67
Mercury (hydrargyrum)	Hg.	100 07
Molybdenum	Mo.	47·88
Nickel	Ni.	29·57
Niobium	No.	?
Norium	Nr.	?
*Nitrogen, or Azote...	N.	14·
Osmium...	Os	99·56
*Oxygen	O.	8·
Palladium...	Pd.	53·27
Pelopium	Pe.	?

* The atomic numbers are from the last edition of Graham's Chemistry, and give the latest corrections.

NAMES OF THE ELEMENTS.	Symbols.	Atomic numbers Hydrogen=1
*Phosphorus	P.	32·02
Platinum	Pt.	98·68
*Potassium (kalium)	K.	39·
Rhodium	R.	52·11
Ruthenium	Ru.	52·11
Selenium	Se.	39·57
*Silicon	Si.	21 85
Silver (argentum)	Ag	108·
*Sodium (natrium)	Na.	22 97
Strontium	Sr.	43·84
*Sulphur	S.	16·
Tantalum, or Columbium	Ta.	92·80
Tellurium	Te.	66·14
Terbium	Tb.	?
Thorium	Th.	59·59
Tin (stannum)	Sn.	58·82
Titanium	Ti.	24 29
Tungsten (Wolfram)	W.	94·64
Uranium	U.	60·
Vanadium	V.	68·55
Yttrium	Y.	32 20
Zinc	Zn.	32·52
Zirconium	Zr.	33 62

11. *Organic and Inorganic Chemistry.*—Animals and plants grow and continue their being by means of what are called *Organs*, as leaves, roots, lungs, stomach, &c., and the products which they form are hence called *Organized* or *Organic* substances. The chemistry of plants and animals is therefore termed *Organic Chemistry.* On the contrary, minerals, water, and air are not produced by organs, do not grow; and the chemistry of these substances is therefore called *Inorganic Chemistry.* This branch of Chemistry opens to us the study of all the elements, and of the compounds which they form, *independent of the influence of life.* In pursuing Organic Chemistry, however, our studies are

What are organized substances? What is Organic Chemistry? What is Inorganic Chemistry? How many elements does Inorganic Chemistry consider? Of how many simple bodies are organic substances composed?

limited to about sixteen elements, which compose the entire vegetable and animal kingdoms, together with all the great rocky masses which constitute the earth's crust.

12. These elements are marked by stars in the preceding table. As they embrace the most important relations of the science—physiological, dietetical, and agricultural, together with numerous arts and manufactures which derive their material from the organic world—we shall be chiefly employed with them in the following pages.

13. The names of these sixteen elementary substances form the left column of the Chart, and they are each represented by a squaie, colored diagram. Single squares stand foi simple bodies, but when joined together they represent compounds. As a separate color is thus assigned to each element of a compound body, its exact composition is shown at a glance.*

AFFINITY, OR CHEMICAL ATTRACTION.

14. Elementary bodies possess the property of uniting to form compound bodies. The power or force by which

---

* Chlorine, Carbon, Sulphur, and Phosphorus are represented upon the Chart by their natural colors. Fluorine, from its supposed resemblance to oxygen in properties, has an analogous tint; Nitrogen is of the color of the air (sky-blue), of which it is the chief ingredient. Oxygen, as the sustainer of combustion, and the agent which changes the blood from a purple to a florid tint, is represented of a crimson color. The bases of the alkalies have various shades of blue, corresponding to the strength of the alkalies which they form. (The alkalies restore the blue vegetable colors discharged by acids.) Aluminum, the basis of clay, is of a clay-color. Silicon, which is said somewhat to resemble carbon, is of a dark color. Iron forms green-colored salt, and manganese those of a rose color.

What is said of the importance of the organic elements? What are their names? How are the simple bodies or elements represented upon the Chart?

What is chemical attraction or affinity? How does it differ from the attraction of gravitation and the attraction of cohesion? Do we study chemical affinity in its causes or its effects?

this union is effected, is called *chemical attraction*, or *affinity*. Chemical attraction is exerted to draw together or unite the particles of matter at insensible distances. It differs from the attraction of gravitation, which operates upon masses, and at all distances. It also differs from the attraction of cohesion, by uniting different kinds of matter; while cohesion binds together only particles of the same kind. Rain falls to the ground by the force of gravitation, the particles of iron are united by the force of cohesion, but in lime, the atoms of calcium and oxygen are held together by the force of affinity. Of the cause of this force we know nothing, and can study it only by its effects, which are to produce compounds differing totally in their properties from the elements which unite to form them.

15. Chemical combination is to be distinguished from mechanical mixture. Sand and sawdust may be intimately mixed, but they do not unite to form a new compound. So the two gases which compose the air, nitrogen and oxygen, are mixed together, but not chemically combined into one substance.

16. The simple bodies unite in pairs to form compounds, which are termed *binary*, because they contain but two different kinds of matter. The lines upon the Chart, converging from the left column to the right, represent the affinities of the elements. Thus *hydrogen* and *oxygen* have an affinity for each other, and combine, as the lines passing from them show,—*water* being the product of their union : *potassium* and *oxygen* are also seen to unite, forming potash : the lines from nitrogen and hydrogen meet at ammonia, also those from *oxygen* and *sodium* at *soda*. Compounds formed by

the union of plain lines are solids; of broken lin ., liquids: of dotted lines, gases.

LAWS OF AFFINITY.

17. *Definite Proportions.*—Affinity is governed by several highly interesting laws, which constitute the groundwork of modern Chemistry. It is a law of affinity, that all chemical combination takes place in definite, unchangeable proportions of quantity. The gases which form water unite in the proportion of 8 to 1, by weight: 8 ounces of oxygen unite with 1 of hydrogen to form 9 ounces of water. - One ounce of hydrogen will not combine with 6, 7, 10, or 12 of oxygen. Eight to one are the proportions for pure water, at all places and seasons; nor is it possible to produce it from any other proportion of its elements. Eight parts of oxygen unite with thirty-nine of potassium to form potash, with twenty-three of sodium to form soda, with twenty of calcium to form lime, and with twenty-eight of iron to form protoxide of iron. Analysis never discovers any other proportions in these compounds.

18. This law of definite proportions governs the formation of all chemical substances whatever; it is universal. All stones and minerals, the dirt of which soil consists, every vegetable product, and all parts of animal structures, consist of elements which are united in definite, unalterable proportions.

19. *Combining Numbers.*—These combining quantities, being fixed, may be expressed by permanent numbers, which are hence called *combining* numbers Relatively, these numbers are always the same, although they are written differently upon different scales. Hydrogen, as is evident upon

Do chemical substances combine in all proportions? What is said of the elements of water? of potash? of soda? of lime? of protoxide of iron?
What is said of the extent of this law?
What are combining numbers? Are they always the same?

the Chart, combines in the smallest proportion by weight of any known body, and is adopted as the unit upon the scale generally used. Hydrogen being assumed as 1, oxygen is 8, sulphur 16, carbon 6, and so on; but if oxygen were taken as 1, the whole scale would have to be divided by eight; or oxygen at 100 multiplies the scale by 12·5.

20. This great law of Chemistry is exhibited upon the Chart in the clearest manner. The sizes or areas of the colored diagrams correspond to the combining numbers, and thus represent relative quantities to the eye. The hydrogen square being the smallest, the oxygen square is 8 times larger, the sulphur square 16, the carbon square 6, and the chlorine square 35 times larger. Observe that diagrams of the same color have exactly the same size throughout the Chart. This could not be otherwise, as the combining proportions are always the same. Thus, oxygen, wherever found, whether in an acid or an alkali, a mineral or a vegetable substance, is seen obeying the law of its fixed proportion; its square is always of the same size; and so with all the other elements. This great law of Chemistry, so admirably illustrated by these diagrams, gives remarkable simplicity to the science; enabling the mind both to comprehend and to retain its facts with readiness and ease.

21. *Multiple Proportions.*—When combination occurs between two elements in more proportions than one, the larger quantities are multiples of the smaller by a whole number. Thus carbon and oxygen form two different compounds, carbonic oxide and carbonic acid. In carbonic oxide, as the

By what method is this great law of definite proportions exhibited upon the Chart? Why are diagrams of the same color always of the same size? What is he effect of this law upon the acquisition of the science?

When the same elements form two or more different compounds, in what proportions do they unite? Give examples. What is said of the nitrogen and oxygen group? What is this law called?

Chart shows, oxygen exists in but one proportion; in carbonic acid the quantity is doubled. In the nitrogen and oxygen group, we see a series of five compounds, which differ essentially from each other in their properties. The amount of nitrogen is constant, but the quantity of oxygen varies as the numbers 8, 16, 24, 32, 40—a simple numerical ratio. This is called the law of *multiple proportions*.

22. When two bodies unite with each other chemically, the proportions which are taken satisfy their mutual affinities, and the quantities are therefore said to be equivalent to each other. Thus the affinity of one grain of hydrogen is exactly equal or equivalent to that of eight grains of oxygen, or thirty-five grains of chlorine. Combining numbers are hence sometimes called equivalent numbers, equivalent proportions, or equivalents; they are also termed combining weights, atomic weights, combining proportions, &c. The atomic numbers should always be associated in the mind with the names to which they are attached, because to the chemist no such thing as abstract hydrogen, oxygen, or carbon exists. It is of their atoms that he invariably speaks. The word hydrogen signifies an atom which weighs 1, the word carbon an atom which weighs 6, and the word oxygen an atom which weighs 8.

23. The law of definite proportions extends to the union of compounds, as well as of elements. The combining proportion of a compound body is the sum of the combining numbers of its several elements. The combining number for lime is calcium 20, oxygen 8=28 : for water it is oxygen 8,

What are chemical equivalents? What are combining numbers sometimes called? Why should the atomic numbers be always associated with the names to which they are attached? What does the chemist understand by the words hydrogen, carbon, oxygen?

How do we learn the combining proportions of a compound body? How does it appear that 37 is the number for hydrate of lime?

hydrogen $1 = 9$. When water and newly burned lime unite, as in the process of slaking, the quantities are therefore 9 of water to 28 of lime, giving 37 for hydrate of lime: thus each acid and alkali has its fixed equivalent number. It is important that the combining numbers of the elements upon the Chart should be learned and remembered; the pupil should then be required to compute the numbers for the compounds which they form. Fractions have been omitted, whole numbers being more easily retained in the memory.

24. The term *gas* is applied to bodies which are neither solid nor liquid, but resemble air. Gases unite in definite proportions by *bulk* or *volume*, as well as by weight. Thus water is formed by one volume or measure of oxygen to two of hydrogen, and like simple proportions govern all gaseous combinations. But as weighing is the grand process by which all the important laws and facts of Chemistry have been established, and as the whole language and nomenclature of the science, as recognized by all chemists, has been conformed to results by weight, these alone are represented upon the Chart. Says Prof. Liebig, "The great distinction between the manner of proceeding in Chemistry and Natural Philosophy is, that one *weighs*, while the other *measures*. The natural philosopher has applied his measures to nature for many centuries, but only for fifty years have we attempted to advance our philosophy by weighing. For all great discoveries Chemistry is indebted to the balance, that incomparable instrument which gives permanence to every observation, dispels all ambiguity, establishes truth, detects error, and guides in the true path of inductive science."

What is a gas? How do gases combine? Why does not the Chart represent combination by volume? What is said of the great distinction between Natural Philosophy and Chemistry?

، CAUSES WHICH CONTROL AFFINITY.

25. *Bodies combine with unequal degrees of power.*—Chem‧cal attraction acts among different substances with different degrees of force. Thus carbonic acid will combine with soda, forming carbonate of soda; but if vinegar be brought in contact with this compound, it will drive off the carbonic acid, and take its place, forming acetate of soda. Again, the affinity of hydrochloric acid for the soda is superior to that of the acetic acid; it will therefore expel it, and form a new substance. Nitric acid serves hydrochloric in the same way, and it is in turn treated in a similar manner by sulphuric acid. It has been attempted to construct tables representing the order of affinities among different substances; but so many causes disturb the play of this force, that such tables are of little value.

26. *Relation of Heat to Affinity*—Heat is the great antagonist of affinity. As this force draws the particles of matter together, heat tends to drive them asunder. By thus separating the atoms, and removing them beyond the sphere of each other's attraction, it weakens and overcomes chemical union. But when the affinities which bind together a compound have been destroyed by the application of a given degree of heat, other affinities of a stronger kind are brought into action, and the elements arrange themselves into new combinations. Thus, heat destroys all organic substances, but at the same time other compounds are formed, which

---

Is the force of chemical attraction equal among all substances? How does vinegar affect carbonate of soda? Why does hydrochloric acid destroy this com pound? What acid expels the hydrochloric? What the nitric? Why are tables showing the order of affinities of little value?

How does heat overcome chemical union? When heat destroys the affinities of a compound, what follows?

resist the decomposing power of combustion. Heat, by melting solid substances, and thus bringing them into a state of liquidity (29), also calls new affinities into exercise, as in glass-making (296, 303).

27. *Influence of Light.*—Light exerts a powerful agency in modifying affinity. Hydrogen and chlorine gases mingled together in the dark do not unite; but if brought into the sunshine they combine explosively. The daguerreotype process depends upon the chemical action of light, exerted upon metallic plates coated with various substances. Light is also the great agent which controls the growth of vegetation, as all vegetable fabrics are built up under its direct influence (329).

28. *Effect of Electricity.*—Affinity is also controlled by electricity, which by many is supposed to be the basis of all chemical action. Atoms which are attracted together are assumed to be in different electrical states, as opposite electricities are known to attract each other. If two slips of different metals have their lower ends dipped into an acid, corrosion (chemical action) immediately takes place ; and if their upper ends are connected, either by being inclined together or by a third slip of metal, an electrical current is created. This is called a simple voltaic circuit, and involves the principle of the galvanic battery. Electrical currents are among the most powerful means of producing chemical decomposition.

29. *Cohesion.*—As affinity only takes place among particles of different kinds of matter at insensible distances (14),

What is said of the effect of light upon affinity? Upon what does the da guerreotype process depend? How does light influence vegetation?

How is electricity supposed to act in controlling chemical action? In the voltaic circuit and galvanic battery, to what is the electrical current due?

Why is cohesion opposed to chemical action? How is cohesion best over come?

cohesion, which holds together atoms of the same kind in masses, must be opposed to chemical action. Substances when in the solid state, even if ground to a fine powder and mixed, very rarely combine chemically. To afford full scope for affinity, cohesion must be completely overcome; and this is best done by melting or dissolving the bodies in a liquid, that their particles may be brought into the most intimate contact.

30. *Effect of the Nascent State.*—Elements at the very moment they are liberated from union, in what is called the growing or nascent state, often enter into new combinations which cannot be formed under other circumstances. Nitrogen and hydrogen, if mingled in the same vessel, do not unite; but when these two gases are set free at the same time, by the decomposition of vegetable matter, they readily combine to form ammonia.

31. *Catalysis.*—Chemical union is also sometimes influenced in a peculiar manner by what is called *presence-action,* or *contact-action,* or *catalysis.* In this case, a body, by its presence or contact, *induces* changes in another, in which it takes no part. Thus if starch is boiled in a little weak sulphuric acid, it is converted into sugar; and if at the termination of the process the acid be examined, it will be found to remain unaltered, both in properties and quantity; so that the smallest proportion of the acid is sufficient to convert into sugar an indefinitely large quantity of starch. The phenomena of catalysis are not well understood.

What is said of the combination of elements just liberated from union? Give an example.
What is the mode of action of catalysis? Are the phenomena well understood?

THE ATOMIC THEORY.

32. It has been proposed to explain the laws of chemical combination by what is called the *atomic theory*. This theory assumes, first, that the ultimate particles or molecules of which all matter is composed are indivisible, unchangeable atoms; second, that atoms of the same element are uniform in weight, but that in different elements they have different weights; third, that the combining numbers represent these relative weights; and fourth, that chemical compounds are formed by the union of these atoms with each other. When these propositions are admitted, the known laws of combination follow necessarily. If bodies unite by atoms, atom to atom, their proportions must be *definite*, and always the same. If several similar atoms unite, as each is indivisible, they must be *multiples* of each other (*multiple proportions*); and as one atom may replace another in a compound, their relation must be that of *equivalents*. This theory has been so universally received by chemists, that its terms have become incorporated with the language of the science; so that to say an atom of iron combines with an atom of oxygen, is as common as to say that a proportion or equivalent of iron combines with an equivalent proportion of oxygen.

33. Of the form or figure of atoms nothing whatever is known. It is therefore no matter in what shape they are represented, as the object is not to indicate their *figure*, but their relations.

34. If each square upon the Chart is considered to represent

Upon what assumed grounds is the atomic theory based? Do the laws of combination result from these propositions? What is said of the reception of this theory by chemists?

Is any thing known of the form of atoms?

How does the Chart give a clear idea of the atomic theory?

an atom, we shall then have a clear view of the atomic theory. Single atoms are seen to combine to form compound atoms: thus an atom of water contains two elementary atoms, of silica four, and an atom of gluten eighty-four simple atoms. Until the announcement of the atomic theory, we had no adequate explanation of the uniformity of the proportions of chemical combination, or of the nature of the cause which renders combination in other proportions impossible.

35. *Crystallization.*—When certain solid substances are dissolved in liquids or melted, so that their particles are free to move among each other, upon the evaporation of the liquid, or the cooling of the melted mass, the atoms arrange themselves together in certain regular geometrical forms, called *crystals.* The process by which crystals are formed is called *crystallization.* Thus, when common salt crystallizes, its atoms arrange themselves in the form of dice or cubes. Alum assumes the form of a double pyramid placed base to base.

36. Attraction, in causing atoms to cohere so as to form solid masses, seems not to act equally all around each atom, but between certain sides or parts of one atom, and corresponding parts of another; so that when allowed to unite according to their natural tendencies, they always assume a certain definite arrangement. This property of atoms has been called their *polarity*, because in these circumstances they seem to resemble magnets, which attract each other only by their poles. When the arrangement of its atoms is not crystalline, a body is said to be *amorphous.* Any change which tends to permit freedom of motion among the atoms of amorphous bodies, favors the reaction of the polar forces, and promotes crystallization.

What are crystals? What is crystallization? What form do the crystals of common salt assume? What those of alum?

What is said of the polarity of atoms? In this property, what do they resemble? What is an amorphous body?

37. The power with which atoms arrange themselves in the crystalline order is seen in the freezing of water; as the particles assume their new position, the water expands with a force sufficient to burst the strongest iron vessels, or to rend solid rocks.

38. Blows, continued vibration, friction, and variations of temperature produce changes in the molecular arrangement of metals; and it is thought that the axles of railroad-cars, though at first constructed of tough and fibrous wrought-iron, may from these causes acquire that crystalline and brittle structure which they often exhibit upon breaking. Crystals of the salts often contain water, called the water of crystallization. These, when exposed to the air or to heat, part with this water, lose their transparency, turn white, and fall to powder: this is called *efflorescence*. Others attract water from the air, and this is known as *deliquescence*.

39. The primitive geometrical forms which crystals assume are divided into six classes or systems, and in each of these classes there is a vast number of secondary forms. Thus in carbonate of lime, 680 modifications of crystalline form have been described. As the subject of crystalline forms, to be made interesting, requires full details, we must refer the inquiring student to the complete treatises upon Mineralogy and Crystalography.

40. When the same body possesses the property of being crystallized in two different systems, it is said to be *dimorphous*. *Isomorphous* bodies are such as have the property

---

What is said of the force with which atoms arrange themselves in the crystalline form? Give an example.

What is said of the effect of blows, friction, and vibration of the axles of rail-cars?
What is efflorescence? What is deliquescence?

How many primitive geometrical forms do crystals possess? How many secondary forms of carbonate of lime have been enumerated?

What is a dimorphous body? What are isomorphous bodies?

of replacing each other in crystals, without giving rise to new figures. Ten groups of isomorphous bodies have been discovered.

41. *Isomeric compounds* are such as contain the same elements, in the same proportions, and yet have different properties. Formerly it was supposed that compounds having the same chemical constitution must necessarily have the same qualities, but such is now proved not to be the fact. Spirits of turpentine, the oil of lemons, oil of juniper, oil of black pepper, and oil of bergamot, as is seen upon the Chart, contain equal amounts of carbon and hydrogen, yet their properties are very different. Oil of roses and illuminating gas are also identical in composition The difference of properties in isomeric bodies is accounted for by supposing that the atoms or molecules are differently arranged in the different cases, as is represented by the Chart.

42. *Allotropism.*—Chemists have lately shown that many of the elements may exist under two or more different conditions, called *allotropic states.* In one state they readily exert their usual active properties; in the other they seem passive, and as it were torpid. Thus the diamond is the passive form of carbon, and it can hardly be made to burn in oxygen gas; while lamp-black, which is one of its active forms, is so highly combustible that it often takes fire spontaneously in the open air. It has been suggested that these conditions of the elements are retained when they enter into combination.

What are isomeric compounds? Give examples. How is the difference of prop
erties in these compounds accounted for?
What are allotropic states? What examples are offered?

THE NOMENCLATURE.

43. The chemical nomenclature is a system of naming, in which the structure of the terms employed expresses the composition of the substances to which they are applied. This nomenclature is the most perfect to be found in any of the sciences. It is very simple, and gives the mind great power over the subject.

44. In the case of simple bodies, the rule is to retain the old established terms; but when a new element is discovered, to give it a name expressive of some leading property. Thus, chlorine takes its name from its greenish color, and iodine from its purple vapor. All the lately discovered metals are distinguished by a common termination, as potassium, sodium, platinum, &c.

45. Compound bodies are of three kinds, *acids, bases*, and *neutral* bodies, or those which possess neither acid nor basic properties. Acids are usually known by the following properties. a sour taste, a power of altering vegetable colors (changing blues to red), and the property of combining with and neutralizing or destroying the properties of the bases or alkalies.

46. A large number of the acids are formed by the union of oxygen with other bodies; they are then named from the element with which the oxygen unites. Thus, sulphur with oxygen gives sulphuric acid, carbon with oxygen gives carbonic acid, phosphorus with oxygen forms phosphoric acid. Acids in which there is no oxygen are named from both their

---

What is the chemical nomenclature? What is said of it?
What is the rule in the case of simple bodies? Give examples.
How are compound bodies divided? What are acids?
How are a large number of the acids formed? How are these named? Give examples How are acids named which contain no oxygen? When the same

elements: thus, hydrogen and chlorine form hydrochloric acid, hydrogen and fluorine hydrofluoric acid. When different acids are formed by the union of the same elements in different proportions, they are distinguished by terminations and prefixes. The termination *ic* describes the strongest, *ous* a weaker, and the prefix *hypo*, which means under, a still weaker acid. Thus nit*ric* acid contains a higher proportion of oxygen than nit*rous* acid, and this more than *hypo*nitrous acid (see Chart). The prefix *hyper* means more, as *hyper*chloric acid, or more commonly *per*chloric, which contains more oxygen than chloric acid.

47. *Bases* are distinguished by their power of combining with and neutralizing acids. They include the alkalies, which have a peculiar acrid taste, as lime, called the alkaline taste; and have also the power of restoring vegetable blues when destroyed by an acid. Besides the alkalies, bases also comprehend those metallic oxides which do not exhibit these alkaline properties, but yet unite with acids.

48. Most of the bases are formed by the union of oxygen with another element, commonly a metal; as oxygen with iron, termed oxide of iron, oxygen with potassium, oxide of potassium, &c. When oxygen combines with the same element in different proportions, forming several oxides, its quantity is indicated by the use of prefixes. Thus *proto* indicates one equivalent or the lowest proportion of oxygen; *deuto*, two, and *trito*, three, equivalents of oxygen. *Per* is used to express the highest degree of oxidation, and is often applied

---

elements form different acids, how are they distinguished? What is the meaning of *ic*, of *ous*, of *hypo*, of *hyper*, or *per* ?

How are bases distinguished? What bodies are comprehended by the term bases?

How are most of the bases formed? How is the quantity of oxygen in an oxide denoted? What does *proto* indicate? *Deuto*? *Trito*? How is *per* used? What are *sub*oxides? What are *sesqui*oxides?

to the deutoxide and tritoxide. Some oxides, which have such inferior basic properties as not to combine with acids, are termed *sub*oxides. *Bin*oxide is equivalent to deutoxide; and *sesqui*oxides are those in which the oxygen is in the proportion of one and a half to one, of the element with which it is combined. (See Chart, Binary Compounds.)

49. The acids and alkalies, although possessing opposite properties, have a powerful attraction for each other, and combine to form salts. By this union the properties of both the acids and bases are completely lost, and a neutral salt is the result. If, however, there is not sufficient base completely to saturate the acid, an *acid*-salt, or *super*-salt, results; while if the base is in excess, a *basic*-salt, or *sub*-salt, is formed. Salts are named after both their elements, as phosphate of lime, from phosphoric acid and lime. But as several acids of the same general name may combine with one base, the salts are distinguished by turning the *ic* of the acid into *ate* of the salt, and *ous* into *ite*: thus nitric acid forms nitrates, nitrous acid nitrites, and hyposulphurous acid hyposulphites. The basic element of a salt is indicated by its usual prefixes; thus, protosulphate of iron is a sulphate of the protoxide of iron. (See Chart.) Salts formed from elements containing oxygen are termed oxygen-acid salts; those containing no oxygen are named *haloid* salts, from their resemblance to sea-salt— chloride of sodium (291).

50. As oxygen forms oxides, so chlorine forms chlorides, bromine bromides, iodine iodides, fluorine fluorides, sulphur sulphides, phosphorus phosphides, and carbon carbides. The

When acids and alkalies unite, what is the result? What is a *super*-salt? What a *sub*-salt? How are salts named? Example? When several acids of the same general name combine with one base, how are the salts distinguished? Examples? How is the degree of oxidation of the base of a salt represented? What are oxygen-acid salts? What are haloid salts?

To what compounds are *ide* and *uret* attached?

compounds of these last three substances are known most generally by the termination *uret*, as sulphuret of iron, carburetted hydrogen.

51. *Chemical Symbols.*—In the case of most organic compounds the nomenclature fails, and cannot be made to express composition. Another expedient has been happily resorted to, which meets the difficulty: it is the use of what are known as chemical symbols. For the symbol of an elementary substance we take the first letter of its name; but as several substances may have the same initial letter, to distinguish between them, we either employ the first letter of their Latin names, or add a second small letter. Thus, C stands for carbon, Cl for chlorine; and as P is taken for phosphorus, K, from *kalium*, the Latin for potash, is taken for potassium. A symbolic letter represents not only an element, but *one atom* or *proportion of that element*. Thus, N O stands for one atom of nitrogen and one of oxygen, which forms nitrous oxide. If more proportions than one are to be expressed, a small figure is added in the same manner as the powers of roots are expressed arithmetically by exponents. Thus, $N O_5$ represents nitric acid, which contains five equivalents of oxygen. A large figure placed before a parenthesis indicates that all included within it is to be multiplied; thus, $3(S O_3 + H O)$ represents three atoms of hydrated sulphuric acid. Some writers dispense with the parenthesis. A collection of symbols is called a formula.

52. *Equations and Diagrams.*—Chemical changes are shown by means of formulæ arranged in the manner of an equation. The separation of carbonic acid, and the formation

of plaster of Paris, when sulphuric is added to carbonate of lime, is thus represented: Ca O C O$_2$ + S O$_3$ = Ca O S O$_3$ + C O$_2$. The substances to be changed, carbonate of lime and sulphuric acid, are placed at the left; the products of the change, sulphate of lime and free carbonic acid, are seen at

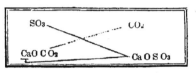

the right. A still better way of illustrating decomposition is by means of lines, such as are shown upon the Chart. By this method the foregoing changes appear as in the above diagram. Here the substances to be changed and the products of change are not only arranged opposite each other, as in the equation, but the character of the change is exhibited more clearly. The plain lines show that one of the products is a solid, and the dotted line that the other escapes as a gas (16). As there is nothing lost during the change, the equivalents upon each side, if added together, will produce equal amounts.

53. It is very important that the nomenclature and the use of symbols should be well learned; and as the common way of teaching this part of the subject is difficult, tedious, and unattractive, it is desirable that beginners should have the Chart constantly before them while attending to it. Much time and labor will thus be saved, while clear, and therefore the most lasting ideas are acquired.

MANIPULATION, OR THE OPERATIONS OF CHEMISTRY.

54. Manipulation means hand-work: it is a term applied to all the practical operations of Chemistry. To become an

---

How are chemical changes shown? How are the substances arranged? What is said to be a still better way of illustrating chemical changes? What is chemical manipulation?

expert manipulator requires great experience, tact, and a high perfection of bodily senses; but many useful operations may be executed with but slight practice and few instruments. The object of all chemical investigation is to ascertain something unknown in reference to the properties of bodies, and this is done in various ways.

55. We determine by taste if bodies are sweet, like sugar; sour, like vinegar; bitter, as epsom salts; saline, as common salt; burning, as alcohol, insipid, as water which has just been boiled, or entirely tasteless. The properties of many substances are revealed by the odors they emit. Thus the peculiar smell of burnt feathers, woollen rags, &c., indicates animal substances. Color is an important property of bodies, and should always be noticed   Some experience is necessary to identify different shades from description; and the pupil will do well to procure slips of paper of a large variety of tints, and paste them in a book with the name of the color opposite each.

56. The property of hardness, which is very important in reference to minerals, is determined in a comparative way, by rubbing or rasping one body against another, and observing which is scratched. Thus talc is scratched by gypsum, and gypsum by calcareous spar. The diamond scratches all bodies and is itself scratched by none. The finger nail also affords a good indication in this way; soapstone and plaster of Paris yield readily to it, while limestone is but slightly affected.

57. Weight is a fundamental property of all bodies; to ascertain it accurately is therefore a matter of great impor-

---

How are the properties of many bodies easily determined? What is said of color?

How do we ascertain the comparative hardness of bodies?

What is said of weight? How is weighing performed?

tance. When we take a piece of wood in one hand, and a piece of lead of the same size in the other, we say that one is heavy and the other light. We mean that they are heavy and light compared one with the other; these terms, then, always express the comparative weight of *equal bulks* of different substances. We have standards or units of weight with which all bodies may be compared, as troy weight, apothecaries' weight, &c. Weighing is performed by means of an instrument called the balance or scales. No balance should be used, even for the roughest chemical work, that will not turn with the tenth of a grain.

58. *Specific Gravity.*—The specific gravity of a body is its weight compared with either water or air. Solids and liquids are usually compared with distilled water, gases with common air. A cubic foot of water weighs about 1000 ounces; a cubic foot of iron weighs 7800 ounces; it is therefore 7 and $\frac{8}{10}$ times heavier than water, hence we say its specific gravity is 7·8. Gold is $19\frac{1}{2}$ times heavier than water; its specific gravity is 19·5. The specific gravity of a solid is obtained by first weighing the body out of the water, and then weighing it suspended in the water, when it will be found to weigh less. The weight in air is divided by the loss in water, and the quotient gives the specific gravity of the substance. The specific gravity of a liquid may be obtained by filling with it a bottle which will hold just 1000 grains of pure water, and then weighing it. Such a bottle will hold just 1340 grains of molasses, 1840 grains of oil of vitriol, 13,500 grains of quicksilver, and only 840 grains of alcohol : these numbers, divided by 1000, give the specific gravities of these several substances.

What is meant by the specific gravity of a body? What are solids and liquids compared with? Gases? How do we determine the specific gravity of a solid? How of a liquid?

59. Pulverization, trituration, or comminution is the break-ing or grinding down of hard substances into powder. It is effected usually in a strong vessel termed a mortar, made of Wedgwood's ware, or porcelain, Fig. 1. This operation must be performed upon most solid bodies before they can be dissolved.

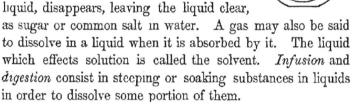

Fig. 1.

60. *Solution.*—The act of dissolving, by which a solid substance, when placed in a liquid, disappears, leaving the liquid clear, as sugar or common salt in water. A gas may also be said to dissolve in a liquid when it is absorbed by it. The liquid which effects solution is called the solvent. *Infusion* and *digestion* consist in steeping or soaking substances in liquids in order to dissolve some portion of them.

61. *Precipitation* consists in the separation of a dissolved substance from the liquid solvent. Spirits of camphor is a solution of camphor in alcohol. If water be added to it, the camphor separates from the alcohol as a white cloud, which soon settles to the bottom : it is precipitated. The substance separated from the solution is called the precipitate, the sub-stance added the precipitant.

62. *Filtering.*—The act of straining, by which solid sub-stances (usually precipitates) are separated from liquids. Coarse sand or cloth is sometimes used to form a filter, but most commonly porous or unsized paper (blotting paper). The paper is cut into pieces of a circular form, Fig. 2, and folded over, as the cross lines represent. It then readily assumes the form Fig. 3, when it is placed within a funnel

How is trituration performed ?
What is meant by solution? What by infusion and digestion ?
What is precipitation ? Give an example. Which is the precipitate ? Which the precipitant ?
What is filtering ? What substances are used as filters ?

which rests upon a stand,* Fig. 4. The filtered liquid is called the *filtrate*.

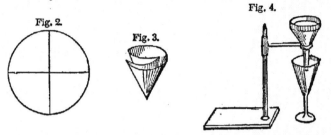

Fig. 2.

Fig. 3.

Fig. 4.

63. *Decantation* is the act of gently pouring off a liquid from its sediment, as when a precipitate has settled to the bottom. Mix some chalk and water in a tumbler, let it rest until the chalk is deposited, carefully *cant* the tumbler over to one side, and you will *decant* the water.

64. *Distillation* is the process by which a liquid is evaporated in one vessel by heat, the vapor conveyed to another

Fig. 5.

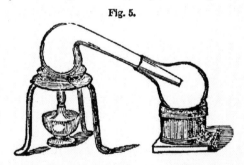

vessel by means of a tube or otherwise, and there condensed by cold into its original liquid form. Fig. 5 represents the

* For minute directions in experimenting, see "Griffin's Chemical Recreations," or "Faraday's Manipulations of Chemistry."

What is decantation?
What is distillation? What is dry distillation? Destructive distillation?

retort and receiver which are commonly used for distillation. The object may be either to separate a liquid from substances dissolved in it which will not evaporate; or to separate two liquids which evaporate at different temperatures, as alcohol and water (380). *Dry distillation* is the distillation of substances without the addition of water. *Destructive distillation* is the distillation of substances at a high temperature, so that their elements are separated and form new combinations.

65. *Heat* is the great agent made use of by the chemist to produce changes in matter, hence Chemistry has been defined as "philosophy by fire." The spirit-lamp is the most convenient means of producing heat, as alcohol when burning produces a very high temperature, but little light and no smoke. In the absence of the common spirit-lamp, the student may make one by inserting the tin or brass tubes of an oil-lamp through a cork, and fitting the cork tightly to a wide-mouthed vial. A common cotton wick is employed, but when not in use it should be closely capped to prevent evaporation.

MEASUREMENT OF HEAT.

66. Variations of temperature are shown by an instrument called a thermometer or heat-measurer. It acts upon the general principle that heat expands all bodies and cold contracts them. A narrow tube of glass terminating at its lower extremity in a bulb, filled with colored alcohol, or most commonly with quicksilver, is attached to a frame or case. The bulb being dipped into water in which ice is

Why is the spirit-lamp the best means of producing heat for the chemist?
What is the principle of the thermometer? How is the freezing point obtained? How the boiling point?

5

melting, the position of the mercury is marked, and called the freezing point, or, more properly, the point of melting ice. The bulb is then dipped into boiling water, the mercury expands, and the height to which it rises is marked as the boiling point.

67. In the centigrade thermometer, which is used in France, the space upon the scale that intervenes between the freezing and boiling points is marked into 100 equal divisions, called degrees. The *zero*, or cipher from which we begin to count, is therefore the freezing point, and 100° the boiling point. This is the most natural and perfect scale. Reaumer's thermometer, used in the east of Europe, has the same space upon the scale divided into 80°; and Fahrenheit's thermometer, the one used in this country and England, has the same portion of the scale divided into 180°; but what is very singular, it has the zero, or point at which we commence counting, fixed at 32° below the freezing point; so that from zero to the boiling point we have 180° + 32° = 212°. The centigrade thermometer is represented by the letter (C), Reaumer's by (R.), and Fahrenheit's by (F.). The degrees above zero are marked with the sign (+), those below with the sign (—): see Fig. 6.

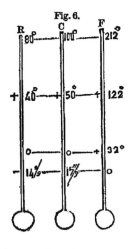

Fig. 6.

The following table exhibits several interesting facts in regard to temperature:

Greatest artificial cold measured (Faraday)........−166° F.
Greatest natural cold observed by a "verified" ther-
   mometer (Sabine)..................................... 56°
Estimated temperature of the planetary spaces
   (Fourier) .... 58°
Mercury (quicksilver) freezes...................... 39°
A mixture of equal parts of alcohol and water freezes 7°
Ice melts ....+ 32°
Greatest density of water .... 39·8°
Mean temperature at the equator .... 81 5°
·Heat of human blood .... 98°
Highest natural temperature observed (of a hot wind
   in Upper Egypt.—Burkhardt) .... 117·8°
Alcohol boils..................................... 172·94°
Water boils .... 212°
Tin melts... 442°
Lead melts .... 612°
Mercury boils .... 660°
Red heat (Daniel) . ... 980°
Heat of a common fire (Daniel) .... 1141°
Brass melts .... 1869°
Silver melts. .... 2283°
Cast-iron melts................................... 8479°

68. Thermometers should never be suddenly plunged into very cold or very hot water, as the glass is liable to crack; and the indications of thermometers bought at the shops or instrument-makers ought not to be trusted, unless they are at first carefully compared with some well-known standard instrument. The mercurial thermometer is capable of measuring accurately only about 600 degrees of heat; temperatures higher than this are shown by instruments called pyrometers, which operate by the expansion and contraction of solid bodies.

What precautions should be observed in using thermometers? In buying them? What is the limit of the indications of the mercurial thermometer? How are higher temperatures measured?

OF THE CHEMICAL ELEMENTS, AND THEIR COMPOUNDS.

OXYGEN.

Symbol O, *equivalent* 8.

69. THIS is the most important of the elements. It is in some way concerned in nearly all chemical changes, and in most of them it takes a very prominent share. As we shall be much in its company in the following pages, it will be well to make its acquaintance first.

70. *Properties* —The condition of oxygen is that of a gas; that is, it resembles common air, which is a mixture of several gases. Some gases when exposed to great cold are brought down to the liquid, and even the solid state (168), and others are condensed into liquids by pressure: but no degree of cold or pressure ever yet applied has been able to overcome or destroy the gaseous properties of oxygen; chemical force alone can do this. Oxygen is transparent, colorless, tasteless, and inodorous, like common air; it is about one-tenth heavier than that body, and possesses the same mechanical properties. It acts neither as an acid nor an alkali, and is dissolved sparingly by water, 100 gallons absorbing about $4\frac{1}{2}$ of the gas. The term oxygen signifies acid-former. It was applied by Lavoisier, who supposed it to be the active principle of all acids, an opinion now known to be false. There is reason to believe that oxygen is capable of existing in two allotropic states (42), a passive or quiescent state, and an active condition, in which its affinities are

greatly exalted. The *ozone*, discovered in the atmosphere by Prof. Schonbein, concerning which much has been said, is supposed to be the active form of oxygen.

71. *Preparation.*—We prepare the purest oxygen, and in the readiest way, from chlorate of potash. A portion of this salt is powdered, dried, and mixed with about one-fourth its weight of black oxide of manganese, or oxide of copper, and heated in a flask, retort, or tube, over a spirit-lamp. The gas comes off copiously, and is collected in jars over water. The pneumatic trough, which is used for this purpose, may be any convenient vessel, containing a shelf, and holding sufficient water readily to fill a jar placed within it, which is then inverted and put upon the shelf. The water in the trough must cover the mouth of the jar. The gas is delivered by the tube at the open end of the jar, through which it rises, displacing the water, and gradually filling the vessel. This arrangement is shown in Fig. 7. The oxide of manganese or copper is not in any way changed; it acts by catalysis (31), promoting in a very high degree the decomposition of the chlorate. Chlorate of potash costs about one dollar per pound, and one ounce will yield about two gallons of the gas. Oxygen may also be prepared by exposing a mixture of bichromate of potash and sulphuric acid, or peroxide of manganese and

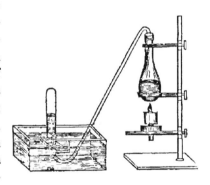

How is pure oxygen gas best obtained? What is a pneumatic trough? How is the oxygen collected? How does the manganese act in promoting decomposition?

5*

sulphuric acid, to heat.
When chlorate of potash
is used, the decomposition
may be thus expressed.

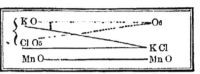

72. *Extent of its Diffusion.*—Oxygen is by far the most widely diffused of all the elements. It constitutes one-fifth by weight of the atmosphere, eight-ninths of the ocean and all other waters, nearly one-half of the solid rocks that compose the crust of the globe,—of every solid substance we see around us, the houses in which we live, the stones and soils upon which we tread, and much more than one-half of the bodies of all living animals and plants. This is shown by the predominance of the red color upon the Chart.

73. The discovery of oxygen was made by Dr. Priestley, in 1774, and it has been justly pronounced " the capital discovery of the last century, rivalling in importance the great discovery of gravitation by Newton in the preceding century." It disclosed the phenomena of nature in an entirely new aspect, exploded the old theories, and laid the foundations of modern chemical science. A glance at the Chart shows that oxygen has a very wide range of combination. It unites with all the elements except fluorine, forming compounds termed oxides. The act of combination is called *oxidation ;* the separation of oxygen from a compound is termed *deoxidation.*

74. *Oxygen a Sustainer of Combustion.*—The leading property of oxygen is the intense energy with which it unites

---

What is said of the diffusion of oxygen ?

What effect did the discovery of this gas produce upon science ?   What striking fact concerning oxygen does a glance at the Chart reveal ?   What is oxidation ? What is deoxidation ?

What is the most important property of oxygen ?   What is said of oxygen as a supporter of combustion ?   Give examples.   What causes the light and heat in combustion ?   Why are they less intense when combustion takes place in the air ?

with other substances. So vehement is this action that fire is produced, and hence oxygen is the great supporter of combustion. All substances which burn in the air, burn in pure oxygen gas with greatly increased brilliancy. An extinguished candle plunged into it is instantly relighted if the least spark of fire remain upon the wick. Iron wire burns in it with vivid scintillations, and phosphorus with a light so brilliant that the eyes cannot endure it. In all these cases the light and heat are produced by the chemical union of the oxygen with the burning body, the weight of which is increased exactly in proportion to the amount of oxygen consumed. All the common cases of combustion which take place in the air are due to the same cause—the combination of its oxygen with combustible substances. It here proceeds in a more subdued and regulated way, because atmospheric oxygen is diluted with four times its bulk of another gas, which if taken alone extinguishes fire altogether.

75. *Illumination.*—Two conditions are necessary for illumination: a sufficiently high temperature, and the presence of solid matter within the heated space. Neither of these conditions alone answers the purpose. The burning of pure oxygen and hydrogen gases together produces intense heat, but is without sufficient light to be even visible in the daytime; and a fire of charcoal which contains no gas, also yields very little light. But if solid carbon be placed within the oxy-hydrogen flame, a brilliant illumination at once ensues. The elements of oil, tallow, wood, &c., with which oxygen unites in ordinary burning are chiefly hydrogen and carbon, the hydrogen it burns to water (90), and the carbon to carbonic acid (167), both escaping away into the atmosphere.

What two conditions are essential for illumination? What is said of the burning of hydrogen and charcoal? How can the oxy-hydrogen flame be made to give a brilliant light? In the ordinary burning of oil, &c., what takes place?

76. The affinity of oxygen for hydrogen is superior to its affinity for carbon. It therefore seizes upon the hydrogen first, where it is present in sufficient quantity, burning it with the production of intense heat. The solid carbon is at the same time set free, and its particles being heated to a luminous whiteness, produce the light which is emitted from the flame. The luminous particles of carbon, floating forward as they are liberated to the surface of the flame, come in contact with atmospheric oxygen, and are there consumed. When the burning body contains both elements, but a disproportionate amount of carbon, as in spirits of turpentine, more of it is set free than can be consumed by the oxygen, and the flame smokes. When the hydrogen is in excess, as with alcohol, there is much heat, but little light, and no smoke; when mingled, these liquids correct each other's defects, and form the basis of "burning mixtures."

77. *Structure of Flame.*—Common flame is not, as it appears, a solid cone of fire, but a hollow luminous shell, as is shown by holding a piece of metallic wire gauze over the flame of a common lamp, Fig. 8.

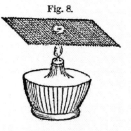

Fig. 8.

In the centre there appears a dark space, surrounded by a ring of light. This dark central portion is constantly filled with gases, formed from the tallow or oil by heat, in precisely the same manner that they are distilled from coal and resin by the gas-manufacturer. The inclosed gases generated at *b*, Fig. 9, cannot, of course, be burned up until they pass to the surface of

---

Why is the hydrogen burned first? What produces the light? When will flame smoke? When will the light be deficient? How are burning mixtures formed?

How is common flame shown to be hollow? What is contained in this hollow space? What is said of the argand lamp? Why is the flame pointed?

the flame at *a*, for want of oxygen. In argand lamps the wick is circular and hollow, and a stream of air is admitted to the interior of the flame, which thus has a double burning surface. A tall glass chimney is placed over the flame, which secures a strong upward current, and hence an abundant supply of oxygen to the flame. The conical or pointed form of the flame is caused by the rising currents of heated air.

Fig. 9.

78. Despritz has shown that the heat evolved in all common cases of combustion, depends upon the quantity of oxygen consumed, and not upon the amount of the combustible with which it unites. Thus a pound of oxygen combining with hydrogen, charcoal, and alcohol, gives in each case very nearly the same quantity of heat; each raising 29 pounds of water from the freezing to the boiling point. The amount of heat produced by equal weights of different combustibles, combining with oxygen, he found to be as follows:

1 pound of charcoal . . raised from 32° to 212°, 78 lbs. of water.
" wood holding 20 pr. ct. } of water " " 27 "
" alcohol . . . . " " 68 "
" oil or wax . . . . " " 90 "
" hydrogen . . . . " " 236 "

The quantity of oxygen consumed in these cases varies greatly.

79. *Oxidation at Low Temperatures.*—But the affinity of

Upon what does the heat of combustion depend? What is the example offered ? How much water does 1 lb. of charcoal by union with oxygen raise from the freezing to the boiling point? Of wood holding 20 per cent. of water ? Of alcohol ? Of oil or wax? Of hydrogen ?

Does oxidation take place at low temperatures? Does oxygen ever combine with bodies without the production of sensible heat ? Is the heat produced the same, whether the iron is burned in oxygen gas or rusted in the air?

oxygen is exerted at low temperatures as well as at high ones
its activity never ceases. It exists in a free state throughout
the atmosphere which envelops the globe, and is in constant
contact with all forms of matter; attacking every thing with
which it is not already combined. This slow combustion,
though unaccompanied by light, is always attended with
heat, although it may not be in sufficint quantity to be measured. An ounce of iron rusted in the air, or burnt in
oxygen gas, produces exactly the same amount of heat in
both cases; the difference being, that in the former instance
the heat is developed so slowly as to take years, while in the
latter case the same effect is produced in as many minutes.

80. The cause of decay in vegetable and animal substances is the action of oxygen upon the elements of which they
consist. They are oxidized, or undergo a slow combustion,
called by Liebig *eremacausis,* which breaks them up into
simpler and more permanent compounds. Oxidation is also
the grand process by which air, earth, and sea are cleansed
and purified from innumerable contaminations. Putrid vapors and pestilential effluvia are destroyed by a process of
burning, more slow, indeed, but as really as if it were done
in a furnace. The offensive impurities which constantly pour
into rivers, lakes, and oceans are perpetually oxidized by the
dissolved gas, and the water is thus kept pure and sweet.
This is the reason why waters that have become foul and
putrid by absence of air, are sweetened and purified when
freely exposed to its action.

81. *Relation of Oxygen to Life.*—But the most interesting
relations of oxygen are to the animal kingdom. It is the
universal supporter of respiration; and, as this is a vital process, it is a supporter of life. The lungs of land animals

(565) and the gills of fish (559) are both adapted to the same purpose—to absorb oxygen; the one from the air, the other from water. An animal confined in a given bulk of air, having consumed its oxygen, dies. If confined in the same bulk of free oxygen, it lives about thrice as long, and more than ten times as fast. A mouse placed in a jar of oxygen breathes very quick, becomes highly excited, and springs about with the greatest activity. But the effect is too powerful: over-action, fever, and in a short time death, are the result.

82. The chemical action that here takes place is simple oxidation, the same that occurs in the open combustion of fuel, except in a less intense degree. The oxygen combines with the elements of the body, oxidizing or burning them, and the products of the combustion pass from the system by the various channels. Its action upon the living system is the same as upon dead matter, purely destructive. It enters the lungs, is absorbed by the blood, and carried to every part where blood-vessels are to be found. Every organ, tissue, muscle, nerve, and membrane is wasted away, burnt to poisonous gases and ashes, and thrown from the system as dead and useless matter; and if these constant losses are not repaired by the due supply of food, emaciation ensues. The fat being most combustible, is burnt first; the muscles then soften, shrink, and decay; and lastly, the brain is attacked, delirium results, and life ceases. This is called starvation: it is oxidation, absolute burning to death.

83. Such is the relation of oxygen to all the animal races which inhabit the earth. Its action is essentially and always

How is oxygen related to the animal kingdom? If an animal is confined in a given bulk of air, what results? If in the same bulk of oxygen gas, what ensues? Describe the effects of placing a mouse in a jar of oxygen.

What is the nature of the action of oxygen in this case? How does it affect the system? If food be not taken to repair the waste, what follows? What, then, is starvation?

destructive ; and yet it is the sustainer of life—the mainspring of all vital activity. But if this agent enshrouds the globe, and its office be thus only to burn and destroy, it may be asked why it does not speedily reduce all combustible things to ashes, and the earth to desolation. This question will be more properly answered when we come to the chemistry of light and vegetation (337).

84. *Oxidation a Source of Mechanical Power.*—The chemical properties of oxygen are a source of power, which is made use of to produce the greatest mechanical effects. When we say that the affinities of oxygen are energetic, it is meant that, in combining with bodies, it gives rise to vast force. A bushel of coals properly consumed in a steam-engine, produces a power sufficient to raise 70 millions of pounds weight a foot high (J. HERSCHEL). The origin of this prodigious force is the chemical union of almost 200 pounds of oxygen with the carbon of the coal. Oxidation, or the affinity of oxygen for the elements of fuel, is thus the ultimate source of all steam power. Electric currents and the force of electro-magnetism are caused by the combination of oxygen with the metals of the galvanic battery ; and in proportion to the activity of this chemical action is the intensity of the effect. In like manner, all muscular force in animals is produced by the oxidation of carbon and hydrogen within the living system (582). Every stroke of the piston—every telegraphic transmission—every motion of the hand—is an exhibition of force which began in chemical changes. Cut off the supply of oxygen, and the steam-engine comes to rest, the galvanic battery ceases to act, and the animal dies.

Are the chemical properties of oxygen a source of power ? How much power is produced by the combustion of a bushel of coals? What is the origin of this force ? What, then, is the ultimate source of all steam-power ? To what are the forces of electricity and electro-magnetism owing ? To what is muscular force also due ? Remove the oxygen, and what follows?

HYDROGEN.

Symbol H, equivalent 1.

85. *Properties.*—Hydrogen is a transparent, tasteless gas, the lightest of all known substances, having about $\frac{1}{14}$th the weight of common air. When pure it is devoid of smell, although, as commonly prepared, it contains impurities, which give to it a disagreeable odor. Hydrogen is never found free in nature, but exists in water, constituting $\frac{1}{9}$th of its weight. It is an essential constituent of all organized substances, vegetable and animal, and is abundantly supplied to plants in water, which they possess the power of decomposing. From its extreme lightness, hydrogen is better fitted than any other substance to inflate balloons, though for this purpose coal-gas, from its greater cheapness, is generally used.

86. *Preparation.*—It is best prepared by the action of dilute sulphuric acid upon bits of zinc. These are placed in a bottle, Fig. 10, to which a cork is tightly fitted. The cork has two tubes inserted. The one for admitting the acid dips beneath the water; the other leads to a pneumatic trough, where the gas is collected in tumblers or jars, in the same manner as oxygen (71). In this case the zinc decomposes the water, and unites with its oxygen, while the hydrogen is set free and escapes. The sulphuric acid dissolves the oxide of zinc as fast as it is formed—thus maintaining a clear metallic surface con-

Fig. 10.

tinually in contact with the water. The diagram exhibits these changes. The portions first collected are not to be used,

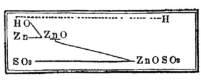

as when mixed with air, hydrogen gas is always explosive. Hydrogen is also obtained by passing vapor of water (steam) through a red-hot gun-barrel, when the oxygen unites with the iron, and the hydrogen is set free. In the same manner, when a blacksmith sprinkles water upon his forge-fire, the red-hot coals decompose it, forming carbonic acid with its oxygen, while the liberated hydrogen burns with the production of increased heat (88).

87. From its extreme tenuity, hydrogen passes through crevices and pores with greater facility than any other substance. Dr. Faraday, in his attempts to liquefy it by pressure, found that it would leak and escape through apertures that were quite tight to other gases; its atoms must therefore be comparatively much smaller. A bell rung in hydrogen is scarcely audible, and when breathed (which, without precaution, is a dangerous experiment) the voice becomes remarkably shrill. Although a gas, and the lightest of all bodies, hydrogen is inferred, from its chemical relationships, to be a metal. Its gaseous form is no objection to this idea, as metallic mercury takes the form of invisible vapor at common temperatures, and other metals may be vaporized by heat.

88. A burning body plunged into hydrogen is extinguished; it is, therefore, a non-supporter of combustion; but, in contact with oxygen, it burns, emits a feeble blue light, and produces an intense degree of heat. The oxy-hydrogen

What was the result of Dr. Faraday's attempts to liquefy hydrogen? What does this prove? Why is hydrogen gas inferred to be a metal?

Does it support combustion? What is said of the oxy-hydrogen blow-pipe? How

blow-pipe is a contrivance for mingling a continuous stream of these gases in an inflamed jet; the light produced by this flame is faint, but the heat is very great. Substances that do not fuse in the hottest blast-furnaces melt in this heat like wax. A small bit of lime of the size of a pea placed within the oxy-hydrogen jet glows with extraordinary intensity (75), producing what is called the Drummond light. This is the light made use of, as a substitute for the sun's rays, in the solar microscope; it is also employed in coast surveys for night-signals. In one case the light emitted by the ball o lime was distinctly visible at a distance of 96 miles (*D. B. Reid*). The heating power of the oxy-hydrogen flame is ac-counted for by the fact that it is solid, and not hollow like ordinary flame (77), and also that a larger amount of oxygen is condensed by union with hydrogen than with any other element (78).

89. Soap-bubbles blown with hydrogen rise in the air, and may be set on fire with a candle. With a mixture of three parts air and one of hydrogen, when fired, they explode with a loud report; if two parts of hydrogen is mixed with one of pure oxygen, the explosion is very violent and deafening.

90. The term hydrogen signifies *water-former*. If a jet of hydrogen be set fire to, and a cold dry tumbler be held over the flame, the inside of the glass will be instantly covered with a film of dew, which rapidly increases, and at last con-denses into drops of water. In all cases where hydrogen is burned with oxygen, water is the product.

Is the Drummond light produced? For what is it used? How far has it been seen? How is the heating power of the oxy-hydrogen flame accounted for?

In what condition does hydrogen explode?

What is the meaning of the term hydrogen? Describe the experiment with the tumbler.

OXYGEN AND HYDROGEN—WATER.

H O = 9

91. *Properties.*—This substance, though familiar to all possesses very remarkable properties, and should be carefully studied. Water is composed of the two gases, oxygen and hydrogen, in the proportion by weight of 8 parts oxygen to one part hydrogen; or by measure, 1 part oxygen to 2 of hydrogen. When pure, it is a tasteless, inodorous liquid; colorless in small quantities, but in large quantities of a splendid ultramarine blue, as when it forms lakes from the melting of Alpine glaciers, and as seen by Parry in the polar regions. It is the most abundant and widely diffused of all chemical compounds. It readily assumes either the solid, liquid, or vaporous state; and with equal facility becomes sweet, sour, salt, astringent, bitter, nauseous, or poisonous, as the substances which it dissolves possess any of these properties. The importance of water, both in the laboratory of the chemist and of Nature, is due to this universal solvent power.

92. *Hydrates.*—Water unites with acids and bases, forming a class of compounds called *hydrates.* These combinations are often attended with heat; water combining with lime develops sufficient heat to ignite wood. Ships at sea have been fired by the accidental wetting of lime in their holds. This heat is caused by the passage of the water from a liquid to a solid state.

93. *The Water-Atmosphere.*—All natural water contains dissolved a certain amount of various gases, which may be expelled by boiling. It then has an insipid, disagreeable

Why should water be carefully studied? Of what is it composed? In what proportions? What is its color? What is said of its solvent power?

What are hydrates? What is said of the heat produced by these combinations? How is it caused? What is said to be dissolved in all natural waters? What is

taste ; but upon being exposed to the air a sufficient length
of time, the gases are redissolved, and the water regains its
palatable flavor. Oxygen gas is thus absorbed to the extent of about four per cent., and the respiratory apparatus
of fish (branchea, or gills) is so arranged (559) that a current of water is constantly flowing in contact with a network
of delicate vascular membranes, by which the gas is im-
bibed : hence, strictly speaking, aquatic as well as land animals breathe air. On the summits of high mountains, where
the air is rarer and more attenuated, less oxygen is absorbed,
and hence the lakes in the mountainous valleys of Switzerland and the Andes are destitute of fish.—(*Brande.*)

94. A small quantity of air dissolved in water greatly
diminishes its power of dissolving other gases. If water,
already saturated with one gas, be exposed to another, the
second is absorbed only in proportion as the first escapes.
The proportion of different gases taken up by pure water is
very variable. Of ammonia it absorbs 780 times its bulk,
of hydrochloric acid gas 480, and of carbonic acid an
amount only equal to its own volume. Of olefiant gas it
dissolves 12·5 per cent., and of nitrogen and hydrogen but
1·6 per cent. of its volume.

95. *Constituents of Common Water.*—Water which has
fallen from the clouds as rain, in the country, away from
cities and large towns, is the purest we meet with, being
contaminated only with the gases which exist in air. But
when filtering through the soil and crevices of the rocky
strata, it dissolves various earthy salts, which, in many
cases, modify its properties very much. River and creek

the effect of boiling? How much oxygen gas does water contain? Do fish breathe
this gas? Why are lakes on high mountains destitute of fish? When water contains one gas and absorbs another, what takes place?

What is the purest water? How does it become impure? What water contains
most of these salts?

waters usually contain the least of these salts, spring and
well water more, and sea-water and mineral waters the
largest quantity.

96. *Hard Water.*—Water derives its quality of hardness
from the presence of these substances, chiefly salts of lime
(the carbonate and sulphate). A single grain of sulphate
of lime will convert 2000 grains of soft into hard water.
When common soap is put into hard water, instead of dissolving in it as it does in soft water, it curdles, or is decomposed,
and a new soap is formed, which contains lime instead of potash or soda. This new soap will not dissolve, and may often
be seen upon the surface in the form of a greasy scum. It
adheres to whatever is washed in it, and gives that unpleasant
sensation called hardness when we wash our hands. To test
this quality of water, dissolve a little soap in alcohol, and place
a few drops of it in the water which it is wished to examine.
If it remains clear, the water is perfectly soft; if it becomes
muddy or opaque, the water is ranked as hard.

97. *Hard Water for Kitchen Use.*—Hard water is a much
less perfect solvent than soft water; that is, being already
partially saturated, it dissolves additional substances but imperfectly. It is therefore inferior to it for all domestic uses,
as tea and coffee making, where solution is to be effected.

98. *Its Effects as a Drink.*—The use of hard water as a
drink is unfavorable in dyspeptic affections.—(*Pereira.*) The
bad effects of hard water upon the animal system are also
seen in the horse. "Hard water drawn fresh from the well
will assuredly make the coat of a horse unaccustomed to it
stare, and it will not unfrequently gripe and otherwise injure him."—(*Youatt.*)

_____

To what does water owe its hardness? What is the effect when soap is put into
hard water? How may we test this quality?
Why is hard water inferior to soft for domestic purposes?

99. *Sea-Water.*—The solid constituents of sea-water amount to about $3\frac{1}{2}$ per cent. of its weight, or nearly half an ounce to the pound. Its saltness may be considered as a necessary result of the present order of things. Rivers which are constantly flowing into the ocean contain salts varying in amount from 10 to 50 and even 100 grains per gallon. They are chiefly common salt, sulphate and carbonate of lime, magnesia, soda, potash, and iron; and these are found to be the main constituents of sea-water. The water which evaporates from the sea is nearly pure, containing but very minute traces of salts. Falling as rain upon the land it washes the soil, percolates through the rocky layers, and becomes charged with saline substances which are borne seaward by the returning currents. The ocean, therefore, is the great depository of every thing that water can dissolve and carry down from the surface of the continents; and as there is no channel for their escape, they of course constantly accumulate.

100. The continuance of this process for numberless ages must inevitably have produced a highly saline condition of the ocean. "The case of the sea is but a magnified representation of what occurs in every lake into which rivers flow, but from which there is no outlet except by evaporation. Such a lake is invariably a salt lake. It is impossible that it can be otherwise; and it is curious to observe that this condition disappears when an artificial outlet is produced for the waters."—(*Fownes.*)

101. *The waters of the Dead Sea* are much more salt than those of the ocean. It is situated at the bottom of an

What proportion of solid matter is contained in sea-water? From whence is it derived? What are these salts chiefly? Why do these salts accumulate in the sea? What is the condition of lakes that have no outlet but by evaporation? What is the effect of creating an artificial outlet?

What is said of the Dead Sea?

immense basin or valley several hundred feet low. ᾽ the Mediterranean Sea, and has no outlet. The stream of water which flow into it do not raise its level, in consequence of excessive evaporation. Its condition is well described by a recent traveller. "When bathing in its waters I floated upon the surface like a log of wood, without stirring hand or foot. With much exertion I could dive sufficiently deep to cover all my body, when I was thrown out again to the surface, in spite of all my efforts to descend lower. On coming out of the water, I found my body covered over with an incrustation of salt the thickness of a sixpence."

102. *Mineral Waters.*—These are such as contain saline substances in the largest proportion. Those which abound in the salts of iron (carbonates and sulphates of iron) are called *chalybeate* or *ferruginous* waters. If the waters are brisk and sparkling, carbonic acid gas is present, and they are called *carbonated* or *acidulous* waters. If the active ingredient be sulphur, the spring is termed *sulphurous*. If the odor of decayed eggs, or the scourings of a foul gun-barrel is exhaled, the waters are charged with sulphuretted hydrogen. The water of the celebrated Congress Spring, at Saratoga, contains, according to Allen's analysis, the following ingredients in a gallon :

Chloride of sodium	390,246 grs.
Hydriodate of soda and bromide of potassium	6,000 "
Carbonate of soda	9,213 "
Carbonate of magnesia	100,941 "
Carbonate of lime	103,418 "
Carbonate of iron	1,000 "
Silex and alumina	1,036 "
Total solid contents	611,852 grs.

What are chalybeate waters? What are acidulous? What sulphurous? What are the main constituents of Congress water?

Carbonic acid............ ....386,188 grs.

Atmospheric air............................... .. 3,261 "

Total gaseous contents................. 389,449 grs

103. *Organic Impurities in Water.*—All natural waters, even those which fall from the clouds according to Liebig, contain traces of decomposing organic matters in variable quantity. To this they owe the quality of becoming putrid when kept. In many cases, it is present in such quantity as to injure health, derange the bowels, and often produce violent dysentery. Stagnant waters, abounding in putrescent matter, contain numberless minute animals (*animalcula*), which are sometimes exhibited by means of the solar microscope; they are not found in the waters commonly used for drink.

104. *Purification of Water.*—The best method of purifying water is by *distillation* (64). This is effected by passing the steam from one vessel into another, which, being kept cool, condenses it: to render it perfectly pure, it must be redistilled at a low temperature in silver vessels. By filtration through sand, or other closely porous media, water may be deprived of suspended impurities, and of all living beings. Boiling kills all animals and vegetables, expels the gases, and precipitates carbonate of lime, which constitutes the fur or crust often seen lining tea-kettles and boilers. Alum (two or three grains to the quart) cleanses turbid or muddy water. The alum is decomposed by carbonate of lime, and the alumina set free, carries down the impurities mechanically; but the sulphuric acid of the alum, combining with the lime, forms sulphate of lime, and makes the water harder than

What is said of the organic matters contained in water? Does common drinking water contain animalcula?

How is water best purified? What is the effect of filtration? Of boiling? Of alum? Of the alkalies potash and soda?

before. The alkalies, potash or soda, soften water. They decompose and precipitate the earthy salts, leaving in solution an alkaline salt, which does not harden it.

105. *Effect of Leaden Vessels upon Water.*—Water sometimes becomes poisonous by contact with lead, as when lead pipes, cisterns, roofs, gutters, &c., are used. The purer the water, the more liable it is to become impregnated with lead, as the presence of earthy salts in solution exerts a protecting influence. Spring and well waters are, therefore, less liable to this contamination than rain-water, which is purer. Water which tarnishes polished lead, when left at rest upon it in a glass vessel for a few hours, or which contains less than about $\frac{1}{8000}$th its weight of salts in solution, cannot be safely transmitted through lead pipes without certain precautions. The best remedy, where there is danger, is to leave the pipes full of water at rest for three or four months, or to substitute for the water a weak solution of phosphate of soda.—(*Christison.*)

106. *Necessity of Water to Organized Beings.*—To the organic kingdom water is an agent of the first necessity, as its abundance and scarcity regulate the distribution of animals and plants over the globe. Its properties seem to mark out the plan of animated nature. From the highest animal, to the meanest vegetable that can grow on a bare rock, this ingredient is absolutely required. It is an essential constituent of all parts of living bodies, forming upwards of one-half the weight of all newly gathered vegetable substances cultivated by man.

Is pure or impure water most liable to become poisoned by contact with lead? How can we determine whether lead will be acted on by water? What is the best remedy where there is danger?

What is said of the importance of water to the organic kingdom?

In what two states does water exist in organic bodies?

What is the office of water in the growth of plants? What is the proportion of water in blood? In flesh?

107. Water exists in most organized bodies in two separate states. In one it may be regarded as an essential portion of the substance, as of sugar or starch in their dryest state (349), from which it cannot be separated without breaking up the compound. In the other state, it is associated with bodies so loosely that it may be removed by drying. The quantity that may be thus separated from various articles of diet, without injury to the compound, is as follows: Wheat 14·5 per cent., rye 16·6, oats 20·8, barley 13·2, Indian corn 18, peas 16, beans 14·11, potatoes 75·9, turnips 92·5, carrots 87·6, beet-root 87·8, white cabbage 92·3, blood 80, muscle of beef 74, of veal 75, of mutton 71, of pork 76, of chicken 73, trout 80·5 per cent.—(*Pereira.*)

108. Both gases and the mineral elements of soils enter the roots of plants dissolved in water. As sap, this water circulates through the various organs, carrying and depositing the newly formed substances, yielding up its own elements, and ministering perpetually to the growth of the plant.

109. In animal systems the use of water is equally important (495). It is the natural drink of- all adults, being the liquid employed in the body to dissolve and distribute the food. Eighty per cent. of the blood (*Liebig*) and seventy-four per cent. of flesh (*Brande*) consist of water; while, to repair the constant waste and loss from the system, an adult man requires about three-fourths of a ton per year (*Draper*). The softness, pliancy, and symmetrical fulness of the animal body, is produced by the liquids of which it is chiefly composed. The tendency of flesh or fresh meat to putrefaction, is caused by the large quantity of watery

How much does a man consume annually? What gives symmetry and fulness to the animal form? How does water cause putrefaction in flesh? How is it checked?

juices it contains. As solution favors chemical action (29), putrefactive changes readily set in; but are checked if the flesh be dried, as is-often done for the preservation of meats.

110. Under ordinary circumstances, water freezes at 32°, and boils at 212°; it retains its liquid condition, therefore, through a range of 180°; and, as in this state only it can exist in animals and plants, these limits mark the thermal conditions upon which living beings can continue on the earth.

111. A cubic inch of water forms very nearly a cubic foot of steam. Water occupies the smallest space, or is most dense at 39.83° F.; if its temperature varies from this point, in either direction, it expands in bulk; this is called the point of maximum density of water. In freezing, water expands very much, and exerts so great a force as to burst the strongest vessels in which it is contained. It is thus that the surface of the hardest rocks is crumbled down into soil fit for the support of vegetable life; the water, percolating into minute crevices and fissures in summer, freezes in winter, and expands with a force which breaks the solid stone.

112. Snow does not quench thirst, but rather increases it; and the natives of the arctic regions "prefer enduring the utmost extremity of this feeling, rather than attempt to remove it by the eating of snow."—(*Capt. Ross.*)

113. The specific gravity of ice is 0.92 (*Silliman*); it therefore floats upon the surface of water. If it sank as fast as it is formed, whole bodies of water would be con-

Within what limits does water maintain its humidity ? What relation has this property of water to life ?

A cubic inch of water forms how much steam? At what temperature is it most dense ? Does water expand in freezing? At what temperature is it most dense ? How does this property of water affect rocks ?

What is the specific gravity of ice? If it were heavier than water, what would

verted into solid ice. During freezing the substances dissolved in water are expelled, hence the ice of sea-water (as is well known to sailors), when melted, forms fresh-water. Water from melted snow, for the same reason, contains no air or gas; hence fish cannot live in it (*Pereira*). One imperial gallon of water weighs 70,000 grains, or just ten pounds. The American standard gallon holds 58,372 American Troy grains of pure distilled water, at the maximum density. One cubic inch weighs 252·458 grains, which is 815 times as much as an equal bulk of atmospheric air (*Silliman*). A cubic foot of water weighs very nearly 1000 ounces avoirdupois (998 2 oz. *Brande*).

DEUTOXIDE OF HYDROGEN.

$$H\ O_2 = 17.$$

114. This curious compound is formed by chemists, with difficulty, by adding to water another equivalent of oxygen. It is a syrupy liquid, of a disagreeable odor, a nauseous, bitter, astringent taste, and is not frozen by intense cold. It is easily decomposed, often with an explosion, and sometimes with a flash of light. As yet, it is of no use.

NITROGEN (*Azote*)

Symbol N, equivalent 14.

115. *Properties and Sources.*—Nitrogen is a permanently elastic gas, destitute of either taste, smell, or color; slightly lighter than the air, and remarkable for its negative

---

be the result? What is said of the ice of sea-water? Of water from melted snow? What is the weight of a gallon of water? Of a cubic inch? A cubic foot? What is the composition of deutoxide of hydrogen? Its properties? Uses?

properties, entering reluctantly into union, and, from its proneness to escape, forming very unstable compounds. It supports neither combustion nor respiration; a lighted taper introduced into it is instantly quenched, and animals placed within it immediately die. It  has from the latter circumstance been called azote (life-destroyer). The term nitrogen refers to its origin from nitre. It constitutes nearly four-fifths of the air (see Chart). It is best obtained by burning phosphorus in a confined portion of air over water (Fig. 11); the phosphorus takes the oxygen forming phos-

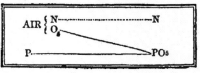

phoric acid, which is soon removed by the water, and nitrogen is left. The accompanying diagram illustrates the change.

116. Nitrogen is not found in any of the mineral formations of the earth's crust, except in some varieties of coal which are of vegetable origin. It is an important element of the vegetable kingdom, to which it is probably supplied by ammonia and nitric acid, which contain it, and exert a very favorable effect upon plants (123). It exists in the tissues or muscle of the animal body to the amount of 17 per cent. Whether plants derive their nitrogen directly from the air through their leaves, or dissolved in water through their roots, and whether the animal system has the power of using or assimilating it when absorbed from the air by the lungs, are questions not yet settled by chemists.

What are the properties of nitrogen?   Why has it been called azote?   What was the origin of its present name? · How is it best obtained?
Is it found in minerals?   How is it supplied to vegetables?

OXYGEN AND NITROGEN.—NITROUS OXIDE.

(Protoxide of Nitrogen, Laughing Gas, Exhilarating Gas.)

$$N O = 22.$$

117 *Properties and Preparation.*—Oxygen combines with nitrogen to form a series of five compounds (see Chart, Binary Compounds), remarkable as illustrating in a perfect manner the law of multiple combination (21). The first in the series is protoxide of nitrogen or nitrous oxide, called also, from its peculiar effects when inspired, laughing gas, or exhilarating gas. It is prepared from nitrate of ammonia, by heating it in a flask, at a moderately low temperature. The gas escapes through a tube, and is collected in jars, over water in the pneumatic trough. Four ounces of the salt produce one cubic foot of the gas. It should be allowed to stand for some time over water, to absorb any nitrous acid that may happen to be formed The change that takes place is shown in the diagram, one atom of nitrate of ammonia yielding two atoms of protoxide of nitrogen and three of water. Protoxide of nitrogen is a
colorless, transparent gas, of a sweetish taste, and very soluble in water; cold water taking up about three-fourths of its volume of the gas. Its specific gravity is 1·52 ; it supports combustion actively, and may be condensed into a liquid by a pressure equal to fifty atmospheres.

118. *Physiological Effects.*—The effect of nitrous oxide upon the system, when taken into the lungs, is peculiar, and

very remarkable. The best method of breathing it is to use a bladder which has been softened in water, or an India-rubber bag filled from the pneumatic trough. A wooden mouth-piece attached to the bladder is placed between the teeth (Fig. 12), the nostrils are closed by the fore-finger and thumb, and the gas inhaled as in common breathing. Its effects are different upon different constitutions: on some it produces symptoms of stupor, which last for a few seconds. Some fall senseless, but recover with confused ideas and headache. The pugnacity of some is excited; all articles which are liable to injury from the violence of the inhaler should therefore be removed. But the most are affected with pleasurable sensations—they laugh and skip about as if intoxicated. "A feverish glow overspreads the system, a thousand delightful visions pass before the mind, the man lives a year in a minute, and that year is in the seventh heavens."

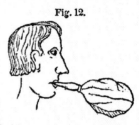

Fig. 12.

119. The celebrated Mr. Wedgwood, "after breathing the gas for some time, threw the bag from him, and kept breathing on laboriously with an open mouth, holding his nose with his fingers, without power to remove them, although aware of the ludicrousness of his situation; he had a violent inclination to jump over the chairs and tables, and seemed so light that he thought he was going to fly."

120. *Mode in which Nitrous Oxide acts upon the System.*—"These effects are undoubtedly due to the oxidizing

---

Does it produce peculiar effects upon the system? What is the best method of breathing it? What effect does it produce upon different constitutions?

What does Mr. Wedgwood say of its effects upon himself?

To what are these effects owing? Why is it more active when breathed than oxygen?

action which the protoxide establishes in the system In this respect it is far more active than even pure oxygen gas, and the reason is obvious : oxygen is but slightly absorbed by watery fluids, but this gas is taken up by them to a very great extent. When it is introduced into the lungs it is rapidly dissolved in the blood, and carried by the circulation to every part of the body, oxidizing whatever is in its path, producing a febrile warmth and an unusual mental disturbance."—(*Draper.*)

121. *Deutoxide of nitrogen*, $N\acute{O}_2$, *hyponitrous acid*, NO_3, and *nitrous acid*, NO_4, are compounds of no general interest, except as illustrating the laws of chemical union; I therefore omit them.

NITRIC ACID (*Azotic Acid, Aqua Fortis*).

$$NO_5 = 54.$$

122. *Preparation and Uses.*—This is the most important of the chemical compounds of oxygen and nitrogen. It is prepared by distilling equal weights of sulphuric acid and nitrate of potash; when on a large scale, retorts of iron or stone-ware are used. The reactions are seen in the diagram. Pure

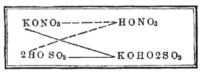

nitric acid is a colorless liquid, of sp. gr. 1·521. It smokes when exposed to the air, and is partially decomposed by the action of light, nitrous acid being formed, which gives it a yellow or orange color. It has an intensely acid taste, and reddens vegetable blues. It stains the skin and nails, and many other animal substances, of a permanent yellow color;

How is nitric acid prepared? Explain the reactions which take place. What are its properties? What its chief uses? Why does it rust the metals so powerfully?

and is hence used to produce yellow patterns upon colored woollen fabrics. It is used for etching on copper, for assaying or testing.metals, and as a solvent for tin by dyers and calico-printers. It is also used in medicine, as a caustic, to cleanse and purify foul ulcers. In consequence of its large proportion of oxygen, it corrodes or rusts the metals with great energy, and hence is the most powerful of oxidizing agents.

123. Nitric acid occurs, in small quantity in rain-water, especially after thunder-storms, and is hence supposed by some to be produced in the air by lightning, which combines the gaseous nitrogen and oxygen ; others suppose it to be produced by the oxidation of ammonia in the air. It is found in nature in combination with the alkalies and earths, in the soil of various localities. Combined with potash or soda, nitric acid is a very valuable fertilizer. Applied to young grass, or to the sprouting shoots of grain, it hastens and increases their growth. It also occasions a larger produce of grain, and this grain, as when ammonia is employed, is richer in gluten, and more nutritious in its quality.—(*Johnston.*)

124. *Aqua Regia.*—A mixture of nitric and muriatic acids is called *aqua regia,* or *royal water,* because it alone is capable of dissolving the royal or noble metals, as they are termed, gold, platinum, &c. The explosive preparation contained in percussion caps (fulminating mercury) is formed by dissolving mercury in nitric acid and adding alcohol.

From what source is it thought to be furnished to rain-water ? What is said of its use in agriculture ?

What is aqua regia ? Whence does it derive its name ? How is the explosive preparation of percussion caps formed ?

NITROGEN AND HYDROGEN—AMMONIA (*Volatile Alkali*).
$H_3 N = 17$.

125. *Properties and Preparation.*—Ammonia is a gas formed by the union of nitrogen and hydrogen. It is colorless, irrespirable, of a pungent, caustic taste, lighter than the air, sp. gr. 0·59, and possesses strong alkaline properties; neutralizing acids, and changing vegetable yellows to brown. Being a gas, it is called *volatile alkali*, to distinguish it from those that are fixed or solid. It is obtained by heating in a flask equal quantities of slaked lime and muriate of ammonia; and as it is lighter than the air, it may be collected, by what is termed the method of *displacement*, in an inverted vessel (Fig. 13). As the gas accumulates in the upper portion of the inverted jar it displaces the air, expelling it downwards. The decomposition is shown in the diagram. The great source of ammonia in commerce is the liquor of the gas-works. Ammonia has a strong affinity for water, which absorbs 780 times its bulk of the gas. This solution is called *aqua ammonia*, and is the common form in which it is sold and used.

Fig. 13.

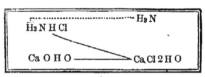

126. *Uses.*—Ammonia is used medicinally in various ways. It is administered internally as a powerful stimulant, and applied externally as a counter-irritant, and for blistering the skin. It is mixed with olive oil (1 part ammo-

What is ammonia? What are its properties? How is it obtained? By what method is it collected? What is its chief commercial source? What proportion of ammonia does water absorb?
What are its uses in medicine?

nia to 2 of oil), and applied externally in sore throat, under the name of volatile liniment. It is applied to the nostrils to recover from fainting, and, if procured in time, is the best antidote to prussic acid. Aqua ammonia, in large doses, is poisonous; the readiest remedy is vinegar.

127. Ammonia is one of the most active elements of manure; it is produced by the putrefaction of all organic substances containing nitrogen, and as it is highly volatile, it constantly tends to escape into the air, where it is lost. The fluid excretions of animals evolve it in large quantities: if these are collected in tanks, and sulphuric acid added, fixed sulphate of ammonia is formed in the liquid, and all the ammonia is thus saved for farm use. Sulphate of lime (plaster) and sulphate of iron (green vitriol) also serve to fix ammonia. Those circumstances of decomposition which give rise to ammonia, produce at the same time carbonic acid, which unites with it, forming carbonate of ammonia. It is in this form that it exists in the atmosphere. The application of ammonia increases the luxuriance of vegetation. It enters the roots of plants dissolved in water, and, according to Liebig, is absorbed by their leaves from the air.

THE ATMOSPHERE.

128. *Its Composition.*—The atmosphere is the thin, transparent, elastic medium which surrounds the globe, extending above its surface to the height of about forty-five miles. It was supposed by the ancients to be a simple body, the different properties which it manifested being caused by ex-

What is said of its use in agriculture? Does it naturally tend to waste? How may it be saved? In what form does it exist in the atmosphere? What are its effects upon plants?

What is the atmosphere? How high does it extend? Of what does it consist? In what proportions?

halations from the ground ; and this opinion prevailed until within about a century. The air is now known to be a compound, consisting, by bulk, of 79 per cent. of nitrogen, and 21 per cent. of oxygen; or by weight, of 77 per cent. of nitrogen, and 23 of oxygen. (See Chart.) It also contains about $\frac{1}{2500}$ its bulk of carbonic acid; and a minute proportion of watery vapor.

129 *Relative Quantities of its Elements.*—A very clear idea of these quantities may be gained, by supposing the air throughout to be of the same density, and its elements separated into strata in the order of their specific gravities. In such a case the air would extend to a height of about five miles.—(*Graham.*) Its greatest quantity of watery vapor, if condensed, would form a stratum of water about five inches deep ; the layer of carbonic acid would be about thirteen feet deep ; that of oxygen about one mile ; and that of nitrogen about four miles in depth.

130. *Constituents and Properties of the Air.*—The chemical properties of the air are chiefly those of the oxygen it contains, this gas being diluted and weakened by four times its bulk of the negative element, nitrogen (115). As atmospheric oxygen is the universal sustainer of animal life (81), its proportion has been admirably adjusted to this object; or rather, the organization of animals may be said to conform to the constitution of the air, because if this were changed, disturbance throughout all the orders of living beings would inevitably ensue. Were the atmosphere wholly composed of nitrogen, life could never have existed, animal

How may we gain a clear idea of the proportion of its elements ?   What would be the thickness of each stratum ?

To what does the air chiefly owe its chemical properties ?   If the proportion of oxygen in the air were changed, what would follow ?   If it were all nitrogen, what would be the result ?   What, were it to consist wholly of oxygen ?

or vegetable: were it wholly to consist of oxygen, other things remaining as they are, the world would run through its career with fearful rapidity; combustion, once excited, would proceed with ungovernable violence; animals would live with hundred-fold intensity, and perish in a few hours. But duly attempered by a large admixture of nitrogen, the grand functions of the animal races, of which it is the mainspring, are carried forward at a measured rate, and within regulated limits.

131. *Carbonic Acid of the Air.*—The proportion of carbonic acid diffused through the air, always minute, varies slightly in different situations. There is less in the air of the country than in that of cities; less over the sea than over the land; less over a moist soil than over a dry one, because it is rapidly absorbed by water. It is furnished to the air by animals, which continually exhale it from their lungs (595). It is produced in vast quantities by combustion, by putrefaction and decay; and it escapes in immense volumes from volcanoes, both active and extinct —(*Fownes.*) On the other hand, it is absorbed by the leaves of all plants, and is necessary to their growth.

132. *Watery Vapor of the Air.*—The atmosphere also contains more or less of watery vapor, which seems to be essential to both animals and plants, as neither of them can live in perfectly dry air. The proportion of moisture in the air depends upon the temperature; the hotter the air, the more it will hold; the cooler, the less: 100 cubic inches of air at 57° contains ·35 of a grain of watery vapor.—(*Brande.*) When the atmosphere is saturated with moisture, that is, contains all it can hold, if its temperature falls, a portion of

---

What is said of the proportion of carbonic acid? From whence is it derived? Does watery vapor in the air perform any useful office? Upon what does its proportion in the air depend? What is the cause of dew?

its water will fall, or be deposited. It is thus cooled at night, which causes the deposit of dew.

133. When two currents of air of different temperatures, saturated with moisture, meet and mingle, the resulting mean temperature falls below the point necessary to hold all the water in a state of vapor; a portion of it, therefore, must fall. This is supposed to be a cause of clouds and rain. Thus southerly winds saturated with humidity, coming in contact with the colder air of northern latitudes, usually give rain. For the same reason, the contact of air in motion with the cold surface of the earth must cause the precipitation of water. This explains the differences in the quantity of rain collected at different elevations in the same place. Thus the annual fall of rain in London, as measured by a rain-gage, was ascertained to be, at a height of 242 feet, 15·9 inches; at 73 feet, 20·4 inches; and upon the ground, 24·4 inches; showing that the air is more cooled near the ground, and, consequently, deposits more rain. The annual fall of rain is greatest at the equator, and diminishes towards the poles. At Granada (lat. 12° north), it falls to the depth of 126 inches; at New York (lat. 40° north), its depth is 40 inches.

134. *Snow-flakes.*—When clouds form, at a temperature below 32°, the vapor freezes into an infinity of delicate needle-like crystals, which deviate from each other at angles of 30°, 60°, or 120°, giving rise to beautiful hexagonal and star-like figures. This is the crystalline structure of the snow-flake, shown in Fig. 14. Snow differs very much in the arrangement of these spiculæ; but the flakes are all of the same configuration in the same storm.

What is the cause of clouds and rain? What is said of the difference in the fall of rain at different elevations? What at different latitudes?

What is the origin of snow-flakes? What their crystalline structure? Have they always the same figure?

Fig. 14.

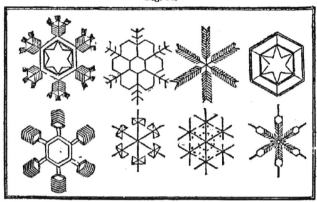

135. *Additional Substances in the Air.*—Liebig has shown that the air also contains minute traces of ammonia, which are washed down, and may be detected in rain-water. Indeed, as the sea contains a little of every thing that is soluble in water (99), so the atmosphere may be conceived to contain a little of every thing that is capable of assuming the gaseous form. The odorous emanations of plants, the miasms of marshes, and principles of contagion, though all producing effects upon the human body, cannot be collected from the air, nor even their presence detected by chemical tests. It is supposed that these substances do not exist in the true gaseous state, but are composed of fixed organized particles, which float about suspended in the atmosphere, like the pollen of flowers. They are all, however, oxidized and destroyed, as the air contains within itself the means of its own purification.

136. *The Law of Gaseous Diffusion.*—The oxygen and

What other substances naturally find their way into the atmosphere ? In what form are many of these substances supposed to exist ?

Is the atmosphere a chemical compound? By what law is the intermixture of the gases regulated ? How is its operation illustrated ?

nitrogen gases, of which the air is chiefly composed, are
not chemically united with each other, but only mixed together mechanically. If we mingle them in a vessel in the
same proportions, we get an artificial air, having the same
properties as the natural air. This uniform intermingling of
the gaseous elements is brought about by what is called the
law of *gaseous diffusion*. Its operation may be thus shown :
two vessels are to be placed one above the other, Fig. 15.
and connected by a narrow tube of any convenient
length (Fig. 15). The lower vessel may be filled
with carbonic acid gas, and the upper vessel with
hydrogen gas. After a short time the carbonic acid,
although twenty times heavier than the hydrogen,
will be found to have ascended into the upper vessel; while hydrogen will have descended into the
lower one,—a complete intermixture of the two gases
in equal proportions having taken place against the action
of gravity.

137. This effect will be produced even though a barrier,
as a membrane of India-rubber, intervene. The force with
which gases thus diffuse into each other is very great.
Dr. Draper has proved that sulphuretted hydrogen will diffuse into atmospheric air, though resisted by a pressure of
fifty atmospheres, equal to the weight of a column of water
more than 1500 feet in height. In like manner, all gases
possess the power of diffusing into each other, although at
different rates of velocity, depending upon their density :
the lighter the gas, the more rapid is the diffusion.

138. This principle is of the utmost importance in relation to the air, because if either of its constituent elements
were to separate from the mass, the extinction of life would

What is said of the force with which gases diffuse into each other ?
Why is this principle of the greatest importance ?

follow. Dr. D. B. Reed assumes that the exhalations from the lungs and skin of a single human body vitiate, or spoil for breathing, ten cubic feet of air per minute, or about 90,000 gallons per day. This foul air, with that formed by innumerable other sources of contamination, is perpetually removed by diffusion, and the atmosphere is thus preserved respirable and pure.

139. *Relations of the Atmosphere to the Living World.*—But it is in its relations to living beings that the atmosphere appears of the highest interest. The vegetable world is derived from the air. It consists of condensed gases that have been reduced from the atmosphere to the solid form, through the agency of the sun's light (329.) On the other hand, animals which derive all the material of their structure from plants, destroy these substances while living, by respiration, and when dead, by putrefaction ; thus returning them again, in the gaseous form, to the air from whence they came. In respect to air, the offices of plants and animals antagonize. What the former derives from the air, the latter restores to it. It is the great link between the two worlds of organization. From the atmosphere all living beings came, and to it they must all return. " It is the cradle of vegetable and the coffin of animal life." We shall study this matter further in Organic Chemistry.

140. *Weight of the Air.*—A column of air one inch square, and extending upward to the limit of the atmosphere, weighs about fifteen pounds; it therefore exerts a pressure on every square inch (at the level of the sea) equal to this weight; but as we pass upward the air expands, becoming more thin

From whence is the vegetable world derived ? What does it consist of? What is said of animals ? What, then, is the relation of plants and animals ?

What is the weight of a column of air, one inch high, extending to the top of the atmosphere ? What do we find as we pass upward? How far must a gal

and light as the elevation increases. A gallon of air, removed from the ground to the height of 11,556 feet, would expand into two (*Brande*); at twice this height its density would be again diminished one-half, and so on. This rarefaction increases so rapidly, that a cubic inch of air at the surface of the earth, if raised to a height of 500 miles, would expand so as to fill a space equal in diameter to the orbit of Saturn.

141. *Curve of Congelation.*—The temperature of the air decreases one degree for every 350 feet of elevation; there is, therefore, over all places, and at all seasons, an altitude at which it falls to the freezing point. At the equator this point is located 15,000 feet above the level of the sea. At latitude 40° it is 9000 feet, at 75° 1000, while at the poles it sinks into the ground. This forms what is called the line or curve of perpetual congelation. Air expands $\frac{1}{480}$ of its bulk for every degree of temperature through which it rises. One hundred cubic inches of pure air weigh 30·829 grains.— (*Regnault.*) Air, assumed as 1, is taken as the standard of the specific gravity of gases—temperature 60°, barometer 30 inches.

(For an account of the physical properties of air, the pupil is referred to the Natural Philosophy.)

CHLORINE.

Symbol Cl, *equivalent* 35·5.

142. *Source and Preparation.*—Chlorine is a gas of a greenish color, as its name implies, and is about two and a half times heavier than air. It supports combustion, though

lon of air be taken upward from the ground to double its bulk ? What is said of the expansion of a cubic inch of air?

In what ratio does the temperature of the air decrease as we ascend ? What is meant by the curve of perpetual congelation ? What is its height at the equator ? At lat. 40° ? What is the rate of expansion of air as we ascend ?

less perfectly than oxygen, and combines directly with the metals, forming a class of bodies called chlorides. It is found abundantly in nature, existing in common salt to the amount of 65 per cent. in union with sodium. Chlorine is best prepared by the action of three parts of hydrochloric acid upon 1 part of black oxide of manganese, in a flask, by the aid of heat. The decomposition may be traced in the accompanying diagram. It may be collected in the pneu-

matic trough over hot water or strong brine, but is absorbed by cold water. It may also be collected by carrying the tube to the bottom of an open vessel; the chlorine rises and expels or displaces the air (Fig. 16).

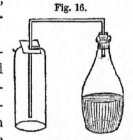

Fig. 16.

143. *Bleaching Properties of Chlorine.*—It is easily dissolved in cold water, and in this state exerts a remarkable bleaching power over vegetable colors. It is principally used in bleaching cotton cloth and paper. The bleaching-powder of commerce is chloride of lime. Chlorine is also a powerful disinfectant, and is used to destroy the bad effluvia of sick rooms; but in these cases it requires to be used with caution, as it is excessively irritating to the lungs. Its bleaching and disinfecting properties are due to its strong affinity for hydrogen, which it takes away from coloring and putrescent substances, thus decomposing them entirely.

What is chlorine? What are its properties? Where is it found? How obtained? How may it be collected? Explain the changes.

How does chlorine affect vegetable colors? To what other use is it applied? To what does it owe its bleaching and disinfectant properties?

144. Humboldt discovered that chlorine possesses the power of quickening the germination of seeds. Old seeds, which could be made to grow by no other process, germinated promptly when steeped in a weak solution of chlorine in water. Chlorine is said, when respired in very minute quantity, to alleviate the symptoms of consumption. It is also stated that workmen employed in bleaching establishments, and other places where chlorine is used, are less liable to this disease than others.

HYDROCHLORIC ACID (*Chlorohydric Acid, Muriatic Acid*).
$$H\,Cl = 36\cdot 5.$$

145. When hydrogen and chlorine gases are mixed in the dark, they do not unite; but exposed to diffused daylight, they gradually unite, and if to direct sunshine they combine explosively, forming hydrochloric acid, which is a transparent, colorless gas, having intense acid properties. It is usually prepared by adding oil of vitriol to common salt, and submitting the mixture to the action of heat. Its ordinary form is a liquid solution, as it very freely dissolves in water. Salts

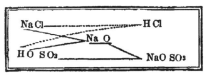

formed from it are called muriates, or hydrochlorates. This acid exists in the gastric juice, and assists in dissolving the food.

For what other purposes has chlorine been used?

What is hydrochloric acid, and how is it formed? What are its salts called? Where is it found?

FLUORINE.

Symbol F, equivalent 18·70.

146. Fluorine exists combined with calcium, as fluoride of calcium, or fluor spar.   In this state it is a minute ingredient of bones, especially of the enamel of the teeth.   It has never yet been separated, but is supposed somewhat to resemble oxygen in its properties, as it does not form a compound with it.   Fluorine combines with hydrogen, forming hydrofluoric acid, which is remarkable for its property of corroding glass.

IODINE.

Symbol I, equivalent 126·36.

147. Iodine is a grayish-black solid, of a metallic appearance, resembling black-lead.   It is obtained chiefly by leaching the ashes of sea-weed (kelp), but it sometimes occurs in the waters of springs.   It dissolves freely in alcohol, but very sparingly in water, has a smell similar to chlorine, and combines with starch, forming a deep blue compound (iodide of starch).   It stains the skin brown, and yields a fine purple vapor when heated.   If a polished silver plate is held over this vapor, it first becomes of a yellow color, then violet, then of a deep blue, owing to the combination of the iodine with the silver.   The iodide of silver thus formed is decomposed by light.   The daguerreotype process depends upon this principle.

What is said of fluorine?

What is iodine?   How is it obtained?   What are its properties?   What is said of its vapors?

BROMINE.

Symbol Br, *equivalent* 78 26.

148. Bromine is a heavy, brownish-red liquid, of a suffocating odor, and is derived, like iodine, from the sea. Both iodine and bromine combine with metals, like chlorine, forming iodides and bromides. They also unite with hydrogen, forming acids—the hydriodic and hydrobromic acids. Iodine and bromine are also used medicinally in the treatment of scrofula and for dispelling tumors.

CARBON.

Symbol C, *equivalent* 6.

149. This important substance is familiarly known as charcoal It is widely diffused in nature, and- is the solidifying element of all living structures. By casting the eye upon the Chart, we see at once that it belongs chiefly to the organized kingdom, constituting about one-half the weight of dry vegetable and animal substances. Carbon exists in several allotropic forms (42), displaying properties remarkably different in each case.

150. *The Diamond* —This is the purest state of carbon. It is a crystal, having the figure of two pyramids applied base to base. The diamond is the hardest substance known, and can only be wrought, or cut, by rubbing one against another, or by the use of diamond dust. Diamonds are ground or cut, usually, into two forms, by means of diamond powder worked with olive oil upon a wheel of soft steel. The *rose diamond* is cut into a hemispherical form, but rises to a point,

---

What is bromine ? For what is it used?

What is carbon ? What fact does a glance at the Chart communicate concerning carbon ?

What is the diamond ? How are diamonds cut? Why cut thus? What is the and has twenty-four flat, triangular faces (facets); these facets reflect the light, and give the gem a glittering appearance. The *brilliant* is cut with a flat face, or table, upon the top, surrounded with facets; it has the finest effect, but requires the sacrifice of a larger portion of the gem. A brilliant-cut diamond is esteemed equal in value to a rough one of twice the weight, besides the cost of working it. Diamonds are of various colors, but the most valuable are colorless and limpid. The snow-white, transparent diamond, is said to be of the *first water*.

151. *Value of Diamonds.*—Diamonds are sold by the carat, a carat being equal to four grains.—(*Ure.*) They increase in value not in proportion to their weight, but in proportion to the *square* of their weight. Thus, the value of three diamonds weighing 1, 2, and 3 carats, is as 1, 4, and 9. The average value of wrought diamonds weighing one carat is $40 (*Brande*); one of two carats will be valued at $160; three carats, $360; 100 carats, $400,000.

152. The largest known diamond is probably that called the *Kooh-i-noor* (mountain of light), of the East Indies. It was discovered in the mines of Golconda just 300 years ago. When rough it is said to have weighed 900 carats. It is of the rose form, and was reduced to 279 carats by cutting. It has caused several wars, and has been six times violently wrested from its possessors. The British have at last seized it, and transferred it to England, that the benighted pagans may stop quarrelling about it (!). It has never been sold, but $10,000,000 is talked of as the price, equal to about seventeen tons of gold.

---

form of the rose diamond? What of the brilliant? What are diamonds of the *first water*?

How are diamonds sold? What determines their value?

What is the history of the Kooh-i-noor?

154. *Uses of the Diamond.*—From its extreme hardness, the dia mond is used for cutting glass, for drilling apertures through other gems, for the pivot-holes of delicate watch-work, also to form the holes through which extremely fine wire is drawn. It refracts light powerfully, and has been used for the lenses of microscopes. The diamond is very difficult of combustion, but may be burned in pure oxygen gas Pepys sealed up a diamond in a piece of pure soft iron, and exposed it for some time to an intense heat; when examined, the diamond had disappeared, and the iron was converted into steel, which is composed of carbon and iron. The diamond is thus known to be pure carbon.

154. *Plumbago, Graphite, or Black-Lead.*—This is another form of carbon, having a metalline appearance, and containing a small proportion of iron. It resists quite a high degree of heat, and is used to make crucibles. It is also used for marking on paper, being sawn into slices and fitted into the grooves of *cedar pencils,* or rounded for *ever-pointed pencils.* It is also employed to relieve the friction of machinery, instead of oil or grease; also for giving lustre to iron, as stove-blacking. In this form it is often adulterated with 50 per cent. of lamp-black, which may be detected by exposing the suspected article for some time to a cherry-red heat, in the open air. The lamp-black will burn away, and its amount may be determined by the loss of weight.

155. Another variety of carbon is *lamp-black.* It is the soot deposited from the flame of pitchy or tarry combustibles. It is usually made by burning the refuse rosin left by the distillation of turpentine. The smoke is conducted

For what is the diamond used? Is it combustible? How is it proved to be pure carbon?

What is plumbago? What are its uses? What is said of stove-blacking? How is the cheat detected?

What is lamp-black? How is it made? For what is it used?

through long horizontal flues, terminating in chambers hung with old sacking, upon which the lamp-black is deposited. It is used for making printers' ink and black paint.

156. *Charcoal* is that species of carbon which is produced by burning vegetable or animal substances out of contact with the air. Every one knows it is a black, inodorous, insipid, insoluble, brittle substance, applied to numerous uses. Common charcoal is made by piling billets of wood together in a conical heap, covering it with earth, and burning the mass slowly, with but a partial access of air. By the usual process of coal-burning in forests, about 18 per cent. of the weight of the wood is obtained (*Ure*), although the amount varies greatly.

157. Charcoal seems to be soft; but if the fine powder, in small quantity, be rubbed between plates of glass, it is found that the little particles are very hard, and able to scratch the glass almost as easily as the diamond itself.—(*Norton.*)

158. *Charcoal as Fuel.*—Charcoal is very combustible, and is extensively used for fuel. When pure, it burns without flame, although it usually contains water, which, during the combustion, is partially decomposed into carburetted hydrogen, which burns with a slight flame. A cubic foot of charcoal from soft wood weighs, upon an average, from eight to nine pounds; and from hard wood, twelve to thirteen pounds. Hence the hard-wood coal is best adapted to produce a high heat in a small space. Yet equal weights of the different charcoals yield equal quantities of heat. Upon an average, a pound of dry charcoal will heat 73 pounds of water from the freezing to the boiling point.—(*Ure.*)

- What is charcoal? What are its properties? How is it made? What per cent. of charcoal is obtained from a given weight of wood by this process?

What is stated concerning the hardness of charcoal?

To what is the slight flame sometimes seen upon burning charcoal due? What is its weight? Upon what does the value of charcoal, as fuel, depend?

159. *Charcoal very indestructible.*—Charcoal is a very un-changeable substance, as it is not affected at common temperatures by air or moisture. The beams of the theatre at Herculaneum were converted into charcoal 1700 years ago, when that city was overwhelmed with lava, and remain as entire as if they had been charred but yesterday Wooden stakes or piles are rendered more durable by charring upon the surface, before driving them into the ground. . Most of the houses in Venice stand upon piles or stakes, the extremities of which are charred for their better preservation. Oaken stakes have been recently found in the bed of the Thames River, where they are supposed to have been driven at the time of the invasion of Julius Cæsar. They were charred to a considerable depth, and were firm at the heart.

160. *Absorbent Property of Charcoal.*—Charcoal possesses, in a remarkable degree, the power of absorbing different gases, and condensing them within its pores. It will absorb 90 times its bulk of ammonia, 35 times its bulk of carbonic acid, of oxygen 9 times, and of nitrogen 7 times its bulk (*Saussure*). When charcoal already saturated with one gas is put into another, it gives out a portion of the gas already absorbed, and takes up a portion of the new gas. Recently burned charcoal imbibes watery vapor from the air very greedily. By a week's exposure to the atmosphere, it thus increases in weight from 10 to 20 per cent. This property of absorption varies with different kinds of charcoal. It is possessed in a higher degree by those containing the most pores, that is, where the pores are finer, and in a lower degree by the more loose and spongy sorts. "A cubic inch

of charcoal," says Liebig, "must have, at the least compu-
tation, a surface of 100 square feet." It is upon this interior
pore-surface that the gases are condensed, and in proportion
to its extent is the quantity absorbed.

161. Other substances besides charcoal, in fact all solids,
porous or otherwise, are supposed to possess, in various degrees, this power of condensing gases upon their surfaces.
The black powder of platinum absorbs 800 times its bulk
of oxygen gas. The gas in this case must be condensed almost to the condition of a liquid. If now a jet of hydrogen
is projected upon the platinum, it unites with the oxygen,
heat is liberated, water formed, and the metal becomes red-
hot. Faraday has lately shown that the porous condition
of the platinum is not necessary, as a similar effect may be
produced by a clean bright slip of the metal.

162. *Preservative Power of Charcoal.*—Connected with
this property is the power which charcoal possesses of removing offensive odors and checking putrefaction. It is
a powerful antiseptic. Charcoal-powder, newly prepared,
when rubbed upon tainted meat, restores it to sweetness.
By charring the inside of casks, water may be kept in
them a long time without spoiling. Vegetable substances
containing much water, as potatoes, are more completely
preserved by the aid of a quantity of charcoal. The bad
odor sometimes acquired by clothes is removed by wrapping
them with charcoal. Filters are constructed for purifying
water, by passing it through layers of charcoal of different
degrees of fineness.

163. *Bone-black.*—The charcoal from bones is called *bone-
black* or *ivory-black*, and is of course loaded with mineral

---

Do other substances possess this power ?

What is stated of the antiseptic or preservative properties of charcoal ? In what
way is it used for this purpose ?

matter (phosphate of lime); but for clarifying purposes, it is superior to wood charcoal. It is extensively used in sugar refining to discharge the color of the raw article. Vinegars, wines, and syrups are also decolorized by the same agent. Payen has recently shown that this power of the charcoals depends upon the more or less complete state of subdivision among their particles, and that animal charcoal is superior to vegetable only because its mineral matter serves to keep the carbon particles further apart. The beneficial use of charcoal upon soils, and in the manufacture of artificial manure (*Poudrette*), is explained by this property of absorption.

164. *Other Uses.*—Charcoal is also used for making gunpowder and fireworks, and, being a bad conductor of heat, for casing iron steam-pipes. Some varieties contain silex (sand), and are used for polishing metals. Charcoal is of great value in separating metals from their oxides in the smelting furnace, as, at a high temperature, it has a powerful affinity for oxygen.

165. *Coke.*—This is a black, porous mass left after heating pit coal with the air excluded, as is done in iron retorts for the manufacture of illuminating gas (177). It ignites with difficulty, but is capable of producing, by its combustion, a higher temperature than any other fuel, bulk for bulk. *Spanish black* is the charcoal of cork. *Black crayons* are made from the charcoal of the willow.

166. *Source of the Carbon of Plants.*—Plants derive their carbon from carbonic acid, most of which they absorb from

What is bone-black? For what is it employed? Why is this superior to vegetable charcoal?

Mention some other uses of charcoal.

What is coke? Its properties? What is Spanish black?

Whence do plants derive their carbon? What was formerly supposed concerning it?

the air through the medium of the leaves. It also comes in through the roots dissolved in water. It was long supposed to be derived from the vegetable mould (*humus*) of the soil, which got into the plant before complete decomposition; but this opinion is now mostly abandoned.

CARBONIC ACID.   (*Fixed Air, Chalk Acid, Mephitic Air, Choak Damp of Miners.*)

$$C O_2 = 22.$$

167. Carbon unites with oxygen in two proportions (see Chart), forming carbonic acid, $C O_2$, and carbonic oxide, $C O$. Of these compounds, the first is by far the most important. Carbonic acid is a colorless gas, with a slightly sour taste, and is about half as heavy again as air. It exists abundantly in the mineral crust of the globe (hence called fixed air), in combination with the earths and alkalies, and is found also in the atmosphere in a pure state (131). It exists in limestone to the extent of 44 per cent. of its weight, and is best obtained by the action of muriatic acid upon powdered marble. Any strong acid will do. The change is exhibited in the diagram. It may be collected by displacement (142), as it is very soluble in water. A cubic inch of marble will yield four gallons of the gas. It extinguishes fire. A candle dipped into it goes out at once; and if poured upon flame, it quenches it as quickly as water.

___

168. *Solid Carbonic Acid.*—Under a pressure of 36 atmospheres (upwards of 500 pounds on the square inch), carbonic acid shrinks into a colorless liquid of sp. gr. 0 83, at 32°. When this pressure is suddenly removed from the liquid acid, it expands into a gas with such rapidity, that one portion absorbing heat from the other, freezes it into a white, filamentous solid. This solid carbonic acid, when dissolved in ether and evaporated, produces the most intense cold known (67).

169. *Sources of Carbonic Acid.*—Carbonic acid is produced very abundantly in nature. The burning of fuel (which always contains carbon) in the open air yields it in vast quantities. The combustion of a bushel of charcoal produces 2500 gallons of this gas. It is also formed within the bodies of all animals, by the union of atmospheric oxygen with the carbon contained in the system, and escapes through the lungs, by respiration, into the air. Each adult man exhales about 140 gallons per day.—(*Davy.*) Its quantity varies at different times, being greatest after a meal, and least during sleep and fasting. Children exhale more carbonic acid, in proportion to their weight, than adults About 4 per cent. of the inspired oxygen is converted into carbonic acid at each respiration; and the bulk of carbonic acid formed is exactly equal to that of the oxygen consumed in producing it.

170. The test of carbonic acid is clear lime-water, which it turns milky, by forming insoluble carbonate of lime. To prove that it is produced both by combustion and respiration, invert an empty jar over a burning candle for a short

What pressure converts it into a liquid? How is this liquid frozen?

Mention some of its sources in nature. How much does an adult man exhale daily? What per cent. of the inspired air is changed to carbonic acid?

What is the test of carbonic acid? How is it proved that it is produced both by combustion and respiration?

time; then agitate in the jar a little lime-water. It will become turbid at once. With a glass tube or tobacco-pipe breathe through another portion of lime-water, and the same effect will be produced.

171. Carbonic acid exists in all natural waters, and from many mineral waters, as those of Saratoga, it constantly escapes, causing them to sparkle, and giving them a lively, pungent taste. Soda-waters are such as have been charged artificially, by various processes, with carbonic acid

172. *Its Physiological Effects.*—Carbonic acid gas, when respired, destroys animal life: this it does in two ways. When breathed pure it produces spasm of the glottis, closes the air-passages, and thus kills suddenly by suffocation. When diluted with even ten times its bulk of air, and taken into the system, it acts as a narcotic poison, gradually producing stupor, insensibility, and death. Its poisonous effects upon the constitution are sensible, though mixed with sufficient air to sustain the combustion of a candle. When respired in the lowest poisonous proportion, the symptoms come on very gradually, and the transition from life to death is usually tranquil. The effects resemble those produced by excess of opium.

173. Persons sleeping in close apartments are sometimes suffocated by the fumes of burning charcoal—carbonic acid gas. It often accumulates at the bottom of wells and in cellars, stifling those who may unwarily descend. To test its presence in such cases, lower a lighted candle into the suspected places: if it is not extinguished, the air may be breathed safely for a short time; if the light goes out, it will be necessary before descending to throw down dry-slaked lime,

In what waters does carbonic acid exist?

Is carbonic acid respirable? What are its effects upon animal life?

What precautions should be taken against the effects of carbonic acid? What

or a considerable quantity of water, or to raise and depress an inverted umbrella in it repeatedly, in order to mingle it with the air. To resuscitate those who have been exposed to the poisonous action of carbonic acid, dash cold water upon them freely, rub the extremities, and, if the body is cold, administer a warm bath. Carbonic acid is used to suffocate insects, as butterflies, when it is desired to preserve the colors perfect. The Lake of Averno, affirmed by the ancients to have been the entrance to the infernal regions, evolves so large a quantity of carbonic acid gas that birds flying over it drop with suffocation. Carbonic acid unites with bases forming a class of salts—the carbonates.

CARBONIC OXIDE.

$$C\ O = 14.$$

174. Carbonic oxide, $C\ O$, is a gas produced by burning carbon with an imperfect supply of air. The blue flame that plays over the surface of coal-fires is caused by the burning of carbonic oxide. It is an unimportant compound.

LIGHT CARBURETTED HYDROGEN.

(*Fire-Damp, Marsh Gas, Heavy Inflammable Air, Carbide of Hydrogen, Dicarburet of Hydrogen.*)

$$H_2\ C = 8.$$

175. Carbon combines with hydrogen to form a very numerous class of compounds, called hydro-carbons (see Chart, Isomeric Group), which are all highly combustible. Carburetted hydrogen is a colorless gas, about half as heavy as

---

treatment when it has been breathed by accident? What is remarked of insects? What of the Lake Averno?

What is the composition of carbonic oxide? How is it produced? Where is it seen?

common air, and not poisonous when respired. It is formed abundantly in the mud of stagnant pools containing decomposing organic matter. It rises in bubbles, mingled with a little carbonic acid, and may be collected in inverted jars. It is often disengaged in large quantities in coal-mines, and, mixed with air, constitutes the fatal *fire-damp*. If the air is more than six times, or less than fourteen times the volume of the gas, the mixture explodes violently when inflamed. Carbonic acid is produced by the combustion; so that those who are not killed by the burning, or shock, are generally suffocated by this gas.

176. *The Davy Lamp.*—To guard against these accidents, which were formerly very common, Davy invented the safety-lamp. The nature of this lamp may be understood by taking a fine wire gauze, and lowering it over the flame of a candle (Fig. 8). It will be seen that the blaze does not pass through the minute openings or meshes of the gauze, which act like short tubes. The metal of the gauze conducts away the heat from the flame so rapidly as to cool it below the luminous point; the gases that pass through are, therefore, not ignited. The Davy lamp is only a common oil-lamp, surrounded by a cage of this gauze (Fig. 17). It is plain that such a lamp, introduced into an explosive mixture, would not fire it, as the flame would be confined within. Since this ingenious contrivance was adopted, explosions in coal-mines have become much more rare, and would probably entirely cease, were it not for neglect in the use of this simple instrument of safety.

Fig. 17.

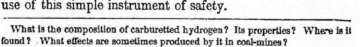

What is the composition of carburetted hydrogen? Its properties? Where is it found? What effects are sometimes produced by it in coal-mines?

What is the principle of the safety-lamp? What is its construction? What effect has it produced?

OLEFIANT GAS.

$$H_4 C_4 = 28.$$

177. *Preparation and Properties.*—This gas is prepared pure, by mixing strong alcohol with five or six times its weight of oil of vitriol, in a retort, and applying heat. It is colorless, tasteless, has a marked odor, and is nearly as heavy as air (sp. gr. ·980). It is very combustible, burning with a bright, intensely luminous flame. When certain varieties of coal, the bituminous, or those containing pitch (*hydrocarbon*), are heated to redness in closed iron vessels (*retorts*), they give off a great number of products, among which are the olefiant and other gases, and several liquids. This is the process by which the illuminating gas of cities is produced.

178. *Coal-gas Manufacture.*—Coal-gas, as it issues from the retort, cannot be directly employed for illumination, because it contains tarry and oily vapors, which would readily condense in the pipes through which the gas must be distributed, and thus create obstructions. The products of distillation are therefore conducted from the retort, by a tube, into a long cast-iron cylinder, called the *hydraulic main*, in which the coal-tar and heavier vapors are deposited. From the hydraulic main a pipe leads away into another vessel, called the *condenser*, which is kept cool by water, and which causes a still further deposit. From the condenser the gases are conveyed to the purifier, where they are passed through milk of lime (one part lime, twenty-five water), in which sulphuretted hydrogen and carbonic acid are separated from it. The purified gas is then carried for-

What is the composition of olefiant gas? Its properties? How is it obtained? Why cannot gas directly from coal be used for illumination? What is the

ward into the gasometer, an immense sheet-iron cylinder, open at bottom and closed at top, which floats in a cistern of water. Gasometers are sometimes fifty feet in diameter, and thirty feet high. From these reservoirs the gas passes into iron pipes, laid down in the streets, called the *mains*, and is thence distributed to the consumers.

179. *Mode of Burning the Gas.*—The quantity of light obtained by the combustion of gas is greatly influenced by the mode in which it is burned. The same quantity of gas, flowing through several small apertures, will yield much more light than if emitted through one large aperture. The argand burner consists of a circle of small holes, of equal size, the centre of the circle being open to admit an upward current of air. Through these holes the gas issues, and is burned in small jets. When the gas passes through an oblong aperture, or slit, it gives a sheet of flame resembling in form the wing of a bat, hence it is called the "bat-wing" jet. There are also other forms, known as the "cockspur," the "fan," and the "fish-tail" or "swallow-tail" jets.

180. *Source of the Light in Illuminating Gas.*—The light emitted by coal-gas is due to olefiant and light carburetted hydrogen gases; its illuminating power is in proportion to the amount of the former, which usually varies from ten to twenty per cent. A natural supply of this gas is used to illuminate the village of Fredonia, N. Y. Gas of better illuminating qualities is obtained by the distillation of oil and rosin, and if well prepared it needs no purification.

181. *Amount of Gas from different Materials.*—Upon an

hydraulic main? What is its use? What is the use of the condenser? What change does the gas undergo in the purifier? What is the gasometer? What are mains?

What is the best mode of burning the gas? Describe the argand burner. How is the bat-wing jet formed? What other jets are mentioned?

To what is the light of coal-gas due? Where is it said to exist naturally? How may better gas be obtained?

average, a pound of good coal yields four cubic feet of gas, a pound of rosin, or pitch, ten cubic feet, and a pound of oil, or fat, fifteen cubic feet.—(*Ure*). The gas from a ton of coal requires about two-thirds of a bushel of lime for its purification.

182. *Comparative Cost of Illumination.*—Coal-gas is by far the cheapest source of artificial light which we possess, although the expense of the apparatus is such that its use is not economical, unless more than 100 lights are required.— (*Brande.*) One pound of tallow in the form of six mould-candles, burned in succession, will last forty hours; $11\frac{1}{2}$ cubic feet of gas, burned at 500 cubic inches per hour, will give the same light for the same time. The comparative expense of different materials of illumination is thus stated by Dr. Ure: An amount of light produced from wax, at a cost of $1.00, costs from tallow $0.28.6, from oil $0.14.3, from coal-gas $0.04.7.

NITROGEN AND CARBON—CYANOGEN.

Symbol Cy, *equivalent* 26.

183. Carbon and nitrogen combine to form a singular gaseous compound, known as cyanogen, having the composition $C_2 N$. It seems to have the properties of an elementary body, uniting with the simple elements, and forming with metals a class of compounds known as cyanides. Thus the paint, prussian-blue, is a cyanide of iron. Cyanogen, uniting with hydrogen, $H C_2 N$, gives rise to that king of poisons, *prussic acid*, or hydrocyanic acid. This substance is a colorless, volatile liquid, possessing the odor of peach-blossoms, and so intensely poisonous that the

What is the product of gas from different materials?

Under what circumstances is the use of gas economical? What is said of the comparative cost of light from gas and other sources?

odors emitted during its preparation often produce fainting It is used in medicine, but so diluted with water that 100 grains of the strongest mixture does not contain more than three grains of the pure acid; and yet a single drop of this diluted acid is a dose, and must be administered with caution. The antidote is caustic ammonia, inhaled.

SULPHUR.

Symbol S, equivalent 16.

184. *Properties and Source.*—Sulphur or brimstone is a yellow, brittle, crystalline solid, which is found in nature both in a state of purity and of combination. The sulphur of commerce is mainly procured from the Island of Sicily, where it is quarried from large deposits, situated in a blue clay formation. When taken out of the ground it is heated in earthen pots, and caused to distil over into water. When melted and poured into wooden moulds, it constitutes *roll-sulphur.* *Flowers of sulphur* is made by heating and subliming it in large apartments, when it is deposited in the form of a fine yellow powder. Sulphur has an extensive range of affinity, and combines with metals, as iron, lead, zinc, &c , forming sulphurets or sulphides. Its specific gravity is 2. It melts at 230° into a pale-yellow liquid; but if the heat be raised to 450°, it changes to a thick, tenacious, molasses-colored body, which, if quenched in cold water, becomes soft and elastic like India-rubber: in this condition it is used to take impressions of medals and coins. From this allotropic condition it gradually returns to its usual state.

What is the composition of cyanogen? What are the properties of prussic acid? For what is it used?

What is sulphur? Where is it chiefly obtained? What is roll-sulphur? How is flowers of sulphur made? What is its range of combination? Its specific gravity? Its melting point? How is it changed by heating to 450°?

185. Sulphur exists in plants, entering their roots as gypsum (265), or in the form of other salts. It is present in an uncombined state in the bodies of animals, chiefly in their muscular parts. It exists in eggs, and discolors the silver spoons with which they are eaten, by forming the black sulphuret of silver. The efficiency of many preparations for staining the hair of a black color depends upon the lead they contain, which unites with the sulphur of the hair. Metallic supports and filling for the teeth are often turned black in the mouth by the action of sulphur. It takes fire at a low temperature, and hence its use in friction matches (196). Powdered and mixed with lead, it forms the sulphur ointment which is applied externally in maladies of the skin, particularly in a disease produced by the itch insect, which burrows in the skin, and delights in filth. It probably acts in this case by being converted into sulphuretted hydrogen.

SULPHUROUS ACID.

$$S O_2 = 32.$$

186. When sulphur is burned in the air, it unites with oxygen, forming a transparent, colorless gas, having a peculiar disagreeable taste, and a most suffocating smell; it is sulphurous acid. It may be liquefied by intense cold, and is very soluble in water. It extinguishes combustion; hence sulphur is often thrown into the fire to quench the burning soot of chimneys. It is respired with difficulty. Sulphurous acid is used in bleaching vegetable and animal colors: the ancients employed fumes of sulphur to bleach wool.— (*Pliny*.) It is used for whitening silk, woollen, and straw

What is said of sulphur in plants? In animals? In eggs? In hair? Why is it used in friction matches? In what maladies is it useful?

How may sulphurous acid be produced? What are its properties? Its uses? How is it obtained? Explain the changes.

goods. If a red rose or dark-colored dahlia be held in the fumes of sulphurous acid, it is blanched; but the colors are restored by weak sulphuric acid. It combines with, instead of destroying, the coloring matters, as chlorine does (141); decomposition, therefore, restores the tint. $S O_2$ may be pro-

cured by boiling in a retort copper clippings with sulphuric acid, $S O_3$. One atom of oxygen of the $S O_3$ unites with cop-

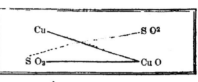

per, and the $S O_2$ escapes, as seen in the diagram, to be collected in jars by displacement.

SULPHURIC ACID. (*Oil of Vitriol.*)

$$S O_3 + H O = 49.$$

187. *Preparation.*—This powerful acid is of great interest to chemists and manufacturers. It was formerly obtained from green vitriol, and was hence called *oil of vitriol.* It is now prepared on the large scale by heating sulphur and nitre in furnaces, and conducting the sulphurous and nitrous acid fumes, which are thus formed, into vast leaden chambers, along with steam and atmospheric air, the floor of the chambers being also covered with water. An atom of nitrous acid, $N O_4$, parts with half its oxygen to the sulphurous acid, $S O_2$, thus forming two atoms of sulphuric acid, $2 S O_3$. Nitrous acid is again formed by the oxygen of the air, and again surrenders its oxygen to the sulphurous acid. A small quantity of $N O_4$ may thus form an endless quantity of $S O_3$. The water at the bottom of the chambers, which soon becomes very acid, is drawn off and boiled down

in platinum stills to a sufficient degree of concentration. The following diagram explains this change very clearly.

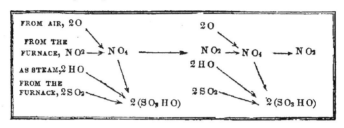

188. When this acid is procured by the distillation of green vitriol, it comes off in a very dry state, and attracts moisture so rapidly as to cause a fuming; it is hence called fuming oil of vitriol, or Nordhausen acid, because it was largely manufactured in a city of this name in Saxony. Common or hydrated sulphuric acid contains a larger proportion of water. The former kind dissolves indigo.

189. *Properties.*—Sulphuric acid has a thick, oily appearance, with at first a greasy or soapy feel; but it speedily corrodes the skin, and causes an intense burning sensation. It has a powerful affinity for water; when a splinter of wood is dipped into it for a short time, it turns black (chars), the acid taking away from it the elements of water, and leaving the carbon. In like manner, it chars and decomposes the skin, and most organic substances, by removing their water. When water and sulphuric acid are mixed, the two liquids shrink into less space, and heat is produced. Pure oil of vitriol is colorless; but slight traces of organic matter, as dust or straws, turn it of a dark shade, as it is usually seen in commerce. It is an active poison, the best antidote being copious draughts of chalk and water, or carbonate of soda or magnesia.

What is the fuming or Nordhausen acid? What are the properties of sulphuric acid? Why does it char and blacken organic bodies? What is the appearance of the sulphuric acid of commerce? Is it poisonous? What is the antidote?

190. *Uses.*—Sulphuric acid is extensively used in the manufacture of soda from common salt; also in the manufacture of chlorine for bleaching; of citric, tartaric, acetic, nitric, and muriatic acids; sulphate of soda, sulphate of magnesia, blacking, soda-water, and various paints; also in dyeing, calico-printing, gold and silver refining, and in purifying oil and tallow. Its chemical uses are innumerable. It is the Hercules of the acids.

191. This acid unites with bases forming the sulphates, and exists in nature both combined, as with lime in gypsum, and free, as in some streams the water of which it renders sour. SO_3 is nearly twice as heavy as water (specific gravity 1·8), a gallon weighing about 18 pounds. The test for sulphuric acid is chloride of barium, with which it forms an insoluble salt. The remaining compounds of sulphur and oxygen are not of general interest.

SULPHURETTED HYDROGEN. (*Hydrosulphuric Acid.*)
$$HS = 17.$$

192. When sulphur and hydrogen are set free together, they unite to form a colorless, transparent gas, having the well-known smell of decaying eggs. It is produced by the putrefaction of all organic substances containing sulphur, as flesh, blood, hair, excrements, albumen of eggs, &c. It is this gas which gives the putrid odor to sulphurous waters. A rotten pump-log standing in a well of hard water (containing gypsum) may render it nauseous by setting free sulphuretted hydrogen. If the well is purified, and a new log introduced, the water may be restored to

---

What are the uses of sulphuric acid?

In what form does it exist in nature? What is its test?

What is the composition of sulphuretted hydrogen? From what substances is it derived? What is said of its odor? What is its effect upon animals?

sweetness. Sulphuretted hydrogen is very deleterious when respired. A small bird dies immediately in air containing $\frac{1}{1500}$ of this gas: $\frac{1}{800}$ killed a middle-sizéd dog, and $\frac{1}{150}$ a horse.—(*Brande.*)

PHOSPHORUS.

Symbol P, *equivalent* 32.

193. *Its Discovery.*—This remarkable substance was first obtained about 200 years ago, by one of the alchemists, while trying to discover the art of making gold. Its mysterious properties were regarded with wonder and awe, and it was shown around among the initiated under the name of the " Son of Satan."

194. *Properties.*—Phosphorus is a solid, of a waxy appearance, easily cut, colorless and transparent, but turning yellow by exposure to the light. It possesses the singular quality of shining in the dark, and is hence called phosphorus, or *light-bearer.* It is highly combustible, often taking fire in the air upon the slightest touch, and burning furiously; it is therefore always kept under water. Great caution is required in experimenting with it. It is a poison.

195. *Source of Phosphorus.*—Bones contain phosphorus— they consist of gelatine, lime, and phosphoric acid. To obtain it, the bones are first burned, which drives off the gelatine. The lime is then separated by adding oil of vitriol, and the oxygen of the remaining phosphoric acid is removed by the action of charcoal at a high heat. The phosphorus distils over by means of a suitable apparatus, and is collected

What is stated of the discovery of phosphorus ?
What are its properties ?
From what source and how is phosphorus obtained ? How much may be extracted from the human skeleton ?

under water.   The skeleton of a man weighs from 10 to 12 pounds, and contains from $1\frac{1}{2}$ to 2 pounds of phosphorus.

196. *Its Use in Matches.*—Phosphorus takes fire at a temperature of about 120º; and as this may be produced by slight friction, it is well adapted to tip the ends of friction matches.   As the phosphorus would be liable to take fire if exposed to the air, it is kneaded with water and gum, or glue, into a paste, which, when dried, serves as a protecting varnish.   Chlorate of potash, nitre, red-lead, or some other substance rich in oxygen, is worked into the paste to insure prompt combustion.   The points of the matches being first coated with sulphur, are dipped into this preparation, and then cautiously dried in a stove.   When the surface is broken by friction, the phosphorus takes fire first, the sulphur next ignites, and then the wood of the match:—200,000 pounds of phosphorus are used annually in London alone for the manufacture of matches.

197. *Its Physiological Relations.*—Phosphorus not only exists as phosphate of lime in the bones of animals, but in a free or unoxidized state it is an essential constituent of the brain and nervous matter.   It is also an ingredient of albumen and fibrin.   The uncombined phosphorus is burned by the oxygen of respiration, forming phosphoric acid, which, united with soda or ammonia, passes from the system by the route of the kidneys.   The uncombined phosphorus of the nervous and cerebral tissue is not in its ordinary form.   It is capable of existing in two allotropic states (42).   In one of these conditions its active properties are suspended   It passes into this torpid state in plants, is consumed by animals in food, passes unchanged through their circulating fluids, and is

How are matches made ?   Is much used for this purpose ?
In what other part of the animal body is phosphorus found ?   In what condi
tion does it here exist ?

thrown into the active state, and oxidized under the influence of the vital force.

198. *Phosphorescence.*—That shining, self-luminous appearance which is sometimes exhibited by putrefying fish, which is also occasionally seen in decaying wood, in the firefly and glow-worm, is termed *phosphorescence*, and is thought to be due to the slow oxidation of phosphorus at low temperatures. It is supposed that the beautiful luminous appearance of the inter-tropical seas is due to the decay of small jelly-fish, or blubber, so abundant in the ocean, and which contain phosphorus.

PHOSPHORIC ACID.

$$P\ O_5 = 72.02$$

199. Phosphorus has an intense affinity for oxygen. Place a bit of phosphorus, of the size of a pea, in a wine-glass, cover it with hot water, and direct against it a current of oxygen gas, it bursts into a violent combustion beneath the surface of the water. When a match is burned, the white smoke that appears is phosphoric acid; it is always produced when phosphorus is burned in dry air or oxygen gas. This acid condenses into solid white flakes of a snowy appearance, and possesses a powerful affinity for water, hissing like a red-hot iron when brought in contact with it. In small quantities it is not poisonous; and when taken medicinally, it must be sucked through a quill or glass tube, as it corrodes the teeth. Phosphoric acid is of great importance in agriculture, as it is principally from its presence in bones that they are so useful as a manure (286) There are

---

What luminous appearances are supposed to be due to phosphorus?
State the composition of phosphoric acid. How may it be formed? What are its properties? To what is the value of bones in agriculture due?

three other compounds of phosphorus and oxygen, but they are of interest only to the scientific chemist.

PHOSPHURETTED HYDROGEN.   (*Phosphide of Hydrogen.*)

$$P\ H_2 = 34 \cdot 02.$$

200. This is a colorless, transparent gas, of a disgusting odor, to which the nauseous smell of putrefying animal substances is partially due. It is more offensive than sulphuretted hydrogen. It may be prepared by boiling phosphorus with a strong solution of potash in a glass retort, the extremity of which dips beneath the surface of water. The bubbles of gas, as they escape into the air, inflame spontaneously, and burn with a bright yellow light. Each bubble, as it explodes, produces a wreath of gray smoke, which dilates, as it rises, with curious rotatory movements of its parts. The singular phenomenon of Will-o'-the-wisp, or Jack-'o-lantern, where a flame or light is said to move at night over marshy places, is supposed to be due to the presence of this self-inflammable phosphuretted hydrogen.

OF THE METALS.

201. The metals are a numerous class of bodies, distinguished by a peculiar brilliancy called the *metallic lustre*, and as being good conductors of both heat and electricity. They, however, exhibit great variations in these, as well as other properties. Authors are not agreed in their classification of the metals.

Give the composition and properties of phosphuretted hydrogen How is it prepared? What effect takes place when it comes in contact with air? How is the Jack-o'-lantern accounted for?

What are the metals?

METALS OF THE ALKALIES.

POTASSIUM. (*Latin, Kalium.*)
Sym. K, *equiv* 39; sp. gr. ·869.

202. *Properties.*—Potassium is a silver-white metal, at common temperatures so soft that it may be moulded in the fingers like wax. It is never found free in nature, but occurs abundantly in rocks and soils combined with oxygen, as potash. It is produced in the metallic state by the action of charcoal upon potash at a very high temperature, which withdraws its oxygen. Davy first separated potassium by means of an electrical current in 1807. It is the lightest of all the metals.

POTASSIUM AND OXYGEN—POTASH.
K O = 47.

203. The affinity of potassium for oxygen is very strong; when exposed to the air, it becomes immediately incrusted with a film of oxide, and can only be preserved under naphtha, a liquid containing no oxygen. Thrown upon the surface of water, it decomposes it, removing its oxygen, and burning with a beautiful pink flame. The same phenomenon appears if the metal be placed in contact with ice, when it instantly bursts into flame. This shows how gunpowder is fired by touching it with an icicle. There is potassium mingled with the powder. When potassium is burned in dry oxygen, pure potash, K O, is formed. This has a very powerful affinity

What is potassium? How did Davy first obtain it?

How is the strength of its affinity for oxygen shown? What is stated of its affinity for water?

for water, which it imbibes as soon as it is exposed to the air, forming the hydrated oxide of potassium, K O, H O, or *caustic potash.*

204. Caustic potash is procured from carbonate of potash, by the action of lime, which deprives it of carbonic acid. It is a white powder, having a powerful affinity for water, which it takes rapidly from the air, and runs into a liquid. Potash possesses all the properties of the alkalies in a pre-eminent degree: it is the type of that class of bodies. It saturates the most powerful acids, changes vegetable yellows to brown, and restores the blues discharged by acids; and also decomposes animal and vegetable substances, whether living or dead. It is used in medicine in the form of small sticks, to cauterize or cleanse ulcers and foul sores; it is hence called *caustic potash.* If a solution of potash be shaken in a bottle with olive oil, or any other fixed oil (404), it will be found to convert it into a soap. This accounts for the soft, greasy feel it has when touched by the finger, as it decomposes the skin, and forms a soap with its oily elements. Its uses in agriculture will be stated when we come to the salts (272). Alkalimetry is the art of measuring the proportion of alkali in an impure mixture or compound.

SODIUM   (*Latin, Natrium.*)

Symbol Na, *equivalent* 22·97.

205. This is a brilliant white metal, very much resembling potassium both in appearance and properties. It has a strong affinity for oxygen, and must be preserved in naphtha. If

---

What is potash? What position does it hold among the alkalies? How is it obtained? What are its properties? How is it used in medicine? Why does it feel greasy to the fingers? What is alkalimetry?

Describe the properties of sodium. What is said of its abundance?

thrown upon the surface of hot water, it bursts into a beautiful yellow flame, and is converted into the oxide of sodium, or soda. It is prepared in the same way as potassium, but with less difficulty. It is perhaps the most abundant metal upon the globe, as it constitutes two-fifths of sea-salt, and is a large ingredient of rocks and soils.—(*Gregory.*)

SODIUM AND OXYGEN—SODA.

$$Na\ O = 30.97.$$

206. This alkali was long confounded with potash, which it greatly resembles, although its properties are less marked. For commercial purposes, it is chiefly derived from sea-salt, and is extensively employed in the manufacture of soap and glass. It is always present in the bodies of animals.

METALS OF THE ALKALINE EARTHS.

CALCIUM.

Symbol Ca, *equivalent* 20.

207. Calcium is a metal but little known. It is obtained with difficulty, and is put to no use. Its name is derived from *calx*, the Latin term for lime; hence also the English word *calcareous.* Calcium combined with oxygen forms lime.

CALCIUM AND OXYGEN—LIME.

$$Ca\ O = 28.$$

208. Lime is produced by burning limestone (carbonate of lime) in large masses, in kilns. The carbonic acid is driven off into the air by the heat, and a white stony substance re-

---

Whence is it derived ?

Describe the metal calcium.

How is lime obtained ? What is the effect of the burning ? What is quick lime, or caustic lime ?

mains, called *quicklime*, or *caustic lime*. It is porous, and sufficiently hard to be transported without falling to pieces. One ton of good limestone yields 11 cwt. of lime.

209. *Hydrate of Lime.*—When water is poured upon quicklime, it absorbs it (every 28 pounds of lime taking 9 pounds of water), swells to thrice its original bulk, crumbles to a fine white powder, and is converted into a *hydrate of lime*, Ca O H O; this process is called slaking. During slaking, heat is produced, often sufficient to ignite wood (92). If water is added too rapidly in slaking, it seems to chill the lime, and produces gritty lumps, which impair its value for building and agricultural purposes.

210. When quicklime is exposed to the air, it first rapidly imbibes moisture, and crumbles to powder; it then gradually absorbs carbonic acid, becoming more and more mild, less and less caustic, and finally regains the neutral condition of the carbonate. Lime exhibits the properties of a strong alkali, decomposing organic tissues, and saturating the strongest acids. It is more soluble in cold than in hot water; 778 pounds of cold water, or 1270 pounds of hot water, are required to dissolve 1 pound of lime. Hence, when a cold saturated solution of lime-water is boiled, a portion of the lime is deposited, which accounts for the crust or fur which lines the interior of tea-kettles and boilers in localities where the water is impregnated with lime. Lime-water is a satu rated solution of lime in water; it is used to counteract acidity of the stomach. *Cream* or *milk* of lime is a thick mix ture of the hydrate with water, such as is used for white-washing. In tanneries, the hides are immersed in milk of

What is the effect of water upon quicklime? What is the effect of adding water too rapidly in slaking?

How is caustic lime changed to the carbonate? What is stated of its solubility? For what is lime-water used? What is milk of lime? Its use?

lime, which partially decomposes them, so that the hair may be easily rubbed off.

211. *Mortar and Cement.*—Lime mixed with sand forms mortar, employed by builders to cement stones and bricks together, as glue is used to join pieces of wood. To make the best mortar, the lime should be perfectly caustic, and the sand sharp and coarse-grained; the presence of clay, even in small proportions, is injurious. The nature of the changes by which the mortar becomes hardened is not satisfactorily explained. *Hydraulic* cement possesses the property of solidifying under water, which ordinary mortar will not do. This property is owing to the presence of sand and clay (silicate of alumina) in the lime of which it is made.

212. *Lime exists in Organized Structures.*—The mineral portion of the skeletons of the higher animals consists of lime combined with phosphoric acid. The shells of the lower animals contain lime, combined chiefly with carbonic acid; and as all parts of animals are derived from the vegetable world, lime must be an essential constituent of plants. Its most extensive use is in agriculture.

213. *Lime in Crops.*—Some soils contain an abundant natural supply of lime; to such its addition is of course useless. Where it does not exist, it must be applied, to enter into the systems of plants. The following table exhibits the amount of lime removed from an acre of land in the following crops; tops, straw, and grain are included.

		Lime.			Lime.
Wheat,	25 bushels,	8·7 lbs.	Turnips,	25 tons,	138·8 lbs.
Barley,	38 "	15·0 "	Potatoes,	9 "	266 0 "
Oats,	50 "	8·2 "	Red Clover,	2 "	126·0 "
					(*Johnston.*)

How is the best mortar made?
In what part of animal structures does lime exist?
Why should lime be added to soils which do not possess it?

These quantities are not always the same ; wheat, especially, contains much more lime than is here stated, when grown upon land to which it has been copiously applied.

214. *Effect of Lime upon the Soil and Plants.*—Lime exerts a very favorable action upon clay soils, by loosening and rendering them less adhesive, and also by setting free the alkalies which are locked up in clay. Soils abounding in vegetable matter are often improved by liming. It changes inert substances in the soil, so as gradually to render them useful to vegetation, decomposes noxious compounds, neutralizes baneful acids, sweetens vegetation, and improves the quality of almost every cultivatable crop. Grain grown upon well-limed land, it is said, has a thinner skin, is heavier, yields more flour, and that richer in gluten than if grown on unlimed land. On flax alone it is said to be injurious, diminishing the strength of the fibre of the stem. Hence in Belgium flax is not grown upon land until seven years after the lime has been applied.—(*Johnston.*)

215. Compounds formed by lime in the soil are insoluble; its action is therefore slow, often requiring from three to six years to produce the best effect. At first it often diminishes the crops, and always does this in overdoses. The hydrate acts most speedily, but good effects may be expected from the carbonate after a longer time. " The more dry, shallow, light, and sandy the soil, the less abundant in vegetable matter ; the milder and warmer the climate in which it is situated, the *less* the quantity of lime which the prudent farmer will venture to mix with it." Lime should never be mixed with fermenting farm-yard

What effect has lime upon clay soils? How does it act upon soils rich in vegetable matter? What is said of grain grown on limed land? What of flax?

Why is its beneficial action so slow? What is the effect of an overdose? Under what circumstances should lime be used with caution? Why should lime never be mixed with farm-yard manure?

manure, as it expels ammonia, a most valuable element of fertility.

MAGNESIUM

Symbol Mg, *equivalent* 12·67.

216. Magnesium is a silver-white metal, like the three preceding. It is of no use, and is prepared only as a curiosity. It unites with oxygen, forming *oxide of magnesium*, or common magnesia, Mg O. Magnesia was first distinguished from lime by Dr. Black, about a hundred years ago. It is a white powder, possessing feeble alkaline properties, and dissolving in about 55,000 times its weight of water.—(*Fresinius*.) Magnesia is found united with acids ; as a sulphate in mineral waters, as a carbonate in magnesian limestone, as a silicate in talc, serpentine, &c. It is prepared by igniting the carbonate. It is used as a mild aperient and corrector of acidity. Magnesia is found in the ash of nearly all plants, but its action upon soils is obscure. Specific gravity, 3·61.

METALS OF THE EARTHS.

ALUMINUM

Symbol Al, *equivalent* 13 69.

217. This metal never occurs free in nature, but always in union with oxygen, forming a sesquioxide of aluminum, $Al_2 O_3$. It absorbs moisture with great avidity. Alumina can neither be pronounced an acid nor an alkali, and yet it seems to possess the properties of both ; towards acids it sometimes

What are the properties of magnesia?
How is alumina obtained? What are its properties? In what forms does it exist pure?

plays the part of a base, while towards bases it behaves as an acid—forming combinations with either. Pure alumina is found crystallized in those precious gems, the ruby and sapphire, which are next in hardness and value to the diamond ; also in a more massive form, as corundum or emery.

218. *Used to fix Colors.*—Alumina has a powerful attraction, both for vegetable coloring matter and the fibre of cloth ; it is hence used by dyers to fix the color upon their fabrics. It is then said to act as a *mordant* (479). When a solution of alum is mixed with an alkali, the coloring matter is carried down, and forms what is called a *lake*. *Carmine* is a lake of cochineal. Alumina also absorbs and combines with oily matters ; hence a certain kind of clay called fullers' earth is used to extract grease-spots from wood, paper, &c.

219. *Composition of Soils.*—Alumina is the basis of clay in soils ; but it is always mixed with more or less silica or sand. To determine the relative amount of clay and sand in a specimen of soil, agitate it thoroughly with a considerable quantity of water, and pour the mixture into a tall glass vessel or wide tube. When left at rest, the coarser particles of sand will first fall to the bottom, then the finer sand, and lastly the clay. By observing the relative thicknesses of the different layers, we get a tolerably correct idea of their proportional quantities. By pouring off the turbid water, after the sand has settled, the clay may be separated from it. It is, however, to be remembered that the purest clay we can obtain by repeated washings and separations, still contains from four to six per cent. of very fine sand,

---

Upon what property does the use of alumina as a mordant depend? What is a *lake*? How does alumina act to extract grease-spots?

How can we determine the relative amount of it in soils? How does Professor Johnston classify soils ?

which can only be removed from it by the refined processes of chemistry. Professor Johnston classifies soils as follows : *pure clay*, or *pipe clay*, that which will allow nothing to subside or separate when diffused through water. The *strongest clay soil* parts with 10 to 15 per cent. of sand by boiling with water and decantation. A *clay loam* loses from 15 to 30 per cent. by the same process. A *loamy soil* deposits from 30 to 60 per cent., a *sandy loam* from 60 to 90 per cent., while a *sandy soil* contains no more than 10 per cent. of pure clay.

220. Clay exhibits in a high degree the power of absorbing and retaining water; hence soils in which clay abounds, after heavy rains suffer the water to evaporate but slowly, and are therefore wet and cold. It is also adhesive, and so compact as to prevent the free extension of the roots. On the contrary, in dry weather it shrinks, hardens, and cracks. Sand possesses the opposite qualities: it retains water but feebly, yields it readily by evaporation, and so completely lacks adhesion that its particles are blown about by the winds. A due admixture of these earths corrects their mutual faults, and forms a productive soil. Clay possesses the valuable property of condensing carbonic acid and ammonia from the atmosphere Porcelain, pottery, bricks, &c., are chemical combinations of alumina with silica, and will be noticed among the silicates (309).

SILICON.

Symbol Si, *equivalent* 21·35.

221. This is a brown powder which does not occur in nature. It is difficult to produce, and is of no importance ex-

---

Why are strong clay soils wet and cold ? What effect has dry weather upon them ? What are the disadvantages of a sandy soil ?

What is said of silicon ? What is stated of the abundance of silica upon the globe ?

cept to the scientific chemist.   It holds an equivocal position in systems of classification.   Brande ranks it among the metals ; and although it may have affinities elsewhere, I adopt his arrangement in this respect, and associate it with aluminum : these form the bases of the two principal earths.   Silica, or oxide of silicon, is estimated to form one-sixth part of the surface of the globe.—(*Silliman*).   In extent it seems to occupy a similar place in the mineral world with carbon in the organic world.   (See Chart).

SILICA   (*Silicic Acid—Silex—Sand.*)

Si O_3 = 45·35.

222. *Preparation and Varieties.*—This abundant compound may be prepared by heating rock-crystal (*quartz*) to redness, and quenching it in water, when it may be easily reduced to a fine, white, tasteless, gritty powder, which is nearly pure silica.   In some of its forms this mineral is found everywhere.   It constitutes a large portion of the rocks in many mountain ranges, the sand and gravel of soils, and the pebbles upon the sea-shore.   It forms gun-flints, grindstones, and the porous burr-stones used in flouring-mills for grinding grain.   Crystallized silica, when colorless, forms quartz or rock-crystal ; when violet-colored, it is the *amethyst ;* when green, *chrysoprase ;* when red, *rose-quartz ;* when possessing red veins or spots, *blood-stone ;* when of a flesh-color, *carnelian ;* when deposited from water, *chalcedony.*   *Sard* is a reddish-brown variety of chalcedony.   *Onyx* is a milk-white variety.   *Sardonyx* consists of the two in plates or layers, giving rise to a beautiful arrangement of colors, and when cut forms *cameos.*   *Agate, jasper,* and *opal* are also forms of

---

silica. Silica, as it occurs in all these forms, is contaminated with certain impurities, usually oxides of iron. Quartz is so hard as to give fire with steel, and scratch glass; and so pure, as to be often used for the eyes of spectacles, under the name of pebbles.

223. *Silica an Acid.*—However strange it may seem that such substances as sand and flint should be ranked among acids, yet such is the fact. At high temperatures, silica exhibits powerful acid properties, and neutralizes numerous bases, forming a class of salts—the silicates. Glass, porcelain, and pottery-ware are all salts—silicates of various bases formed at a high heat (303). Most rocks and minerals are also silicates. (See Chart.)

224. Silica is dissolved by but one acid, the hydrofluoric, which is hence often used for etching glass. Although common quartz and sand are totally insoluble in water, yet they are rendered soluble by the action of the alkalies; hence one reason of applying potash to soils, is to dissolve their silica. When liberated from its combinations by the agency of the air (302), it is soluble in water, and hence is always present in springs, the waters of which trickle through soils and the fissures of rocks. Silica is necessary to the growth of vegetation, and exists abundantly in many plants; particularly in the stalks of the grains and grasses. It is this which communicates stiffness and strength to their stems, as the skeleton does to the bodies of animals. If there is a deficiency of soluble silica in the soil, the grain-stalk will be weak, and liable to break down, or *lodge.* It is silica which gives their quality to scouring-rushes.

When does silica exhibit acid properties? What salts of silica are in common use?

What acid dissolves silica? Under what circumstances does silica become soluble? What office does it perform in plants?

METALS EMPLOYED IN THE ARTS.

I R O N. (*Latin, Ferrum.*)
Symbol Fe, *equivalent* 28.

225. Were we to seek for that circumstance which might best illustrate the peculiarities of ancient and modern civilization, we should perhaps find it in the history of this metal. The ancients, imbued with a martial spirit and passion for conquest, regarded iron as the symbol of war, and gave it the emblem of Mars. And if it were required also to symbolize the pacific tendencies of modern society—its triumphs of industry and victories of mind over matter, its artistic achievements and scientific discoveries—we should be compelled to make use of the same metal, IRON. As gold and jewels have long been the type of ignorant and empty pomp, so iron may now be well regarded as the emblem of beneficent and intelligent industry.

226. *Uses of Iron.*—Iron, in some of its innumerable forms, ministers to the benefit of all. The implements of the miner, the farmer, the carpenter, the mason, the smith, the shipwright, are made *of* iron, and *with* iron. Roads of iron, travelled by "iron steeds," which drag whole townships after them, and outstrip the birds, have become our commonest highways. Ponderous iron ships are afloat upon the ocean, with massive iron engines to propel them; iron anchors to stay them in storms; iron needles to guide them; and springs of iron in chronometers, by which they measure the time. Ink, pens, and printing-presses, by which knowledge is scattered over the world, are alike made of iron. It warms us in our apartments; relieves our jolts in the carriage; ministers to our ailments in the chalybeate mineral

How did the ancients regard iron? Of what may it now become the symbol? Enumerate some of the uses that are made of iron.

waters, or the medicinal dose; it gives variety of color to rocks and soils, nourishment to vegetation, and vigor to the blood of man. Such are the powers of a substance which chemists extract from an otherwise worthless stone.

227. *Properties of Iron.*—Iron is of a grayish-white color, and of a perfect lustre when polished. It may be thrown into many conditions, in which it exhibits remarkably different properties. It is malleable, as in bar or wrought iron; and may be forged into any form under the hammer. It is very ductile, and may be drawn out into the finest wire, which is extremely tenacious (tough); an iron wire $\frac{1}{36}$ of an inch in diameter bearing a weight of sixty pounds.

228. *Welding of Iron.*—When wrought-iron is heated to whiteness, it becomes soft, pasty, and adhesive, and two pieces in this condition may be incorporated or hammered together into one. This is called *welding.* During the heating, a film of oxide is formed upon the surface of the metal, which would obstruct the ready cohesion of the separate masses. To prevent this, the smith sprinkles a little sand upon the hot iron, which combines with the oxide, forming a fusible silicate of iron, which is easily forced out by pressure, leaving clean surfaces that unite without difficulty. This important quality is enjoyed only by iron, platinum, and sodium. All the other metals pass suddenly from the solid to the liquid state at their respective melting points, as ice is changed to water.

229. *Wrought and Cast Iron.*—Wrought-iron possesses what is called a *fibrous texture;* that is, it seems to consist of compacted threads, running parallel to each other like the fibres of flax. Another state of the metal is *cast-iron*, which,

What is the appearance of iron? Name some of the conditions it may assume. What is welding? Have all metals this property?
What is the texture of wrought-iron? What of cast-iron? ‘ What is said of the

on the contrary, has a granular texture (consists of grains) it is brittle, cannot be forged, but may be melted and cast in moulds, which wrought-iron cannot. Cast-iron expands when first poured into a mould, so as to copy it perfectly; but it subsequently contracts, so as to be less in size than the original pattern. The *expansion* is caused by the particles assuming a crystalline arrangement while consolidating; the *contraction* by the cooling of the metallic mass, after it has solidified. Wrought-iron is said to lose its tough, fibrous character, by the effect of blows or constant jarring, and to become crystalline.

230. *Ores of Iron—The Per Centage Scale.*—Iron occurs in nature almost universally in a state of combination. The mineral masses which it forms with oxygen, carbon, sulphur, and the metals, and from which it is extracted, are called its ores. They are quite numerous, but are not all equally valuable as sources of the metal. The five principal ores that are wrought for the production of iron, are exhibited upon the Chart by means of a scale marked off into a hundred divisions. The proportions per cent. of iron, and the elements with which it is combined in the ore, are shown in a very clear manner. This method of expressing chemical composition, by proportions per cent., was in general use before the introduction of atomic proportions: it is still much employed.

231. One of the richest ores of iron is loadstone, or the magnetic black oxide. It contains seventy-two per cent. of iron to twenty-eight per cent. of oxygen, and is a mixture of the protoxide and the peroxide. It is of a grayish color, and when rubbed gives a black powder, and is strongly magnetic. This is one of the most valuable ores; it is very widely dif-

---

changes which cast-iron undergoes after being poured into the mould? What causes its expansion and contraction?

What are ores of iron? How is their composition represented upon the Chart?

fused, and furnishes iron of the best quality. The superior iron from Russia, Germany, and Sweden is produced from it. *Specular iron (red iron ore).*—This is very hard, and sometimes resembles polished steel. When coarse, the oxide is of a brown color; but its powder is always red, thus distinguishing it from the magnetic oxide. This oxide contains sixty-three per cent. of iron to thirty-seven of oxygen. It exists in all the red clays, which are termed ores when they yield twenty per cent. of the metal. *Hematite (hydrated oxide of iron).*—*Brown iron-stone* is very abundant all over the world, and particularly in the United States, and is the chief source of the iron of commerce. It usually affords a yellow powder, and is not attracted by the magnet unless it has been burnt or roasted. It contains fifty-nine per cent. of iron, twenty-seven of oxygen, and fourteen of water.

232. *Pyrites,* which signifies fire-stone, is so named because it was used in firelocks, before the introduction of gunflints, to produce sparks with steel. It is a sulphuret of iron, of which there are two principal varieties, the red and white. Yellow pyrites, when it occurs in minute brilliant scales, is sometimes mistaken for gold (*fool's gold*). It is tested at once by heating it, when it gives off a sulphurous smell. Pyrites is chiefly prized as a source of copperas, alum, Spanish brown, sulphur, and sulphuric acid. Yellow pyrites contains forty-seven per cent. of iron and fifty-three of sulphur. *Sparry iron (steel ore)* is of a yellowish-gray or brownish-red color. It is a carbonate of iron, and effervesces slightly with nitric acid. This ore contains sixty-three per cent. of oxide of iron, thirty-four per cent. of carbonic acid, with a

What is said of loadstone? What is its color? What of its powder? What are the properties of specular iron or red ore? Of hematite?

What is the meaning of the term *pyrites?* Its origin? Composition? What is it often mistaken for? What are its chief uses? What is stated concerning sparry iron? What does it produce?

small quantity of lime, magnesia, and manganese. A variety of steel is made directly from this ore, without cementation (236). The cheap German steel is derived from this ore.

233. *Obtaining the Metal.*—The process of separating this metal from its ores is called *reducing* or *reviving* it, and the ores are said to be *smelted.* The operation is conducted in tall chimney-like structures, termed *blast-furnaces.* They are constructed of the most refractory fire-proof bricks, and are from thirty to sixty feet high, and about sixteen feet in internal diameter in the largest place, having the form seen in Fig. 18. The top or mouth of the furnace serves both for charging it and for the escape of smoke: it is both door and chimney. The tubes serve to supply the air, which is driven in by means of a steam-engine and an air-pump, or fanners. A single blast apparatus, connected with an English furnace, propelled 12,588 cubic feet of air per minute.—(*Ure.*) Formerly the air was used at the ordinary temperature (*cold blast*), but within a few years an immense improvement has been effected by heating the air before it enters the furnace (*hot blast*).

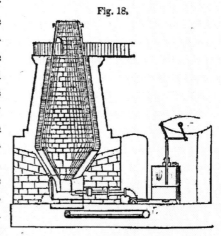

Fig. 18.

234. In some cases, the materials are drawn up an inclined plane, to the mouth of the shaft, by means of the

What is reducing or reviving? In what is the operation of smelting conducted? Describe the blast-furnace. What is the hot blast? The cold blast?

same steam-engine that impels the blast mechanism. The furnace is supplied with ore, coal, and limestone, broken into small fragments. When the heat is sufficiently intense, the carbon of the fuel deoxidizes the iron, and carbonic acid is also expelled from the lime, leaving it caustic. Sand and clay, in greater or less quantities, now remain combined with the iron. The lime, acting as a flux, unites with these, forming the *slag* or *scoria*, a crude semi-vitreous product. The melted iron, falling to the bottom of the furnace, accumulates, and is drawn off by taking out a *tap* or *plug*. It is allowed to run into a bed of sand, containing straight channels, and furrows running at right angles. The former are termed by the workmen the *sow*, and the latter the *pigs*, and hence the origin of the term *pig-iron*. As the contents of the furnace are removed from below, crude ore is constantly supplied above, and the operation goes on day and night uninterruptedly for years, or until the fabric demands repair.

235. The product of the smelting-furnace is *cast-iron*. Its peculiar properties of brittleness and fusibility are due to the presence of a considerable quantity of carbon and some other impurities, the removal of which converts it into wrought-iron. This is done in an oven-shaped furnace (reverberatory furnace), in which the fuel is not mingled with the metal, as in the case of smelting, but heats it by the flame reflected from the low roof. A workman, with a long oar-shaped implement of iron, stirs (puddles) the melted mass until the carbon is burned away, and the metal becomes thick and pasty: this is called *puddling*. The puddler then rolls it up

---

In what form are the materials introduced? What are the first changes which take place? What part does the lime play? What is the origin of the term pig-iron?

What is the product of the smelting-furnace? What impurities does it contain? How is it changed into wrought-iron? Describe the puddling process. How is the iron greatly improved?

into balls, which he transfers to the *tilting-hammer*, where it is beaten by heavy blows into a rude bar, the liquid impurities, consisting principally of silica and alumina, being squeezed out, as water is driven from a compressed sponge. The metal, still hot, is then passed between grooved cylinders, and rolled out into bar-iron. The quality of the metal is greatly improved when these bars are broken up, bound together, reheated to the welding point, and put through the same process repeatedly: this is called *piling* or *fagoting*. In malleable iron there is still retained a small portion of carbon, about $\frac{1}{2}$ per cent.

236. *Steel.*—This remarkable modification of iron is a compound of iron with about one and a half per cent. of carbon. It is made by imbedding bars of the best wrought-iron in powdered charcoal, in boxes or sand-furnaces which exclude the air, and heating it intensely for a week or ten days. The chemical changes that take place are obscure; probably carbonic oxide penetrates the heated metal, is decomposed, surrenders part of its carbon, and escapes as carbonic acid. The steel, when withdrawn, has a peculiar, rough, blistered appearance, and is hence known as *blistered steel*. This method of making steel is called the process of *cementation*. When blistered steel is drawn into smaller bars, under the tilting-hammer, it forms *tilted steel;* and this, broken up, heated, and again drawn out, forms *shear steel*, so called because it was originally thus prepared for making *shears* to dress woollen cloth. English cast-steel is prepared by melting blistered steel, casting it into moulds, and drawing it out into bars. *Case-hardening* consists in forming the surface of iron into steel, by heating it with charcoal for a short time.

What is steel? How is it made? What change occurs? What is tilted steel? What is shear steel? What is case-hardening?

237. In its properties steel combines the fusibility of cast-iron with the malleability of bar-iron. Its value for cutting instruments, springs, &c., depends upon its quality of being tempered. When heated to redness, and suddenly quenched in cold water, it becomes so hard as to scratch glass. If again heated, and cooled slowly, it becomes as soft as ordinary iron ; and, between these two conditions, any required degree of hardness can be obtained. As the metal declines in temperature, the thin film of oxide upon its surface constantly changes its color. The workmen are guided by these tints. Thus a straw yellow indicates the degree of hardness for razors, a deep blue for sword-blades, saws, and watch-springs. Steel receives a higher polish than iron, and has a less tendency to rust.

238. Nitric acid, placed upon steel, corrodes the metal, and leaves the carbon as a dark-gray stain; writing and ornamental shading is thus often produced upon it. A good quality of steel, when its clean surface is washed with dilute nitric acid, should give a uniform tint. If it exhibits a fibrous, streaked, or mottled appearance, we may infer that it has been unequally carbonized, and is not the best. A drop of nitric acid leaves upon iron a whitish-green stain (oxide) ; it may thus be distinguished from steel. Steel may be made magnetic, and retains its magnetism permanently; but soft iron may be charged with magnetism, and deprived of it, at will. Upon this property of iron depends the action of the electro-magnetic telegraph.

239. *Oxides of Iron.*—Iron has a strong affinity for oxygen (74), and unites with it, forming oxides. When metallic

Upon what does its value for cutting instruments depend ? What is said of polishing and rusting ?

What effect has nitric acid upon steel ? What is the test of good steel ? How may iron be distinguished from steel ? What is said of the magnetic properties of iron and steel ?

iron is exposed to moist air, it soon becomes covered with a red crust, which is the sesquioxide of iron, $Fe_2 O_3$; it is also called the peroxide. This oxide gradually absorbs water, turns of a yellowish color, and forms rust, which is hydrated peroxide of iron. These colors are well shown in bricks, which before burning are of a yellow color, owing to the hydrated peroxide of iron in the clay. Heat expels the water from the peroxide, which colors the bricks red.

240. These compounds of iron are the most abundant oxides in nature, existing in numerous stones, rocks, and soils, and are the cause of their red and yellow colors. Protoxide of iron, Fe O, cannot be produced in a separate state, as it attracts oxygen and rapidly passes into the peroxide. In a state of combination it is widely diffused in nature, existing chiefly in those rocks having a greenish or dark tint. The iron in mineral waters (*chalybeate springs*) usually rises to the surface in the form of a protoxide; after a brief exposure to the air more oxygen is absorbed, and a reddish scum is formed upon the surface, which gradually falls to the bottom of the current as a reddish sediment of insoluble peroxide.

241. When iron is heated in the smith's forge, and then beat on the anvil, a scale flies off which is of a black color, and when crushed gives a black powder: this is the black oxide, and is supposed to be a combination of the two other oxides, Fe O + $Fe_2 O_3$. Gallic acid, with $Fe_2 O_3$, gives a black precipitate (writing-ink); chlorine water and oxalic acid remove it.

242. Iron rusts rapidly in water containing air (oxygen),

What gives to brick their yellow color before being burned? Why are they red after they are burned?

What is said of the abundance of these oxides? Why cannot the protoxide of iron be easily obtained in a separate state? Of what is the reddish sediment in chalybeate springs composed?

What is black oxide of iron? What is ink composed of?

or the slightest trace of acidity. But in water which has been deprived of air by boiling, or rendered alkaline by lime, ammonia, potash, or soda, it is not rusted, but retains its polish for years.—(*Brande.*) *Galvanized iron* is made by dipping iron, the surface of which has been cleaned, into a bath of melted zinc, and then into another of melted tin. The coating thus given prevents rust. When cast-iron, as cannon, for example, has been long buried in the sea, it becomes lighter, and is changed into a substance resembling black-lead. The iron in this case has probably been dissolved by chlorine from the sea-salt. Cast-iron is rendered malleable by heating it for a considerable time with iron scales or oxide. It is thrown into the market under the name of malleable iron.

MANGANESE.

Symbol Mn, *equivalent* 27 67.

243. Manganese is a hard, brittle metal, of a grayish-white appearance, much like cast-iron. It never occurs pure in nature, but its oxides are found combined with many ores of iron, a metal which it resembles in many of its properties. Manganese is prepared by making its oxide into a paste with oil and lamp-black, and heating it to whiteness in a covered crucible. It rapidly oxidizes when exposed to the air, and is best preserved in naphtha.

244. It forms no less than seven different compounds with oxygen. Its oxides are diffused in small quantities through nearly all soils, and traces of them may be detected in the ashes of most plants. Protoxide of manganese is of a pale-green color, is a powerful base, giving rise to rose-colored

How is galvanized iron made? What is said of iron long buried in the sea? How is cast-iron rendered malleable?
What is manganese? What metal does it resemble? How is it prepared?

salts. The peroxide, or black oxide, MnO_2, is employed as a cheap method of procuring oxygen gas on a large scale, and for the manufacture of chlorine. It is also used under the name of glass-maker's soap, to destroy the green tinge given to glass by protoxide of iron, and to oxidize carbonaceous impurities. If added to glass in large quantities, it gives it an amethyst or purple color. It has also beer recently made use of in the manufacture of steel.

ZINC.
Symbol Zn, equivalent 32·52,

245. Zinc is a brilliant, bluish-white meta. sp gr. 7, found abundantly in nature in the state of sulphuret (*zinc blende*), and as carbonate, or *calamine*. It exists in immense quantities in the State of New Jersey. At common temperatures it is brittle, but when heated from 212° F. to 300° it may be rolled out into thin sheets, and retains its malleability when cold. At 400° it becomes again quite brittle, at 770° it melts, and when air has access to it, it takes fire, burning with a whitish-green flame It soon tarnishes in moist air, forming a thin film of oxide, which resists change. Zinc is extensively used for roofing, gas-pipes, gasometers, gutters, the lining of refrigerators, for preparing hydrogen, and in galvanic batteries. It is lighter than lead, cheaper than copper, and less liable than iron to be affected by oxidation

COPPER. (*Latin, Cuprum.*)
Symbol Cu, equivalent 31·66, sp. gr. 8 95

246. Copper is a tough, malleable metal, of a red color, and often found native in masses of great magnitude. It is

---

What is said of the oxides of manganese ? What are their uses ?
What is zinc ? What are its properties? Its uses ?

stiffened by hammering, and softened by heating and quenching in water; the reverse of the effect produced upon
steel (237). In moderately dry air copper slowly acquires
a superficial brown tarnish, consisting of a thin film of sub-
oxide, $Cu_2 O$. In damp air it acquires a green crust, from
the formation of the carbonate. Vegetable acids dissolve
copper in the cold state and not in the hot state. Sauces
containing vinegar, and preserved fruits or jellies, should,
therefore, not be allowed to remain in copper vessels, as the
salts produced are poisonous. Being little affected by the
air, copper is better adapted for culinary and many other
utensils than iron.

LEAD. (*Latin, Plumbum.*)

Symbol Pb, *equivalent* 103 56, sp. gr. 11·35.

247. This useful and familiar metal occurs under various
mineral forms, but the most valuable one is galena, a sulphuret. Lead is a soft, blue metal, easily scratched by the nail,
and leaving a stain when rubbed upon paper. It is highly
malleable, but not very ductile. In the air a film of oxide is
rapidly formed, which protects it from further corrosion. It
melts at about 612°, and on the surface of the melted mass
an oxide (dross) rapidly forms It contracts upon solidifying, which renders it unfit for castings. Litharge is a protoxide of lead, Pb O. Minium, or red-lead, consists of
$Pb_3 O_4$. White-lead is a carbonate of the protoxide of lead ;
it is the most important salt of lead, being extensively used
as a white paint, and also to give body to other paints.

What is copper ? What effect has air upon it ? What precautions should be
observed in the use of copper utensils ?
What is lead ? Give its properties. What is litharge ? Red-lead ? White-
lead ?

ANTIMONY. (*Latin, Stibium.*)

Symbol Sb, equivalent 129 03.

248. Antimony occurs in nature united with sulphur. It is a brittle, bluish-white metal, and is but little affected by exposure to the air. The compounds of antimony are used in medicine, the most important being the tartrate of antimony and potash, or tartar emetic.

ARSENIC.

Symbol As, equivalent 75.

249. Arsenic is a brilliant, brittle, steel-gray metal, usually occurring united to iron and sulphur, from which it is separated by heat. The coarse gray powder sold as fly-poison, under the name of cobalt, consists of metallic arsenic. Common arsenic, or arsenious acid, $As\ O_3$, is formed by a union of the metal with oxygen. This is white arsenic, or ratsbane, the well-known poison. Its antidote is iron-rust (hydrated sesquioxide of iron), with which it combines, forming the insoluble arseniate of iron. If this is not at hand, milk, the whites of eggs, soap-suds, or sugar, should be swallowed, and the same observation may be applied to other cases of poisoning. Arsenious acid prevents the decay of organized substances, and it is therefore rubbed on the flesh side of the skins of animals that are to be preserved. When exposed to heat it volatilizes before melting, and its vapor has the odor of garlic.

What are the properties and uses of antimony? What is tartar emetic? What is arsenic? What is said of it? What is the antidote? What is the effect of common arsenic upon flesh?

TIN. (*Latin, Stannum.*)

Symbol Sn, *equivalent* 58·82.

250. Tin is a brilliant, silver-white metal, which occurs most abundantly in Cornwall, England. It has been found in this country only at Jackson, N. H., in small quantities. It is softer than gold, slightly ductile, and very malleable, common tin-leaf or foil being often not more than $\frac{1}{1000}$ of an inch in thickness. It melts at 442°. When a bar of tin is bent it gives a peculiar crackling sound, due to the disturbance of its crystalline structure. It tarnishes but slightly upon exposure to the air, and is therefore very suitable for cooking-vessels. Sheet-iron coated with tin constitutes the common tin-ware

MERCURY. (*Latin, Hydrargyrum.*)

Symbol Hg, *equivalent* 100 07.

251. Mercury is sometimes found in the metallic state, but is principally obtained from the bisulphuret (cinnabar), by distillation with lime or iron filings in iron retorts. It has a silvery-white color, a brilliant lustre, and is distinguished from all other metals by being liquid at ordinary temperatures. It solidifies only when cooled to −40° F., and is then soft and malleable, but if reduced to a much lower temperature it becomes brittle. It boils at about 660°, and emits vapors at all temperatures above −40° F. Its sp. gr. is 13·568.

252. Mercury is extensively used in the construction of

What is the appearance of tin? What are its properties? What is common tin-ware?

Give an account of mercury.

barometers, thermometers, mirrors, &c. When heated nearly to its boiling point, and exposed to the action of air, it absorbs oxygen, and is converted into the peroxide of mercury (red oxide), which; when heated, evolves oxygen, and is reduced to a metallic state. It was from this source that Priestley first obtained oxygen gas. Mercury combines with chlorine in two proportions, forming the protochloride of mercury, Hg Cl (calomel), and the bichloride, Hg Cl₂ (corrosive sublimate). The latter has a disagreeable, acrid, metallic taste, and is very poisonous. The proper antidote is white of egg, which forms with it an insoluble, inert compound.

SILVER. (Latin, Argentum.)
Symbol Ag, equivalent 108.

253. Silver occurs native, both uncombined and as a sulphuret and chloride. It is the whitest of the metals, and has a bright, beautiful lustre. It is very malleable and ductile. It may be extended into leaves not exceeding $\frac{1}{10}$ of an inch in thickness, and one grain may be drawn out into 400 feet of wire. It is used chiefly for coinage and silver plate. Silver does not tarnish in air or water. It forms compounds with oxygen, sulphur, chlorine, iodine, and bromine, all of which are darkened by the action of light, a property which is made use of in the daguerreotype process.

PLATINUM.
Symbol Pt, equivalent 98 68

254. This very valuable metal is of a whitish-gray color, somewhat resembling silver. When pure, it scarcely yields

For what is mercury used? What is the composition of calomel? What is the composition of corrosive sublimate?

Describe silver. What is said of its compounds?

What are the qualities of platinum?

in malleability to gold and silver. It is very ductile, and takes a good polish. But the qualities which render it so useful, and in some cases indispensable to the chemist, are its extreme difficulty of fusion, being unaffected by any furnace heat, and the perfect manner with which it resists the action of almost all acids. It is acted on by chlorine and aqua regia, but less easily than gold, and is not affected by air. Platinum is about half as valuable as gold. Sp. gr. 22·5.

GOLD. (*Latin, Aurum.*)

Symbol Au, *equivalent* 98 23.

255. This is one of the most widely diffused of the metals, being found native in every country, generally in the form of minute grains, though sometimes in masses weighing several pounds. It has a brilliant yellow color and great density. It is so very malleable that it may be extended into leaves $\frac{1}{282000}$ of an inch in thickness, and so ductile that a single grain may be drawn into 500 feet of wire. It does not tarnish or oxidize when exposed to the air or heat, is affected by no single acid, and dissolved only by aqua regia (124). Its specific gravity is 19·2.

METALS COMBINED WITH EACH OTHER—ALLOYS.

256. Metals combine with metals to form alloys—an important class of bodies, as each compound thus produced may be looked upon, for all practical purposes, as a new metal.

257. *Brass* is an alloy of copper and zinc : four parts of the former to three of the latter. When the proportion of zinc is increased we have *pinchbeck*, or *Dutch gold*

What is said of gold? What are its properties?
What are alloys? How may they be considered?
What is brass? Pinchbeck?

258. *German silver* is an alloy of copper, zinc, and nickel, the finer kinds containing most nickel. Bronze consists of 90 parts of copper to 10 of tin; gun-metal, 92 copper to 8 of tin; *bell-metal* and *gong-metal* of 80 parts of copper to 20 of tin. Britannia consists of about 100 parts of tin, 8 of antimony, 2 of bismuth, and 2 of copper.

259. The speculum of Lord Rosse's celebrated telescope is composed of 126·4 of copper to 58·9 of tin.

260. *Type-metal* is an alloy of 3 parts of lead and 1 of antimony. Pewter is composed of tin, with a little antimony, copper, and bismuth. The inferior kinds contain a good deal of lead.

261. Alloys which contain mercury are called *amalgams.* An amalgam of tin is used for silvering the backs of mirrors; and an amalgam of tin and zinc for exciting electrical machines. Gold and silver coin is alloyed with from $\frac{1}{10}$ to $\frac{1}{13}$ of copper, by which its hardness and wearing quality is greatly improved.

SALTS.

262. Salts are combinations of acids with bases (49). They are a very numerous class of bodies. We can here notice but few of them, and those very briefly. The common idea of a salt is that it must have a saline taste, like ordinary kitchen salt, and dissolve in water; but this notion is erroneous, as many salts have no taste at all, and are insoluble in any quantity of water, either cold or hot. There are two ways of classifying or grouping the salts—either by placing

What is German silver? Bell-metal? Bronze? Britannia?
Type-metal? Pewter?
What are amalgams? What is said of coin?
What is a salt? What is the common idea of a salt? How is this wrong?
How are the salts classified?

together those which have a common acid, or those which have a common base. I have adopted the arrangement of D_1. Gregory, and classed together those derived from a common acid. The salts contain variable proportions of water, which are represented upon the Chart by the usual symbolic letters (H O), instead of diagrams.

SULPHATES.

PROTOSULPHATE OF IRON.   (*Copperas, Green Vitriol*)

$$Fe\ O, S\ O_3 + 7\ H\ O.—(Silliman.)$$

263. This salt, composed of sulphuric acid and protoxide of iron, is largely manufactured at Stafford, Vt., by the decomposition of iron pyrites, which furnishes, by oxidation, both the acid and the base (see Chart). It is used for dyeing dark colors, for making ink, and in medicine as a tonic in nervous diseases, and where the blood is supposed to be deficient in iron. It often exists in soils to a pernicious extent, but is decomposed by lime; gypsum or plaster being formed.

SULPHATE OF LIME.   (*Plaster of Paris, Gypsum, Alabaster.*)

$$Ca\ O, S\ O_3 + 2\ H\ O = 86. \quad Sp.\ gr.\ 2\cdot3.—(Graham.)$$

264. This salt is easily made artificially, by dropping sulphuric acid upon lime. It occurs in many parts of the world, forming extensive rocky beds. It is so soft as to be scratched with the nail. The white varieties are turned in lathes, and worked with edge tools into various ornamental

---

What is the composition of protosulphate of iron? For what is it used?

What is the composition of sulphate of lime? What are its common names? Where is it found? What is alabaster? What property adapts it for taking casts? What is stucco-work?

forms, constituting the common *alabaster*. When powdered gypsum is heated to nearly 300° F., it parts with its water of crystallization. If now it is made into a liquid paste with water, it again combines with it, and speedily hardens or sets, resuming its stony aspect. Owing to this property, it is used to take impressions and make casts, by being run into hollow moulds. It is also used in architecture for making ornamental figures and designs upon walls and ceilings, called *stucco-work*.

265. Ground gypsum is of extensive use in agriculture. It is supposed to act by furnishing lime and sulphur to plants, and by absorbing carbonate of ammonia from the air and rain-water. It is said to *fix* the ammonia, that is, it is decomposed, forming sulphate of ammonia and carbonate of lime. It dissolves in 468 times its weight of water, and is a constituent of most springs, the water of which it renders hard (96).

SULPHATE OF MAGNESIA. (*Epsom Salts.*)

$$Mg\,O,\,S\,O_3 + 7\,H\,O - (Graham.)$$

266. This well-known salt is made by dissolving magnesian limestone or serpentine rock in strong sulphuric acid. It exists in some natural waters, as in the Epsom springs, whence its name. It is used in medicine as an aperient, and as an antidote to the salts of lead, which are poisonous.

SULPHATE OF SODA. (*Glauber's Salt.*)

$$Na\,O,\,S\,O_3 + 10\,H\,O = 71 + 90. - (Graham.)$$

267. This salt is made by the action of sulphuric acid upon soda or common salt. It was introduced into medicine by

What is said of the use of gypsum in agriculture ?
Give the composition and uses of Epsom salts.
Of Glauber's salt.

Glauber, and is therefore called Glauber's salt. Its chief use is as a cathartic for horses and cattle.

SULPHATE OF ALUMINA AND POTASH. (*Alum.*)

$$K O\ S O_3 + Al_2 O_3\ 3 S O_3 + 24 H O.$$

268. Alum is a double salt, consisting of two bases united to one acid. It has a sweetish, astringent taste, and is dissolved in 18 times its weight of cold water, and in its weight of boiling water.—(*Fownes.*) It is extensively used in dyeing, the alumina it contains being the active agent (218). It is also used in tanning, and in clarifying liquors, &c. The potash of alum may be replaced by soda (soda alum) and ammonia (ammonia alum), without altering the form of its crystals.

THE CARBONATES.

269. These are very abundant in nature. . Carbonic acid, being always present in the air and in natural waters, is ever ready to seize upon free bases. The union of carbonic acid in salts is very weak, owing to its elastic property, by which it constantly tends to escape into the condition of a gas. It is expelled from its combinations by most other acids, and always with effervescence, a property which distinguishes the carbonates.

What are the properties of alum?

Why are carbonates so abundant? Why are they easily decomposed? How are they distinguished?

CARBONATE OF SODA.

$$Na\ O,\ C\ O_2 + 10\ H\ O = 53 + 90.\ —(Graham.)$$

270. The form of the soda of commerce is soda-ash. It was formerly procured by leaching the ashes of marine plants. It is now chiefly made from sea-salt, by the action of sulphuric acid; sulphate of soda is formed, which is converted into the carbonate by means of lime and sawdust, under the influence of heat. The discovery of this process by Leblanc, of France, at the close of the last century, produced immense results upon the manufactures and commerce of the world. (See Liebig's Letters on Chemistry.) Carbonate of soda, being both cheaper and purer than ordinary potash, is largely employed in the manufacture of soap and glass. It is also much used by washerwomen as a detergent, and to render hard water soft. Soda replaces potash in the ashes of plants grown near the sea.

271. Bicarbonate of soda is formed by passing a stream of carbonic acid through a saturated solution of the carbonate of soda, which unites with a second equivalent of the acid. It forms the effervescing soda-powders, and is used in bread-making instead of yeast, to render the dough light and spongy.

CARBONATE OF POTASH.

$$K\ O\ C\ O_2 = 69.$$

272. This is a highly alkaline and very soluble salt. It is prepared on a large scale by leaching wood-ashes, and

---

Give the composition of carbonate of soda. How is it obtained? What are its properties? What are its uses?

How is the bicarbonate formed? For what is it used?

What is the equivalent of carbonate of potash? How is it prepared? What is said of the ashes of different plants?

evaporating the solution in iron pots ; the product is hence called *potash*. When this crude potash is heated to redness, its carbonaceous impurities burn away, and *pearlash* is formed. Potash, or pearlash, therefore, represents the readily soluble portion of wood-ashes, and consists chiefly of carbonate of potash, with small amounts of carbonate of soda and common salt. Ashes are said usually to yield about $\frac{1}{15}$ their weight of potash (*Watson*); but different plants, and even different parts of the same plant, yield ashes of a very different composition. Thus the ashes from one ton of pine wood give of pure potash, 0·90 lbs. ; beech, 2·90 lbs. ; oak, 3·6 lbs. ; common wheat straw, 7 80 lbs. ; dry straw of wheat before earing, 34 lbs. ; bean-stalks, 40 lbs. ; stalks of Indian corn, 35 lbs. ; thistles in full growth, 70 lbs. ; wormwood, 146 lbs.—(*Ure.*)

273. This explains at once the great value of potash in agriculture. It is carried away by crops, and must be restored to the soil, or the land will be exhausted. Certain plants, as Indian corn, potatoes, the grape-vine, &c., flourish only where potash is abundant; they are hence called *potash plants.*

274. *Leached ashes* are far from being worthless to the farmer. Besides a small amount of potash, they contain other valuable elements of fertility, calculated to have a permanently beneficial effect upon the land. Applied at the rate of two tons an acre, their effects have been observed to continue for fifteen or twenty years. They are most beneficial upon clay soils, and are said especially to promote the growth of oats.—(*Johnston.*)

275. Potash exists in vegetation in combination with or-

What plants require potash ?

What is said of leached ashes ?   Upon what soils are they most beneficial ?

What plants and what parts of plants contain most potash ?

ganic acids (463), which are converted into carbonic acid by burning. It is usually more abundant in herbs than in shrubs, trees, or the grains, and abounds in the bark, twigs, and leaves, more than in the solid wood.

CARBONATE OF LIME. (*Limestone, Marble.*)

Ca O, CO_2 = 50; sp. gr. 2 9.—(*Graham.*)

276. Vast deposits of this salt are distributed all over the globe, in the form of limestones, marbles, chalks, marls, coral reefs, shells, &c. Carbonate of lime dissolves in water, containing free carbonic acid ; hence the well and spring water of lime districts becomes impregnated with it, and is hard. When the hardness of water is due to this cause, it may be *softened* by the addition of lime-water, which neutral‐izes the excess of carbonic acid, and all the carbonate is pre cipitated.

277. *Animal Origin of Limestone.*—Numerous and extensive as are the limestone deposits, it is conjectured that they are all of animal origin. The densest limestone and the softest chalk are found to consist of the aggregated skele‐tons or shells of myriads of tribes of the lower animals, which have existed in some former period of the world's history.—(*Kane*) The formation of coral reefs, which are sea-islands of carbonate of lime, built up from the depths of the ocean by minute aquatic animals, is an example of similar deposits now in process of formation.

What is the composition and equivalent number for carbonate of lime? When the hardness of water is owing to the presence of this substance, how may it be softened?

What is said of its origin?

CARBONATE OF AMMONIA.—$N H_3 C O_2 + H O = 48$;

OR,

CARBONATE OF OXIDE OF AMMONIUM—$N H_4 O, C O_2 = 48$

278. When organic substances containing nitrogen, as flesh, and the liquid excretions of animals, decay or putrefy, carbonic acid and ammonia, an acid and a base, are simultaneously set free. These unite, and escape into the air as carbonate of ammonia. The elements of this salt are both gases, and the salt itself is a gas ; but the alkali is so much stronger than the acid, that the compound still retains pungent alkaline properties. It was formerly procured by distilling the horns of harts; hence it was called *Spirits of Hartshorn.* The base of this salt is supposed not to be really ammonia, but an oxide of a peculiar compound, $N H_4$, termed *ammonium*. It has not been obtained separate, but is said to form an amalgam with mercury. According to this view, carbonate of ammonia becomes carbonate of oxide of ammonium, and muriate of ammonia chloride of ammonium.

HYDROCHLORATE OF AMMONIA. (*Sal Ammoniac, Muriate of Ammonia.*)

$N H_3 H Cl = 53.5.$

OR, CHLORIDE OF AMMONIUM. $N H_4 Cl.$

279. Ammonia, saturated with muriatic acid and crystallized, forms an inodorous salt, sal ammoniac. It is used in soldering, to cleanse metallic surfaces, the muriatic acid dissolving the coat of oxide. Mixed with lime, which de-

What is the equivalent for carbonate of ammonia ? How is it produced ? Why was it called spirits of hartshorn ? What is ammonium ?
What is the composition of sal ammoniac? For what is it used ?

composes it and expels the ammonia, it is used to fill smelling-bottles, and is volatilized by heat.

NITRATES.

NITRATE OF POTASH. (*Nitre, Saltpetre.*)

$$K O, N O_5 = 101.$$

280. Nitre is naturally formed in the soils of certain dry, hot countries, which abound in organic matters and potash. It has a cooling taste, and dissolves in its own weight of boiling water. Nitre preserves animal substances from putrefaction, and it is hence used in packing meat, to which it imparts a ruddy color.

281. The large quantity of oxygen contained in nitre, and the feeble affinity by which it is held, adapt it for sudden and rapid combustion; it is, therefore, the chief ingredient in gunpowder and fire-works.

282. *Gunpowder* is a mechanical mixture of nitre, charcoal, and sulphur, in variable proportions. These elements are moistened with water, ground and pressed through sieves perforated with holes, and dried at a steam-heat. The force of the explosion depends upon the sudden production of gases when the powder is fired. One volume of the gunpowder produces about 2000 volumes of the gas.—(*Gregory.*)

283. *Composition of Gunpowder.*—Common gunpowder consists of 76 parts nitre, 12 carbon, and 12 sulphur. More

---

What is the composition and combining number for nitrate of potash? What are its properties?

Why is it adapted for fire-works?

What is gunpowder? How is it made?

What is its composition? What effect has the charcoal? What the sulphur? How do we determine its quality?

charcoal gives it more power, but also causes it to attract moisture from the air, which injures its quality. For blasting rocks, where a sustained force rather than an instantaneous one is required, the powder contains more sulphur, and is even then often mixed with sawdust to retard the explosion. Good gunpowder should resist pressure between the fingers, give no dust by rubbing, and have a slight glossy aspect.

284. *Composition of Fire-works.*—Fire-works contain nitre as a chief ingredient, mixed with charcoal, sulphur, ground gunpowder, and various coloring substances. The splendid combinations of colored light seen at pyrotechnic exhibitions are thus produced : filings and borings of iron and steel give white and red sparks ; copper filings give the flame a greenish tint, and those of zinc a fine blue color. Amber, resin, and dry common salt, afford a yellow flame ; acetate of copper (verdigris) imparts a pale green ; and camphor yields a very white flame. *Gold-rain*, that descends from rockets like a shower of stars, is made by mixing 16 parts nitre, 4 ground gunpowder, 4 sulphur, 1 brass filings, $2\frac{1}{4}$ sawdust, and $\frac{1}{2}$ glass-dust.

NITRATE OF SODA. (*Soda-Saltpetre.*)

$$Na O, N O_5 = 85.$$

285. This salt is procured from certain soils in South America. It resembles potash-saltpetre, but does not answer for making gunpowder It is employed as a source of nitric acid. The nitrates are distinguished for their solubility.

What is the composition of fire-works ? What substances produce the different colors ? How is gold-rain made?
What is said of soda-saltpetre ?

PHOSPHATES.

PHOSPHATE OF SODA. $Na O, P O_5 = 103.$—(*Graham.*)

PHOSPHATE OF LIME. $Ca O, P O_5 = 100.$—(*Brande.*)

286. There are two classes of the phosphates, the poly-basic and the monobasic phosphates. The monobasic, of which the above are examples, are the simplest in composition, but not the most common. The phosphate of lime in bones is represented by Berzelius as composed of 8 Ca O, $3 P O_5$, which makes the quantity of acid and base about 50 per cent. each. Phosphate of lime is the mineral portion of bones, and constitutes 54 per cent. of their weight.— (*Berzelius.*)[1] The flesh also contains compounds of phosphoric acid. These are stored up by nature in large quantity in the grain and seeds of plants. Thus the proportion of phosphoric acid in the ashes of wheat is $49\frac{3}{4}$ per cent.; oats, 43 per cent.; Indian corn, $44\frac{3}{4}$; field beans, $37\frac{1}{2}$; field peas, $39\frac{1}{4}$; rye, $49\frac{1}{4}$; stalks or straw contain much less; the ashes of wheat-straw give but 3 per cent.; oat-straw, $2\frac{1}{2}$; rye-straw, $3\frac{3}{4}$; corn-stalks, 17; bean-straw, $7\frac{1}{2}$; and pea-straw, $4\frac{3}{4}$ per cent.—(*Johnston.*)

287. *Exhaustion of the Phosphate of Lime.*—If, therefore, the policy of a farmer be to sell grain and stock, he will gradually remove these phosphates from his soil, and diminish its productiveness. It may seem a trifling source of exhaustion to soil, when cart-loads of manure are returned to it annually; but the absence of this one element, however

What is the composition of phosphate of lime? In what plants is phosphoric acid found?

If a farmer's policy be to sell his grain and stock, what will follow? Is this element essential to the growth of grain?

small, destroys the fertility of land, for it is essential to the healthful growth of grain. A soil may be apparently rich, and produce a luxuriant growth of straw ; but if phosphoric acid and lime be deficient, the wheat will be light and shrunken. A single small cog may be as necessary to the correct movement of a watch as the mainspring, and so the earthy phosphates are as indispensable to first-rate crops as the rains of heaven.

288. *Restoration of Bone-earth.*—The phosphates are chiefly applied to the soil in the form of bones, which are reduced to powder by crushing, burning, dissolving in oil of vitriol, or softening by steam at high pressure. The finer the bones are divided, the more prompt is their action; when in coarse lumps they decompose slowly, but are more lasting in their effects. Phosphate of lime occurs native in the minerals *apatite* and *phosphorite.* Massive beds of phosphate of lime are said to have been recently discovered near Crown Point, N. Y., and in Morristown, N. J. The mineral is reputed to be nearly pure, containing 92 per cent. of phosphate of lime.

HYPO-SULPHITES.

HYPO-SULPHITE OF SODA. $Na O, S_2 O_2 = 79$ —(*Brande.*)

HYPO-SULPHITE OF LIME. $Ca O, S_2 O_2 = 76.$—(*Brande*)

289. These salts are of no interest, being used only in the daguerreotype process, to decompose the salts of silver upon the surface of the plates.

How are phosphates applied to the soil ? How are the bones prepared ? What discovery has recently been made ?

What is said of the hypo-sulphites ?

OF THE HALOID SALTS.

290. The compounds that we have been considering be-long to the class of oxygen acid salts. There is another group called the *haloid* salts, from their resemblance to common salt (chloride of sodium). They consist of simple bodies, as chlorine, fluorine, &c., united directly with the metals.

CHLORIDE OF SODIUM. (*Common salt, Sea-salt, Rock-salt, Kitchen-salt.*)

$$Na\, Cl = 58\cdot47,\ sp.\ gr.\ 2\cdot5.$$

291. This well-known substance crystallizes in the form of cubes, which dissolve in $2\cdot7$ times their weight of water, alike hot or cold. Salt is obtained either from the earth, in the form of blocks (rock-salt); or, if it occurs impure, by digging holes in the salt-beds, and filling them with water, which, when it will dissolve no more, is pumped out and evaporated in shallow pans. It is also largely produced from brine springs, and by the evaporation of sea-water; the latter, however, has a bitter taste, from the salts of magnesia, which also exist in the sea. Sea-water contains about one-thirtieth its weight of salt (about 5 oz. to the gallon). Estimating the ocean at an average depth of two miles (*Lyell*), the salt it holds in solution, if separated, would form a solid stratum 140 feet thick.

292. Salt exists in plants in small quantities, and some-times promotes their growth by being applied to the soil. It is also an ingredient of animal bodies; it exists in the blood,

What of the haloid salts ?
How is common salt obtained ? What amount of salt is contained in sea-water ?

and is eaten with relish by both man and beast. It has been calculated that the average annual consumption of salt by an adult amounts to sixteen pounds, or about five ounces per week.—(*Pereira*.) Salt is used for packing and preserving meat; it prevents putrefaction by absorbing water from the flesh (504).

CHLORIDE OF CALCIUM.

$$Ca\,Cl = 55\,5.$$

293. This is a substance having a strong affinity for water. Chemists use it for drying gases.

294. Chlorine combines with iron, forming two compounds, the protochloride, $Fe\,Cl$, and the sesquichloride, or perchloride, $Fe_2\,Cl_3$, which are seen to correspond with the oxides of iron.

FLUORIDE OF CALCIUM. (*Fluor Spar.*)

$$Ca\,Fl = 39.$$

295. This salt is found in minute quantity in the teeth and bones of animals.—(*Berzelius*.) The native fluor spar is used as a source of hydrofluoric acid. It is so soft as to be readily cut into various forms; and from its beautiful variety of colors it is employed for ornamental articles.

Is salt useful to plants? How much salt is consumed by an adult annually?
What is chloride of calcium?   .
What is said of the compounds of chlorine and iron?
What of fluoride of calcium?

MINERALS.

QUARTZ.

$Si O_3$.

296. Quartz is silica crystallized. When broken down into fine grains, it forms sand, and this, consolidated or cemented with oxides of iron, constitutes sandstones. The United States Capitol is built of sandstone; it is called *freestone*, because it is easily wrought. When silica is fused with bases it unites with them, playing the part of an acid (223), and forming salts—the silicates. Most rock formations consist of minerals which are composed of these silicates. Their constitution is represented upon the Chart in the same manner as the other salts: figures placed above the diagrams signify that the *compound atoms* with which they are connected are to be multiplied by them. Thus feldspar is seen to contain three atoms of alumina and three of silica.

TALC.

$Mg O, Si O_3$.

297. Talc is a silicate of magnesia. French chalk and soapstone are varieties of talc, and are so soft as to be worked with the same tools as wood. Soapstone does not fracture in the fire, and is used as lining for fireplaces, grates, &c. It has a soapy or greasy feel, hence its name.

SERPENTINE.

$Mg O, Fe O, Si O_3$.

298. Serpentine is a double silicate of magnesia and iron

What is quartz? What is sandstone? How are the silicates formed? What is talc? For what is soapstone used?

It takes its name from its variety of colors, like the serpent; its prevailing tint is green. It forms extensive barren ridges of magnesian rocks, such as that extending from Hoboken, with frequent interruptions, through New Jersey, Pennsylvania, Maryland, into Virginia. The decomposition of these minerals yields magnesia to the soils

HORNBLENDE.

$2 \, Mg \, O, \, Ca \, O, \, Fe \, O, \, 3 \, Si \, O_3.$

299. This mineral is a tersilicate of magnesia, iron, and lime. It is of a dark or black color, and exists abundantly in many rocks, which yield lime to soils when decomposed. It is an element of the slate and trap rocks.

FELDSPAR.

$K \, O, \, 3 \, Al_2 \, O_3, \, 3 \, Si \, O_3.$

300. Feldspar contains a large proportion of clay. It is the chief ingredient of porphyry, the hardest and most enduring of all the rocks. Feldspar, with hornblende and mica, forms syenite, or Quincy stone, of which the Bunker Hill Monument, and Astor House of New York, are constructed. It is a white or flesh-colored mineral, and by decomposition furnishes the potash and clay of soils, and the fine clays of porcelain ware.

MICA.

$Al_2 \, O_3 \, K \, O \, Fe \, O \, 3 \, Si \, O_3.$

301. Mica occurs in semitransparent plates, which may be split into elastic leaves of almost any degree of thinness.

Give the composition and properties of serpentine. Of hornblende. Of feldspar Of mica. What is granite composed of?

It withstands fire, and is used as a substitute for glass in the doors of stoves. It is frequently called isinglass. Quartz, feldspar, and mica compose granite, which underlays all other rock formations. The Rocky Mountains, Andes, Himalayas, Alps, Pyrenees, Carpathian, Ural, and all the highest mountains in the world, are granite.

302. Upon many of the silicates the air exerts a destructive agency; its carbonic acid slowly unites with their bases, thus breaking the bond which united their elements, and setting them free. By absorbing into their pores moisture, which expands in freezing, they are also mechanically crumbled down. These joint forces are constantly active in disintegrating and wearing down (weathering) rocks and stones, and reducing them to the condition of soil.

ARTIFICIAL SILICATES.

303. *Glass.*—The several kinds of glass are composed of silica with the various bases. Its manufacture depends upon the circumstance that, when melted, the material is easily worked into any desirable form, and when cooled it is colorless and does not crystallize. *Silicate of potash and soda* forms a colorless glass, which is soluble in water. This soluble glass is applied to wood, cloth, &c., to render them incombustible. *Silicate of soda and lime* forms windowglass; the soda gives it a slight greenish tinge, which is very obvious when we look through several panes placed together. The lime hardens the glass and adds to its lustre.

304. *Silicates of potash and lime* give *plate-glass* for mirrors, and crown-glass (the finest window-glass).

How are rocks crumbled down?
Upon what does the manufacture of glass depend? How is colorless glass formed? How is window-glass made? How plate-glass?

305. *Silicates of potash and lead* yield flint-glass and crystal-glass. The oxide of lead renders it very soft, so as to be easily scratched, but greatly increases its transparency, brilliancy, and refractive power: it is hence used for girandoles, chandeliers, and optical lenses.

306. Silicates of alumina, of oxide of iron and potash, or soda, produce green or bottle-glass, the color being due to the impurities of the materials.

307. Glass is colored by means of various metallic oxides, which are added to the melted material. The oxides of iron give to glass blue, green, yellow, and brown colors, depending upon the degree of oxidation and the quantity. The oxides of copper give a rich green. The black oxide of manganese, in large quantities, forms a black glass; in smaller quantities, various shades of purple. Oxide of cobalt gives beautiful blues of various tints; and antimony imparts a rich yellow. The artificial gems used by jewellers are only colored glass. The enamel watch-dials, and semi-opaque transparencies, are glass rendered milk-white by oxide of tin or bone-earth.

308. Glass is cut by the diamond, and holes may be easily bored through it by the end of a three-cornered file, if the point of friction is kept wet with spirits of turpentine. *Annealing* is causing the glass to cool by slow degrees, as otherwise it would be very brittle

309. *Earthenware.—Silicate of alumina, or clay,* is the basis of all the varieties of pottery. Its adaptation for this purpose depends upon its plasticity when mixed with water, the readiness with which it may be moulded and shaped,

How is flint-glass made? For what is it used?
Of what is bottle-glass made?
How is glass colored?
How is it cut? How may it be bored? What is annealing?

and also upon its capability of being stiffened and solidified when exposed to a high heat in furnaces or kilns. After burning, the earthenware, though hard, is porous; it adheres to the tongue and absorbs water with avidity, even allowing it to sweat through. To prevent this, the ware is covered with a glassy coating, or *glazed*.

310. *Common red pottery ware* owes its color to oxide of iron, and is glazed with a preparation of clay and oxide of lead. Vessels thus coated are objectionable for domestic use, because the lead glaze is sometimes dissolved by acids, as vinegar, producing poisonous effects. Bricks and flower-pots are unglazed. *Porcelain* is made of the finest clay, and is glazed without lead.

311. *Common porcelain* is most usually colored blue, owing to the facility with which cobalt may be applied. The patterns are first printed upon paper, which is applied to the ware after it has been once heated (*biscuit ware*). When again heated, the coloring matter adheres to the surface. The same materials are used in coloring porcelain as give the tints to colored glass. The more delicate patterns are laid on with a camel's-hair pencil.

What is earthenware composed of? What are the properties of clay that fit it for this purpose? Why is it glazed?

To what is the color of the common red ware due? What is it glazed with? Why is this objectionable? Of what is porcelain made?

How are the colors applied? What is meant by the term biscuit-ware? How are the more delicate patterns applied?

PART II.

ORGANIC CHEMISTRY.

VEGETABLE CHEMISTRY.

GROWTH OF THE PLANT.

312. ORGANIC CHEMISTRY treats of the composition and properties of all those compounds which are formed in the organs of living beings, and which compose their fabric (11). It inquires into the nature of their growth and decay, and into the changes which they may be made to undergo by artificial means.

313. Organic Chemistry is divided into two branches, Vegetable Chemistry and Animal Chemistry, which differ from each other in certain very important respects to be hereafter pointed out. It deals with substances which, in their production, manifest the phenomena of *life* or *vitality* There has been a reluctance to consider the science of organized beings, from a chemical point of view, because it is said that a peculiar force (the vital force) is here brought into action, which refuses to be governed by the laws of inorganic nature. But this is of little consequence: so long as the vital force is governed by any fixed laws, and influences the chemical changes which take place in the living body, it

Of what does Organic Chemistry treat? Into what does it inquire?
How is it divided? Why has there been a reluctance to consider this subject?

14*

must be studied in connection with those changes. We are not to inquire into its *nature* any more than that of heat or magnetism, but only into its *effects*.

314. *The just Scope of Chemistry.*—It is the business of Chemistry to investigate *all* the changes that take place in the nature of compound substances, and to determine the precise conditions in which, and the rules or laws by which such changes occur; and as every species of growth and decay consists in the passage of matter from one condition to another, in the rearrangement and reunion of its elements, the full investigation of the subject belongs most clearly to chemical science.

315. *The Organic Elements.*—All vegetable and animal substances are composed mainly of but four elements—carbon, hydrogen, oxygen, and nitrogen. These, differently united, make up the vast variety of organic forms which we see upon the earth; they are the four letters which compose the alphabet of organic nature, and have been termed *organogens* (generators of organization). These elements, derived by plants from the inorganic or mineral world, are united to form different substances called *proximate principles*, and these are again combined to produce the various organized structures. Thus oil, starch, sugar, gluten, and woody fibre, are proximate principles which are found in the various parts of plants. The separation of an organized substance into its proximate elements is termed *proximate analysis;* into its final or simple elements, *ultimate analysis.*

316. By reference to the Chart it will be seen that inorganic compounds are all *binary*, united in pairs, element to

Does Chemistry inquire into a part or all of the changes which matter undergoes? Of what are all vegetable and animal substances composed? What have they been termed? What do these elements form? Give examples of proximate principles. What is proximate analysis? Ultimate analysis?

In looking at the Chart, what difference is seen between inorganic and organic

element, acid to base, in such a way as to satisfy affinity most completely, and thus form permanent combinations. But, by looking at the organic compounds, we see that they are differently formed. The elements are united, not in pairs, but grouped together, by threes and fours, in such a way that the most powerful attractions of the elements are not satisfied. Thus, in water, oxygen is held by a single force, its affinity for hydrogen: there are no other forces drawing in different directions, and tending to weaken its affinity; the union is therefore stable. But in sugar, the affinity of oxygen is divided between hydrogen and carbon; it is united strongly with neither, but feebly with both. Its tendency to combine with one is, to a degree, counteracted by the affinity of the other. The forces brought into play in this kind of combination are therefore complex; and as in mechanics, complicated machinery is always most easily deranged, so in organization, the more complex the substance, the more readily is it decomposed and broken up into simpler and more permanent compounds. Chemical principles thus account for the instability of all living things.

317. *Plan of Studying the Subject.*—Organic substances have their origin entirely in plants. Here they are first put together, fashioned into innumerable forms, and endowed with all their wonderful qualities. They then pass into the systems of animals, which possess no power of *creating* or *forming* the materials of their own fabric, and can only *transform* and *consume* that which is supplied to them by plants. These facts furnish us with a natural order in which to study the subject; first the formation, and then the de-

---

compounds? What is the mode of union of inorganic compounds? Point out examples of this upon the Chart. What is the mode of union of organic substances? Why are organic compounds less stable than inorganic?

Where do organic substances originate? What is the office of animals? How should the subject be pursued?

struction of organized compounds. This plan is not only recommended for its naturalness and simplicity, but it is calculated to bring out most distinctly those grand and beautiful laws which govern the organic world. Facts, otherwise scattered, are thus linked together in a great system, and, while our views are elevated and expanded, the mind is much aided in its efforts at acquisition.

318. The theory of *compound radicals* is passed over with a bare explanation (391), as it is of no popular importance. It may be serviceable in advanced study, but even there its utility is so doubtful that it is rejected by such authorities as *Brande* and *Silliman*.

319. *Germination of the Seed.*—Vegetable physiology informs us that every perfect seed contains within it the rudiment of a new plant; in some varieties so complete that the microscope reveals its structure, root, stem, and leaves, while in others it is less distinctly developed. This minute plant, the germ or embryo as it is called, lies imbedded within the mass of the seed, surrounded by a substance well adapted to protect and preserve it. Wrapped in this envelope, the embryo remains at the disposal of external agents. In certain conditions it continues at rest and torpid; but when these conditions are changed, it suddenly awakens from its slumber, puts forth a new power, and begins to grow; this is called germination.

320. *Nourishment of the Embryo.*—The embryo, during growth, derives its nourishment from that portion of the seed in which it is inclosed, and which consists chiefly of starch. But no nutriment can enter the germ except in a liquid form, and starch is insoluble in water; it hence cannot accompany the fluid sap when it begins to circulate. To remove this difficulty, nature resorts to a very beautiful pro-

---

What does every perfect seed contain? What is germination?

cess. When a seed is exposed to the joint action of moisture and air, at a proper temperature (which may vary in different cases), it absorbs water and oxygen, swells in bulk, chemical action begins, carbónic acid is given off, its temperature rises, and a new substance is produced within the seed called *diastase*. This substance seems to be a kind of ferment (378), and possesses the remarkable power of converting starch into sugar. It is formed in very small quantity, and at those points where the nourishment passes into the germ: in the potato it is found only in the immediate vicinity of the eyes or young buds. Here it performs its function, transforming the insoluble starch into soluble sugar or gum, as the necessities of the young plant require.

321. The food, thus prepared, is carried into the embryo, which expands; one part, the *radicle*, shooting downward to form a root, while another, the *plumule*, extends upward to the surface, if the seed be buried in the ground. The growth here takes place at the expense of materials previously prepared and stored up in the seed. The germ transforms and appropriates, but has no power to organize the elements which contribute to its nourishment.

322. *Office of the Leaf.*—But when the plumule, or stem, appears above the ground and expands its earliest leaves, which turn of a green color as soon as they emerge into the light (329, 478), the plant passes into another stage of existence; a new order of phenomena are manifested, which, for beauty and sublime interest, are surpassed by nothing in nature. The young plant, no longer depending for nourishment upon ready-made nutriment furnished by the seed, be-

How is the embryo nourished ? What beautiful expedient is resorted to for the nourishment of the germ ? What is diastase?

What is the true function of vegetables?

As the embryo expands, what parts appear?

What are the offices of the leaf?

gins to exert a formative power, the true vegetable function, and produce from the mineral elements of the earth and air such organized compounds as it may require for developing the various parts of its system.

323 The leaf is the seat of these chemical changes, and whether it be an humble blade of grass, or upon the oak that has stood a thousand years, its office is the same: it is at once an organ of exhalation, digestion, and respiration, corresponding to the skin, stomach, and lungs of animals.

324. *The Leaf an Organ of Evaporation.*—Water, containing mineral and gaseous substances in solution, is absorbed by the roots and carried upward, as ascending sap, to the leaves, from the surface of which much of it evaporates, leaving the remainder in a more concentrated state. This process goes forward in the daytime with great activity. Hales found that a sunflower weighing three pounds exhaled from its leaves thirty ounces of water in a day. Evaporation takes place chiefly from the under surface of the leaf, through a multitude of little pores, or slits, called *stomata*, situated in the leaf-skin, or cuticle. These orifices vary in size, and are very numerous; in the apple-tree leaf there are said to be 24,000 upon a square inch—(*Gray.*) They have a valve-like action, by which the rate of evaporation is regulated; contracting when the amount of water supplied by the roots is small, and opening when it is abundant.

325. *Leaves absorb Carbonic Acid from the Air.*—Besides the elements of nutrition furnished by the ascending or crude sap, the leaf possesses the remarkable power of absorbing carbonic acid from the atmosphere. Although the proportion of this gas in the air seems small (but $\frac{1}{2500}$ of its

bulk, or by calculation about seven tons over each acre), yet the structure of the vegetable machine is such as to draw it from the air in a very rapid manner. The leaf, shaped so as to expose the largest surface, is mounted upon a slender foot-stalk, that it may be put in motion by the slightest breeze, and its contact with the air increased; while at the same time, it is constantly covered with a film of moisture, which is highly absorptive of carbonic acid. These conditions enable the foliage to withdraw this gas from moving masses of air in considerable quantity. Boussingault passed a rapid current of air through a glass globe containing a vine-branch, when three-fourths of its carbonic acid was absorbed by the leaves. The little mouths, or absorbent pores, which drink it in from the atmosphere, are situated upon the under surface of the leaf. This may be shown by taking a common cabbage-leaf, and applying the under side to a wound or cut. It will draw quite powerfully, inducing a discharge, while the upper surface will produce no such effect.—(*Norton.*)

326. *Decomposing and Formative Power of the Leaf.*— The carbonic acid absorbed from the air or contained in the sap is decomposed in the leaf; its oxygen being thrown back again into the atmosphere, while its carbon furnishes the solid element of wood, and enters largely into *every compound formed in the vegetable kingdom.* The plant also possesses the power of decomposing water and ammonia, by which hydrogen, nitrogen, and oxygen are also produced, which, with the small proportion of mineral matters brought up with the sap, furnish the materials for all the countless variety of vegetable and animal substances. The food which we con-

---

purpose? Give the experiment of Boussingault. Where are the absorbent pores situated? How is this proved?

How does the leaf dispose of its carbonic acid? What becomes of the oxygen? What of the carbon? What other substances does it decompose? What is thus

sume, the fabric of our clothing, and the wood which forms our houses and fuel, were all put together and endowed with their peculiar properties by the leaves of plants. They are thus the true builders. They organize and construct living substances from the dead mineral matter of the earth and air. Whatever is derived, immediately or remotely, from the vegetable world, was produced by the subtile chemistry of a leaf. The newly formed compounds are carried in the current of descending or elaborated sap, and are deposited in the system of the growing plant, or stored up in the seed.

327. *Flow of the Sap.*—The cause of the flow of sap in plants, and of the circulation of blood in animals, long remained a mystery. It has recently been investigated by Dr. Diaper, and shown in both cases to be immediately due to capillary attraction, and ultimately to electrical forces. The demonstration will be found in his valuable work on the " Chemistry of Plants."

328. *Relation of Plants and Animals.*—We have seen (169) that carbonic acid, from numerous sources, and in immense quantities, is perpetually poured into the air. We now discover that the vegetation of the globe is charged with the grand function of reversing this action. Animals, by respiration and decay, withdraw from the air its oxygen, and return in its place carbonic acid. Plants, on the contrary, absorb carbonic acid, decompose it, and restore again pure oxygen to the air. They thus counteract and compensate each other. What the former does, the latter undoes. If animals tend to vitiate the air, plants tend, in an equal degree, to purify it   So exactly are these antagonizing actions

furnished ?   Out of these what are formed ?   What are the leaves of plants, then ?
What becomes of the compounds formed in the leaf?
What is the cause of the flow of sap ?.
What effects do animals produce upon the air ?   How do plants counteract this ?

balanced in the economy of nature, that the constitution of
the atmosphere remains unchanged from age to age.   How
wonderful, that a few gases condensed from the invisible air,
translated from the systems of plants to those of animals, and
then restored again to the air, should give rise to all the
grand and awful phenomena of life and death upon this
planet !

329. *Light controls Vegetable Growth.*—The motive power
of the vegetable machine is the *light of the sun.*   The chemical changes which take place in the leaf are brought about
by the action of this force.   None can fail to have observed
that light exerts a most favorable influence upon vegetation.
Plants made to grow in the dark are white, watery, and
sickly.   Their products are diseased, and often poisonous,
and they cannot mature or bear seeds.   If but a single beam
of light is admitted, the leaves and branches turn and bend
towards it with eagerness.   Even in the shade they are
feeble and unhealthy ; but when exposed to sunlight, they
speedily acquire a bright green tint, and become thrifty and
vigorous.   A plant was discovered in a mine, which, from
its singular appearance, was supposed to be a new variety.
It was taken up into the light, when in a few days it turned
out to be common *tansy.*

330. The nature of the compounds produced in leaves
depends upon the quantity or intensity of the light.   Tropical plants secrete powerful medicinal, aromatic, and coloring
substances which they cannot be made to yield in the less
brilliant light of higher latitudes, although the temperature
is maintained artificially at the point to which they have been

What force controls changes in plants ?   What is the appearance of plants grown
in the dark ?   When grown in the shade, are they vigorous ?   What is the effect
of sunlight upon plants that have grown in the dark ?   Give an example.

What is said of tropical plants ?   How is this fact applied ?

accustomed. This circumstance is taken advantage of in cultivating vegetables for the table ; for many, if raised under diminished light, may be used for food which are naturally unpleasant, and quite obnoxious to the taste. Thus celery, which is naturally rank, tough, and stringy, if its stems are blanched or made to grow in the absence of light, becomes esculent and palatable. The sides of fruits exposed to the sunlight are of a ruddy color, and of a sweeter taste than those parts that are shaded ; while some leaves are acid in the morning, tasteless at noon, and bitter at night.

331. *Compound Nature of Light.*—A ray of light coming from the sun produces a threefold effect—an illuminating, a heating, and a chemical effect. It is therefore said to be composed of a luminous ray which impresses the eye, a calorific ray which affects the thermometer, and a chemical ray which acts neither upon the thermometer nor the eye, but produces chemical changes, as upon the plate in the daguerreotype process. By passing a ray of light through a prism (see Natural Philosophy), it is decomposed into a series of seven colors—violet, indigo, blue, green, yellow, orange, and red—which are thrown in this order upon an oblong space called the *spectrum.* If passed through a second prism, these rays are united again, and form simple white light. Dr. Draper has determined that the ethereal force which produces changes among chemical atoms, controlling the decompositions and combinations which take place in the leaf, resides in the yellow region of the spectrum

332. *Mode in which Light acts upon the Leaves.*—The science of optics teaches us that light consists of vibratory,

Does a ray of light contain any other than the luminous principle? What are they ? What is the effect of passing light through a prism ? In what part of the spectrum does the force affecting chemical atoms reside ?

Of what does light consist? To what are the different colors owing ? How may a landscape or a bunch of flowers be seen to bear an analogy to a piece of music.

wave-like movements or undulations in an ethereal medium which exists throughout all space, just as sound is the result of undulations propagated by vibrating bodies through the air; and as the different tones of sound are occasioned by variations in the size and rapidity of the aerial undulations which fall upon the ear, so the different colors are also due to diversity in the magnitude of the ethereal waves which impress the eye. And to carry the analogy still further, as a melodious piece of music may be regarded as the result of innumerable air-vibrations of various degrees of intensity, skilfully arranged by the composer to produce a harmonious impression upon the ear; so also a bunch of flowers, or a beautiful landscape, must be looked upon as produced by countless myriads of luminiferous wavelets, originating in the sun, and sent across the abyss of space to act upon chemical atoms, and arrange them into combinations of most exquisite symmetry and beauty.

333. *Wonderful Nature of the Ethereal Action.*—" A forest-tree, from its magnitude, rising perhaps a hundred feet from the ground, and spreading its branches over hundreds of square yards, may impress us with a sense of sublimity. A section of its stem might assure us that it had lived for a thousand years, and its total weight could only be expressed by tons. An object like this may indeed call forth our admiration, but that admiration is expanded into astonishment when we consider minutely the circumstances which have been involved in producing the result. If we conceive a single second of time, the beat of a pendulum, divided into a million of equal parts, and each one of these inconceivably brief periods divided again into a million of other equal parts, a wave of yellow light, during one of the last small intervals,

---

What view of the subject adds surpassing sublimity to the contemplation of a forest-tree ?

has vibrated 535 times; and now that yellow light is the agent which has been mainly involved in building up the parts of the tree, in fabricating its various structures, and during every one of a thousand summers, from sunrise to sunset, the busy rays have been carrying on their operation. Who, then, can conceive, when in the billionth of a second such enormous numbers of movements are accomplished, how many have been spent in erecting an aged forest oak! Who also can conceive the total amount of force employed, from century to century, in arranging the vegetation of the surface of the globe!"

334. *Relation of the Sun to Vegetation.*—" Look also at the sun! Even the magnificent views of the astronomer are here surpassed, and that gigantic star no longer appears as a centre or focus of mere mechanical force, who draws up comets from the abysses of space, and with an inexpressible velocity precipitates them headlong back again—who afar off watches the revolving planet glide on its elliptic path, or makes the tide ebb and flow in the seas; but he appears as the fountain of light and of life, who spreads in the torrid zone a luxuriant vegetation, and in autumn ripens the harvests for our use—whose many-colored rays, during the revolving seasons, are occupied in fashioning and forming food for us, or evaporating pure water from the sea, or condensing clouds in the sky, which give an air of change and life to those regions of eternal repose."—(*Draper.*)

335. *The Sun's Rays a Source of Incalculable Power.*— All force is estimated by the effect it is capable of producing. The power of the solar beams may thus be definitely measured, and it appears almost incredible. They decompose

---

In what relationships does the sun appear?

What examples are given of the chemical power of the sun's rays? Can force be created or destroyed?

carbonic acid at common temperatures—an effect which all the resources of the chemist cannot enable him to imitate. It has been seen (84) that the affinity of oxygen for carbon and hydrogen, the power with which they unite, is very great. The solar beams, in separating them, must necessarily expend an equal amount of force. It is in the chemical union of oxygen with carbon and hydrogen that the muscular power of animals arises. The power of the steam-engine is also due to the combination of atmospheric oxygen with the carbon and hydrogen of wood and coal. But before these elements can unite for the production of power, an equal quantity of force is exerted by the sun's light to separate and arrange them. In nature, it is no more possible to create or destroy *force* than *matter*. It passes from state to state; but its total amount, when we take the universe into the estimate, is unchangeable. Power, which emanated from the sun, and was expended in the formation of vegetable structures, where it remained for a time latent or hidden, reappears through the admirable contrivance of the steam-engine, or the thousand-fold more wonderful mechanism of the human body.

336. *Source of the Power obtained from Coal.*—The great deposits of coal which are scattered over various parts of the earth consist of the carbonized remains of a vegetation which flourished long before man appeared upon the globe, perhaps thousands of centuries ago. The trees of that period were vastly larger than those now upon the earth, and must have been condensed from an atmosphere richer in carbonic acid than ours, and perhaps by a more brilliant sun. And yet this coal, having slumbered in its ancient beds until layer after layer of rocks has been formed above it, now

What is said about the great deposits of coal? Whence was the coal originally derived? Whence came the power by which it was condensed from the air?

comes forth as from a reservoir of power and beneficence, to surrender again its ethereal agents, light and heat, for the use of man, and return as carbonic acid to the air from whence it came. The power which we now derive from it was expended by the sun, millions of years ago, in separating it from the carbonic acid of the ancient atmosphere.

337. *The Solar Rays are the Antagonists of Oxygen.*— We have seen that oxygen gas (82) is the foe of organization and life ; its affinity for the other organic elements being such, that it perpetually rends them from their combinations, thus inducing constant decay and dissolution. We now perceive that the solar rays are the great antagonists of oxygen. Under their influence, the mineral elements are changed to living forms. Under the influence of oxygen, they are returned again to the inorganic world. If oxygen dilapidates, they renovate ; if *that* decomposes and breaks down, *they* construct and build up ; if *that* is seen in the falling leaf of autumn, *they* are proclaimed in the exuberant foliage and blossoms of spring. If oxygen is the mainspring of destruction upon the globe—wasting, burning, consuming, and hastening the dissolution of all things—the solar rays constitute the mighty force of counteraction. They reunite the dissevered elements, substitute development for decay, call forth a glory from desolation, and life and beauty from the very bosom of death.

338. *Nature of the Plant.*—We may therefore regard the green, growing plant as the grand factory of organic nature. It is a machine driven by the power of solar light, whose office is to form and construct the compounds which are to be consumed by animals, for the production of force, loco-

What is said of the relations of oxygen and the solar rays?
How may we look upon the growing plant ? What two kinds of compounds are fashioned in plants ?

motion, and sensation. It obtains carbon from carbonic acid, hydrogen from water, nitrogen from ammonia or nitric acid, and various earthy and alkaline salts from the soil. With these elementary or mineral substances it fabricates organic compounds, which are deposited in its tissues.

We pass now to an examination of some of the more important substances produced by plants.

PRODUCTS OF VEGETABLE GROWTH.

WOODY FIBRE. (*Lignin.*) $C_{12} H_{10} O_{10}$.

339. *Structure of Wood.*—The substance of wood which abounds in the trunk and branches of trees, giving them firmness and strength, is the most abundant product of vegetation. Besides forming the bulk of all trees, it also exists in the straw and stalks of grain, in the membrane which envelops the kernel (bran), in the husk and skin of seeds, and in the rinds, cores, and stones of fruit. It consists of slender fibres or tubes, closely packed together. When first formed, these tubes are hollow, and serve to convey the sap or vegetable juices; but in the heart-wood of trees (*duramen*) they become filled up and consolidated, the circulation of fluids taking place in the white external sap-wood (*alburnum*).

340. In most trees of temperate climates these woody tubes are deposited in external layers or rings, one every year, so that by cutting the trunk across, and counting the

---

What is the most abundant product of vegetables? Where is it found? Of what does it consist? What purposes do these tubes serve when first formed? What is the duramen? What is the alburnum?

How may we determine the age of a tree? What trees have these layers most dense? Upon what does the hardness of wood depend?

rings, we can determine the age of the tree. Those trees which grow on a poor soil, in high situations, exposed to the wind, have these layers of fibres more dense and closely packed together than if grown in a protected spot, or upon a moist, rich soil. Upon the density with which the fibres are imbedded together depends the property which different kinds of wood possess, of hardness or softness, by which they are worked with ease or difficulty.

341. *Value of Wood as Fuel.*—Equal weights of different kinds of wood give out the same amount of heat in burning if they are equally dry. But wood varies greatly in the amount of moisture it contains, and upon this circumstance mainly depends the economy of different samples for fuel. The proportion of water contained in wood may be ascertained by drying the shavings in an oven at 140°, and determining the amount of loss by weighing. Green wood contains from 20 to 50 per cent of water (sap); birch has 30, oak 35, beach and pine 39, elm 44, and poplar 50 per cent. Wood dried in the air (seasoned) for a year, still contains from 20 to 25 per cent. of water. If dried at a strong heat (kiln-dried), it yet retains 10 per cent. of moisture, and begins to carbonize (char) before parting with it all. Thoroughly kiln-dried wood afterwards absorbs from the air 10 or 12 per cent. of water.

342. The presence of water diminishes the value of wood for fuel, by absorbing and carrying off the heat during its conversion into steam, and by causing slow and imperfect combustion. One pound of artificially dried wood will raise

Upon what circumstance does the economy of different kinds of wood for fuel depend ? How is the proportion of water contained in wood ascertained ? Give the per centage in different specimens of green wood. How much water does seasoned wood contain ? When kiln-dried, how much ?

How does water diminish the value of wood for fuel ? What amount of heat will a pound of dried wood produce ? How much oxygen will it consume ?

35 pounds of water from the freezing to the boiling point, and consume the oxygen from 148 cubic feet of air.

343. *The Chemical Properties of Fuel adapted to the Wants of Man.*—" Next to his food, man's most pressing want, even in the rudest state of society, is protection against cold. He employs fire for this purpose ; that is to say, he takes means for developing violent chemical action between the elements of certain combustible substances and the oxygen of the air, and of availing himself of the heat thus disengaged. But does one man in a thousand, while enjoying the warmth of his fire, reflect for a single moment upon the combination of circumstances to which his pleasure is due ? Does he reflect on the very peculiar nature of the fuel provided for him in the forest or the field, or in the black bituminous coal, the relic of a vegetation now passed away ? Does he pause for a moment to consider that the characteristic components of his blazing log, the carbon and the hydrogen, are the *only* elementary substances in existence fitted for the purpose ; the only bodies whose products of combustion are of such a kind as to pass off in invisible and odorless forms, to mingle in the air, and eventually to return again into the very same condition as that which has just been destroyed ? It is most wonderful, when we reflect on these things, to observe how much our physical happiness depends upon what some will call accidental circumstances. Is it by accident that carbonic acid is odorless and harmless unless in considerable quantity, while the oxides of all other combustible substances capable of existing in a gaseous state are pungent and irritating, and insufferable in the smallest doses ?"—(*Fownes.*)

344. *Preservation of Wood from Decay.*—The decay of wood is caused by the action of moisture and oxygen upon

How are wood and coal especially adapted for fuel?

its outer surface and within its pores, and also by albumen (374), a putrefiable substance contained within its sap. It is therefore preserved by covering it with a coating of paint or other prepaiation, which protects it from air and moisture, and also by expelling the sap and filling its pores with unchangeable substances, as solutions of mineral salt. *Kyanized* wood is such as has been thus impregnated with corrosive sublimate (bichloride of mercury), which precipitates the albumen, rendering it insoluble and harmless.

345 Boucherie, of France, impregnated wood with common salt and pyrolignite of iron, by felling the trees in summer, and immersing the lower ends of their trunks in the saline solution; as the water evaporated from the foliage the liquid was drawn up into the trunk, and at length made its appearance in the leaves. He found that green wood required about one-fortieth its weight of the preserving (antiseptic) liquid, and became harder, tougher, more durable, and less combustible than by natural seasoning. Steaming wood, or soaking it in water when newly cut, tends to preserve it by dissolving out its sap.

346. *Cloth and paper are composed of wood.* Linen and cotton consist of woody fibre nearly pure. Flax contains a gray coloring matter, which is removed by bleaching and boiling in ley; it is then perfectly white. The fibres of cotton are white when they come from the pod (except the yellow nankeen cotton), and the goods are bleached only to remove the soil which they have acquired by manufacturing. Paper, as well as the clothing we wear, is therefore composed of woody fibre, being made chiefly from waste cotton

What causes the decay of wood? How does paint preserve it? What is kyanized wood?

Describe Boucherie's method of preparing wood for preservation.

What are linen and cotton composed of? What is said of flax? Of cotton fibres? Of paper? Describe the process of paper-making.

7*

and linen rags; for the coarser kinds, old ropes and cut straw are used. In this process, the rags, after being bleached by chlorine, are boiled in alkali, and reduced to pulp by means of a beating-engine. The pulp, formed into sheets and dried, is blotting paper. To convert it into writing paper it is soaked in a preparation of glue and alum, or of rosin and alumina (sized), and then pressed between hot iron plates.

347. *Wood may be made explosive—Gun-cotton.* When raw cotton is steeped for a few minutes in equal quantities of nitric and sulphuric acids, and then carefully washed with water and dried, it becomes explosive, like gunpowder, and forms *gun-cotton.* Flax, tow, and even purified sawdust, may also be made similarly explosive. The change that takes place consists in separating the elements of water from the woody fibre by sulphuric acid, and their replacement by nitric acid, which is also a large element of gunpowder. The explosive power of gun-cotton is eight times greater than that of gunpowder (*Silliman*), but it is very dangerous, being liable to inflame at low temperatures. It ignites at 350° F.

348. *Collodion* is a solution of gun-cotton in ether. It is applied to wounds; the ether evaporates, leaving a film which excludes the air and favors healing.

349. *Composition of Pure Wood.*—Pure woody fibre is white, tasteless, insoluble in water and alcohol, and has a specific gravity of 1·5; hence all wood, when deprived of the air within its pores, sinks in water. It belongs to a class of bodies called the ternary group—starch, sugar,

How is gun-cotton formed? What change takes place? How does it compare with gunpowder in explosive power? Why is it dangerous?

What is collodion? For what is it used?

What are the properties of pure wood? To what class of bodies does it belong? For what are they remarkable? How do they differ?

and gum (see Chart)—which are remarkable for containing an equal number of oxygen and hydrogen atoms; their composition is therefore simply charcoal and water (*hydrate of carbon*). They all contain the same quantity of carbon, differing only in the proportions of water; they are thus readily transformed one into another, and may all be produced by plants out of simple carbonic acid and water. The formula for woody fibre, obtained from Dr. Prout's analysis, gives C_{12} H_8 O_8. *Cellulose*, a substance associated with woody fibre, has the composition C_{12} H_{10} O_{10}. We have no unobjectionable data from which the atomic equivalent of lignin can be inferred.—(*Brande.*)

350. *Heat changes Woody Fibre into Starch.*—When fine sawdust is boiled in water to separate every thing soluble, and then dried and several times heated in an oven, it becomes hard and crisp, and may be ground into a fine meal, which has a taste and smell similar to that of ground wheat; it ferments when made into a paste with yeast, and produces a uniform spongy, nutritious bread.—(*Autenrieth.*)

351. *Wood may be converted into Sugar and Starch.*— Wood, when dipped in strong sulphuric acid, is charred; that is, the acid attracts from it the elements of water, while the carbon remains. If shreds of old cotton or linen, which consist of nearly pure woody fibre, are boiled for several hours in diluted sulphuric acid, they are converted first into gum, and then into grape-sugar (368). By this process the rags will yield more than their weight of crystallizable sugar. Woody fibre is also converted into starch, by boiling with caustic potash.

352. *Distillation of Wood.*—When wood is burned in

How may woody fibre be converted into starch ?
How may it be changed to sugar ?
What is the result of the distillation of wood ?

close vessels (*destructive distillation*), or with but a partial access of air, it gives rise to a large number of compounds, depending upon the nature of the various substances contained in its tissue. Among these are carbon, olefiant gas, and ammonia, which have already been noticed, and we can glance at but one or two others of the most important.

353. *Pyroligneous Acid* is a crude vinegar distilled from wood: nearly half a pound may be produced from a pound of beech-wood. It is a brown, acid liquid, having a strong, smoky taste and odor. It is cheap, and contains acetic acid. It is extensively employed to manufacture salts, the acetates used by dyers as mordants.

354. *Creosote* is a brown oily liquid, obtained from wood-tar and pyroligneous acid. It has a powerful, smoky, burning taste, corrodes the skin, and mixed with alcohol and oil of cloves, it is used as a remedy for toothache. The term *creosote* means *flesh-preserver*. Meat steeped for a few hours in a solution of 1 part creosote to 100 water remains sweet, and will not putrefy. It preserves the flesh by coagulating its albumen (374). The same effect is produced by vapor of creosote which exists in smoke. Meat and fish, exposed to the smoke of green wood, undergo a like change. It is this vapor in smoke which renders it so irritating to the eyes, causing the flow of tears.

355. *Slow Decay of Wood.*—When wood, straw, or leaves are exposed to the air, they turn of a brown or black color, and undergo a slow burning, or decay (*eremacausis*). The change that here occurs is the same as in active combustion, the only difference being, that in the first case it takes years,

What is pyroligneous acid? For what is it used?
What is the meaning of the word creosote? How does it preserve flesh? Does it exist in smoke?
What is the difference between slow decay and active combustion? To what is the dark color of rich soils owing?

while in the latter it is done in minutes. The hydrogen is oxidized first (76), and most rapidly; the residue, of course, contains an increased and constantly increasing proportion of carbon, which gives it a darker color. It is thus that vegetable matter in different stages of decomposition (humus, ulmine, geine, vegetable mould, &c.) impart a black, rich appearance to soils.

356. Carbonaceous matter constantly accumulates in the soil of forests, which proves that it must be derived from the atmosphere. It is removed from soils by cropping, and may be restored by adding vegetable and animal manures, by ploughing in fresh plants (*green-manuring*), or by cultivating those which leave many roots in the earth. A crop of clover was found to leave in the soil several thousand pounds weight of roots, while wheat did not leave $\frac{1}{5}$ this quantity.

357. *Mineral Coal derived from Vegetation.*—Mineral coal was formed in the earth from an ancient vegetation, by a kind of smouldering decomposition, such as moist vegetable matters, straw, and manure undergo when placed in compost heaps. The trees were collected in basins by floods and covered with mud, where they were gradually carbonized. In anthracite coal, which consists of nearly pure carbon, this decay has reached its last stage; in the bituminous coal it is less advanced, much hydrogen still remaining; the bituminous variety, therefore, burns with flame, while anthracite does not.

How is it shown to be derived from the atmosphere ?   When removed by cropping, how may it be restored ?

How was mineral coal formed ?   What is the difference between anthracite and bituminous coal ?

STARCH. (*Fecula.*)

$C_{12} H_{10} O_{10}$.

358. *Proportion of Starch in different Grains.*—Starch is an abundant vegetable product. It is deposited in the grains, seeds, roots, stems, and fruits of many plants. Potatoes (different varieties) contain from 10 to 20 per cent of starch; buckwheat, 52 per cent. ; barley-meal, 67 ; oatmeal, 59 ; rye flour, 61 ; wheat flour, 56 to 72 ; Indian corn, 80 ; rice, 82 , peas, 32 ; and beans, 35 per cent.—(*Pereira.*)

359. *Appearance of Starch Grains.*—Pure starch is a snow-white powder of a glistening aspect, which makes a crackling noise when pressed with the finger. It is composed of transparent rounded grains, the size of which varies in different plants from $\frac{1}{800}$ to $\frac{1}{3000}$ of an inch in diameter ; being largest in the potato, and smallest in wheat. Examined by a microscope, the whole surface of the grain appears covered by parallel rings, which seem depressed or cut into it. The grains have a laminated texture, consisting of a series of concentric layers or membranes, the outermost of which is the thickest or firmest. Fig. 19 represents several different kinds of starch grains.

Fig. 19

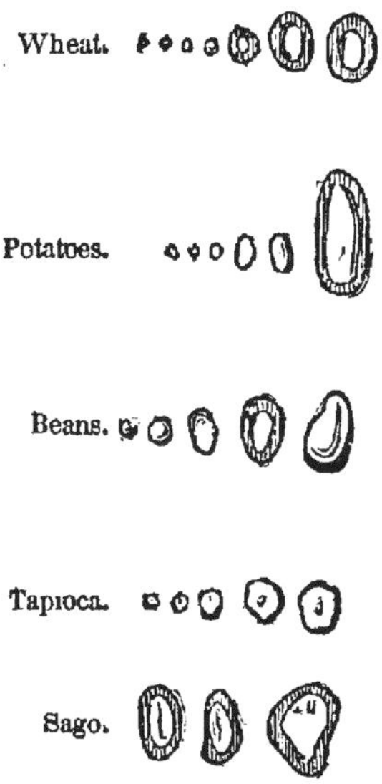

Wheat.

Potatoes.

Beans.

Tapioca.

Sago.

(Starch Granules.)

360. *Preparation and Uses.*— Starch is obtained from potatoes by grating them, and washing the pulp upon a sieve. The

water carries off the starch in suspension, and deposits it on standing. From flour it is procured by making it into a paste with water, and washing it in a similar manner. Starch is insoluble in cold water; but in boiling water the grains swell, the outer membranes burst, and their contents are dissolved out, producing a pasty or jelly-like mass (gelatinous starch, or amadine). This is the reason why starch once dissolved in hot water can never be restored to its original condition. In this state it is employed for stiffening and imparting a gloss (dressing) to various fabrics and articles of wearing apparel. Prussian blue or indigo is usually added to starch, to cover the yellowish hue it obtains by solution, and the tinge which fabrics long worn are apt to acquire. Potato-starch absorbs water much more freely than wheat-starch, and goods that are stiffened with it are hence apt to *give* in damp weather, and to become mouldy, if laid by.

361. *Starch as Food.*—Starch is an important element of food. It belongs to a class of substances (*sugar, gum,* &c.) which contain no nitrogen, and therefore cannot be converted into the fabric or flesh of the animal body, as this always contains nitrogen. They seem designed to be consumed (burned) in the system for the production of animal heat, and are hence called elements of combustion or respiration. Liebig maintains that they are converted into fat, which is also a non-nitrogenized body. Other chemists have denied this. The stomach of man is incapable of digesting starch in the raw state. It cannot break or dissolve the grains; hence the necessity that such food should be previously

How is starch obtained from potatoes and flour? What is the effect of boiling upon starch? For what is the gelatinous starch used? Why is indigo added? What is said of potato-starch?

Why cannot starch be converted into flesh? What is supposed to be its office in the system? Why must starch be cooked before being eaten by man? What is said of the lower animals?

cooked. The inferior animals possess a higher digestive power, and make use of starch in the raw condition ; but it has been found that all is not digested, a considerable quantity of alimentary matter passing through the intestines entirely unaffected as when it, was swallowed. Hence the advantage of boiling potatoes and partially fermenting grain for feeding stock.

362. *Different Kinds of Starch.*—There are several kinds of starch in use for dietetical purposes. *Sago* is a brownish-white variety, obtained from the pith of the palm-tree. It is used to form a light, nutritious, easily digestible article of food for invalids, in febrile and inflammatory cases. *Arrow-root* is a pure white starchy powder, obtained from the tubers of a plant grown in the West Indies. It forms a nutritious jelly, and an agreeable, non-irritating diet. *Tapioca* is another much esteemed variety of starch. It is greatly relished by infants about the time of weaning ; and in them it is less apt to become sour during digestion than any other farinaceous food.—(*Christison.*) These varieties are very often adulterated with potato-starch and ground rice. Such impurities may be easily detected with the microscope, as the grains of each variety are peculiar and distinct in their form and appearance.

363. *Transformations of Starch.*—When starch is heated in an oven to a temperature not exceeding 300° F., it becomes soluble in cold water, and is changed into *gùm.* It is sold under the name of *starch-gum*, or *British gum*, and is successfully substituted for *gum-Arabic* by the calico-printers, in thickening many of their colors. If gelatinous starch is boiled for a few minutes with weak sulphuric acid, it changes

from a viscid mass to a limpid fluid, and a substance is pro-duced called *dextrine*, which resembles gum in its properties. If the boiling is continued for a few hours, and the acid removed by neutralizing it with chalk and filtering it, the liquid will be found to yield upon evaporation a mass of solid *grape-sugar* (368) exceeding in weight the starch from which it was produced. In effecting these transformations the acid suffers neither loss nor change, and may be obtained at the close of the process in the same condition and quantity as at the beginning. Dextrine has precisely the same composition as starch. The grape-sugar contains an increased proportion of the elements of water (see Chart). In the same way *diastase*, a nitrogenized principle formed in seeds during germination (320), acts upon starch, converting it first into dextrine and then into sugar, without itself undergoing any change. It acts by the power of catalysis (31).

364. *Starch changed to Sugar in Fruits.*—Unripe fruit, as apples and pears, contain starch, which as ripening proceeds is gradually changed to sugar. The transformation of starch into sugar seems also to be effected by frost, as frozen potatoes and apples acquire a sweet taste by being thawed. The formation of starch goes on in the vegetable tissue after the functions of the plant have ceased. Thus, it has been stated that 100 lbs. of potatoes contain of starch, in August, 10 lbs.; in September, $14\frac{1}{2}$ lbs.; in November, 17 lbs; in March, 17 lbs.; in April, $13\frac{3}{4}$ lbs.; and in May, 10 lbs. The quantity of starch thus increases during autumn, remains uniform through the winter, and in spring, when the germinating principle begins to be active, it diminishes—is transformed into dextrine and sugar by the agency of diastase.

What is the effect of ripening upon the starch of fruits? What change is produced by frost? What is said of the increase of starch in the vegetable tissue? What example is given?

GUM. (*Mucilage.*)

$C_{12} H_{10} O_{10}$,

3·55. *Properties of Gum.*—The term gum is applied to a class of bodies such as are sometimes seen exuding in small globules or tears from the bark of cherry, plum, and apple trees. They are translucent, tasteless, inodorous, and either dissolve in water, or swell up and form with it a thick mucilage. They are produced quite abundantly in plants, flowing from the bark of several tropical trees in such quantity, as to be collected for commercial purposes. Some articles of diet yield the following proportions of gum: Wheat flour, 2·8 per cent.; rye flour, 11; Indian corn, 2 2; peas, 6·3; kidney beans, 19; potatoes, 3·3; cabbage, 2·8. It is considered to be nutritive, but not easy of digestion. It is a hydrate of carbon (349), and ranks with the elements of respiration (361).

366. *Gum-Arabic,* perhaps the best known of the gums, is a hard, brittle substance, the finer kinds being white, the more common of a yellow or brown color.. Its solution is very adhesive, and is used to form pastes. Pieces of it are also slowly dissolved in the mouth, to allay troublesome cough and irritation of the throat. It is collected from the bark of trees in Arabia and Senegal. *Gum-Senegal* is essentially the same thing.

SUGAR.

367. *Proportions in different Substances.*—This is the sweet substance of plants, and is a very common product of vegetable growth. It is found in various articles used for

What are the properties of gum? Where is it found?
What is gum-Arabic? For what is it used? Where is it obtained?
What are the proportions of sugar in different articles of food?

food, in the following proportions: Wheat flour, 4·2 to 8·4 per cent. ; wheat bread, 3·6 ; rye flour, 3·2 ; Indian corn, 1·4 ; figs, 6·2 ; ripe pears, 6 4—kept for some time, 11·5 ; ripe gooseberries, 6 2 ; cherries, 18 ; peaches, 16 ; melons, 1·5 ; cow's milk, 4·7 per cent.

368. *Cane-Sugar and Grape-Sugar.*—There are two principal varieties of sugar. That which is extracted from the juice of the sugar-cane, green corn-stalks, beet-roots, and the maple-tree, is called cane-sugar. It is the kind in common use. The other is obtained by the transformation of starch and dextrine, and is abundant in fruits, as the apple, pear, plum, cherry, and fig. It is especially abundant in grapes, and is hence called grape-sugar—also *starch-sugar*, or *glucose.* The white, sweet grains in raisins are grape-sugar. It also forms that portion of honey which solidifies. These two kinds of sugar differ in composition and properties. Cane-sugar has the formula $C_{12} H_{11} O_{11}$, and is dissolved freely by one-third its weight of cold water. Grape-sugar is represented by $C_{12} H_{14} O_{14}$, and dissolves slowly, requiring one and a half times its weight of water. Two ounces of cane-sugar are equal in sweetening power to five ounces of grape-sugar.

369. *Mode of obtaining Sugar.*—The annual production of sugar in various parts of the world is estimated at about one million of tons.—(*Dr. Carpenter.*) This is chiefly obtained from the sugar-cane; the beet-root and the maple yielding but a small proportion. It is procured by crushing the cane-stalks between cylinders, collecting the juice, and evaporating it by boiling in large open vessels. When re-

What are the principal varieties of sugar ? Which has the greatest sweetening power ?

What is the annual produce of sugar throughout the world ? From what is it chiefly obtained ? How is it procured from the cane-stalks ? How is the crude sugar refined ? - How is it whitened ?

duced to a proper consistency, the syrup is transferred into *coolers*, where a portion of it crystallizes, forming *raw* or *brown sugar*. The uncrystallizable portion is drawn off as molasses. The juice, when first expressed, is liable to run into rapid decomposition, from the heat of the climate. This is prevented by the addition of a small quantity of lime, which neutralizes acids and coagulates the impurities. Hence traces of lime are always to be detected in crude or brown sugar. The raw sugar is refined by dissolving it in water mixed with some albuminous substance—white of eggs, or serum of blood, and heating again. The albumen coagulates, and thus removes the impurities. One gallon of cane-juice, upon an average, yields a pound of sugar. To whiten or decolorize the syrup, it is filtered through a bed of coarsely powdered animal charcoal (163). It is then evaporated in vacuum-pans (the air being exhausted so that it will boil at a lower temperature), and recrystallized, forming the glistening white loaf-sugar. Beet-roots are treated in a similar manner—100 pounds yielding four or five pounds of purified white sugar, besides a quantity of syrup.

370. *Uses of Sugar.*—Sugar is made use of by everybody as a delicious and healthful element of diet. As it belongs to the ternary group of bodies, it is considered to act as fuel for the system, being directly consumed in respiration (361). Sugar is extensively used in domestic economy as an antiseptic—that is, to prevent the decomposition or putrefaction of organic substances. It preserves fruits by separating their water, and fixing it in an unchangeable syrup, and by excluding the air. It is employed by many for the preservation of meat and fish, as a much smaller quantity of it is required to prevent putrefaction than of

How is sugar supposed to act in the system? How does it preserve fruits? Why is it said to be superior to salt in preserving meat?

salt, while the meat is said to be equally savory and nutritious.

371. *White syrup* is the thick, oil-like solution of sugar
in water. If this is set by, and allowed slowly to evaporate,
the sugar gradually deposits itself (crystallizes) in the form
of *sugar-candy.* The liquid sugar of honey is thus, after a
time, deposited as a granular solid, forming candied honey.
Candied sweetmeats are produced in the same way. When
sufficiently heated, sugar becomes brown, loses its sweet
taste, and acquires bitterness. In this state it is called *caramel,* or *burnt sugar.* When dissolved in water, it is used to
color soups and sauces, and also various liquors.

OF THE ALBUMINOUS COMPOUNDS.

372. *Their Similarity of Composition.*—The bodies we
have just been studying are associated in plants with another class of substances, less abundant, but equally important—the albuminous or nitrogenized compounds. They
consist of the four organic elements, carbon, hydrogen, oxygen, and nitrogen (hence called *quaternary compounds*),
together with a small quantity of sulphur and phosphorus,
although it is too minute to be determined in atomic proportions, for this reason these substances are not represented
upon the Chart. This group consists of albumen, gluten or
vegetable fibrine, and caseine, all having the same chemical
composition $(C_{48} H_{36} O_{14} N_6)$.—(*Liebig.*) It has hitherto been
assumed that these compounds contain, as basis, a common
principle called *proteine,* hence they have been called *pro-

What is white syrup? How are candied honey and candied sweetmeats produced? What is caramel? For what is it used?

What are the albuminous compounds composed of? Why are not the sulphur
and phosphorus represented upon the Chart?

teinaceous compounds; but recent researches have rendered it doubtful if such a principle can be obtained.

373. *Vegetable Albumen.*—When the water which has been used to wash starch from wheat flour or rasped potatoes is allowed to stand until it becomes clear, and then boiled, it assumes a turbid appearance, and deposits a flaky, white substance, known as *vegetable albumen.* This substance is identical in composition and properties with white of eggs, and is named albumen from *albus,* white. When dried it forms a brittle, yellow, gummy mass. It dissolves in cold water, forming a glairy, tasteless, and nearly colorless fluid; but if heated to 160° it *coagulates,* that is, becomes solid, and will not again dissolve in water, either cold or hot. Liquid albumen is not only coagulated by heat, but also by alcohol, creosote, and corrosive sublimate. It is also coagulated by most acids, with which it unites as a base, forming definite compounds. Coagulated albumen is dissolved by the alkalies, towards which it acts as an acid, combining with and neutralizing them. Boiled eggs furnish a familiar example of coagulated albumen.

374. *Albumen easily putrefies.*—A most remarkable property of albumen is its instability, or tendency to decomposition. This is due to the complexity of its composition (316), as it consists of six elements and a large number of atoms ($C_{48} H_{36} O_{14} N_6 + S P$), and also to the fickle nature of its nitrogen (115). Dissolved in water, and at common temperatures, it is speedily broken up, and runs into putrefaction; this property is destroyed by coagulation. Decay in the starch group gives rise only to carbonic acid and water; but in albumen, in addition to these, hydrogen combines

How is vegetable albumen obtained? Whence does it derive its name? What are its properties? By what agencies is it coagulated? How do alkalies affect it? Why is albumen so unstable? What are the products of decay in this group?

with nitrogen, sulphur, and phosphorus, forming ammonia, sulphuretted hydrogen, and phosphuretted hydrogen. The disgusting odor emitted by putrefying animal substances is thus caused by the decomposition of albumen and its congeners. The sap and juices of all plants contain more or less of dissolved albumen, which is an active cause of fermentation, and of decay in wood. It is also a constituent of the blood and flesh of animals, and, in the same manner, induces in them rapid putrefactive changes. Any process, therefore, which coagulates or fixes the albumen in an insoluble compound, or which removes it from the living tissues, tends to preserve them, by arresting decomposition. Substances which act in any of these ways to prevent putrefaction are called *antiseptics*.

375. *Vegetable Caseine.*—When pea or bean meal is soaked in water, and the albumen removed by coagulating with heat, if a little acid be added to the clear liquid, a white, filmy substance is deposited, known as vegetable caseine, from its resemblance to the caseine or *curd* of milk. It contains nitrogen, and has the same composition as albumen, but differs from it in not being coagulated by heat. It contains no free phosphorus, but a large proportion of phosphate of lime.

376. *Vegetable Fibrine.*—If the flour of wheat or other grain be made into a paste, and kneaded in a linen cloth, with the addition of water, until the starch is all removed, there remains a gray, tough, adhesive, elastic substance, which may be drawn out into strings, known as *gluten* or *vegetable fibrine*, from its identity of composition with the muscular fibre of flesh or lean meat. Gluten also contains

---

To what is the unpleasant smell of putrefying animal substances due? How may decay be obviated? What are antiseptics?

w is vegetable caseine obtained? How does it differ from albumen?

nitrogen, and has the same formula as albumen and caseine. Gluten is odorless and tasteless; it swells up in water without being dissolved. When dried, it shrinks and hardens into a yellowish substance resembling horn or glue. In the moist state, gluten, like albumen and caseine, putrefies rapidly. Wheat contains from 8 to 35 per cent. of gluten, Indian corn 12 per cent., rye 9 to 13, barley 3 to 6, oats 2 to 5, beans 10, potatoes 3 to 4, red beets 1·3, turnips 0·1, and cabbage 0·8 per cent.

377. *Elements* of *Nutrition.*—These nitrogenized compounds are of very great interest, as they exist in all foods that are adapted for the support of animals. They are the flesh-forming principles—the true elements of nutrition, out of which the animal fibres and tissues are constructed. The nutritive value of food thus depends greatly upon the proportion of its albuminous constituents; and as wheat contains a larger share than any other grain, it is ranked as the most nutritive. But the same kind of grain differs very much in the relative quantity of its nitrogenized principles when grown in different conditions. Manures abounding in nitrogen increase the albuminous products of vegetation. Thus unmanured wheat gave 9 per cent. of gluten, that manured with solid excrements of the cow gave 11·9, of the horse 13·6, of the sheep 32, with ox blood 34, and with the fluid excretions of man 35 per cent. The wheat of warm climates is said to abound more in gluten than that grown in colder regions. Those fertilizers which produce the largest proportion of gluten are richest in nitrogen, and, as a necessary consequence (115), are very liable to decomposition, the ni

---

What is gluten? What are its properties?

What is said of the nitrogenized compounds? Upon what does the nutritive value of food depend? What is the effect of the nitrogenized manures upon grain Why is precaution needed to save them?

trogen escaping into the air as ammonia. This will be prevented (127) by the skilful farmer.

ACTION OF THE ALBUMINOUS PRINCIPLES UPON THE STARCH GROUP.—PRODUCTION OF ALCOHOL.

378. *Nature of Fermentation.*—A solution of sugar in
pure water remains unchanged; exposed to the air it gradually evaporates, the sugar crystallizes, and may be obtained
again in the same state as it was before being dissolved.
But if to the saccharine solution there be added a little putrefying flesh, blood, cheese, flour, milk, white of egg, or
any albuminous substance in the act of decomposition, this
action is communicated to the sugar, which is decomposed
and broken up into new compounds. The substance thus
added is called *ferment,* and the process *fermentation.* The
conditions of this fermentation are the presence of sugar in
solution, or in a moist state, the presence of an albuminous
substance in a state of putrescence, and a favorable temperature, from 70° to 80° F. If the juices of plants which
contain sugar, as that of apples, grapes, &c., are extracted
and preserved, without the contact of air, they remain sweet;
but if the air is admitted, its oxygen soon induces a putrefactive change in the albuminous substances, and this in turn
is communicated to the sugar. This is known as the vinous
fermentation.

379. *Mode of Action of Ferment.*—The way in which
ferment acts upon sugar is not well understood; but there
is no combination between the elements of the two substances. From the small quantity that may be employed,

What is ferment? What is fermentation? What are the conditions of fermentation? What is vinous fermentation?
How does the ferment act in producing change?

it has been supposed by some to act by its presence (31); others think that the atoms of the decomposing ferment being in a state of motion, communicate motion also to the atoms which compose the sugar, and thus overturn their nicely balanced affinities. It is probably a kind of infection, such as is propagated to a sound apple by placing a rotten one in contact with it.

380. *Production of Alcohol.*—By fermentation, sugar is converted into *carbonic acid* and *alcohol.* An atom of grape-sugar, $C_{12} H_{12} O_{12} + 2 H O$, having parted with its two atoms of water by heat, gives rise to four atoms of carbonic acid and two of alcohol, $C_4 H_6 O_2$. (See Chart.) Cane-sugar is always converted into grape-sugar before it undergoes fermentation. Commercial alcohol is obtained chiefly from grains which abound in starch; this is converted by the albuminous principle of malt (diastase) into grape-sugar, and the fermentation being continued, alcohol is produced. The glutinous portion of the grain employed is converted into *yeast,* which possesses the same property of inducing fermentation in other bodies. Alcohol is separated from the watery solution in which it is generated by *distillation.* It boils, and is converted into vapor at a much lower temperature than water (173° F.). It may therefore be obtained by vaporizing and condensing in separate vessels; but it still retains a portion of water, which may be removed by quick-lime.

381. *Properties of Alcohol.*—Pure alcohol is a colorless, mobile fluid, of a pleasant, fruity smell, a burning taste, and has never been frozen. Its sp. gr. is 0·795; it is therefore

Give the changes which an atom of grape-sugar undergoes during its conversion into alcohol. What becomes of the starch in grain? What of the gluten? How 'e the alcohol obtained pure?
What are the properties of alcohol? For what is it used?

about one-fifth lighter than water. It is very volatile, and has a strong affinity for water, on which account, together with its property of coagulating or hardening albumen, it acts as a powerful antiseptic (374), and is used to preserve organic substances from putrefaction. This is also the reason why alcoholic liquids, when exposed to the air, attract moisture and increase their quantity of water. It is very combustible, burning without smoke, and producing an intense heat; it is therefore much used in lamps by chemists; it is also extensively employed as a solvent. It is a powerful stimulant, and produces remarkable effects upon the human constitution (614.)

382. *Quantity of Alcohol produced from different Substances.*—Equal weights of the different grains give nearly equal quantities of alcohol. 100 lbs. of wheat, rye, barley, oats, and Indian corn yield, upon distillation, an average of $4\frac{1}{2}$ gallons of spirits, containing 45 per cent of absolute alcohol; 100 lbs. of beet-roots produce $1\frac{1}{3}$, and 100 lbs. of potatoes, $1\frac{2}{3}$ gallons. By adding together the equivalents of the alcohol and the carbonic acid produced by an atom of sugar in the vinous fermentation, they will be found to be nearly equal (92 to 88). About one-half the weight of the grain consumed in distillation passes off as carbonic acid. To every gallon of pure alcohol there is formed nearly 450 gallons of carbonic acid. The per centage of strong alcohol contained in common spirituous liquors is as follows: Irish whisky, 53·9; gin, 57 6; rum, 53·6; brandy, 53 3; London porter, 4·2; cider, 5 to 9; champagne, 12·6 per cent.— (*Pereira.*)

383. *Loss of Substance in the Production of Alcohol.*—

What grains yield most alcohol? What becomes of half the weight of the grain?

Of what is alcohol always a product?

We thus understand that alcohol is not one of the principles formed by nature and stored up in plants, but is always a product of rotting and putrefaction—the result of a process in its nature destructive. It is obtained from grain at the expense of its starchy and saccharine elements, one-half of which are converted directly into carbonic acid, and returned to the inorganic world, while the nitrogenized elements of the grain are destroyed as food for man.

384. *Of the Lactic Acid Fermentation.*—When certain saccharine juices, such as those of beet-roots, carrots, or onions, are exposed to the air at moderately high temperatures (from 86° to 104°), fermentation takes place, the sugar disappears, but, instead of carbonic acid and alcohol, *lactic acid, mannite,* and a mucilaginous, gummy substance, are formed, which render the liquid viscid and ropy. It is hence also called the *viscous* fermentation. This well illustrates the difference of products arising from the decomposition of the same organic substances at different temperatures. The gum produced in this species of fermentation has the same composition as the sugar. *Mannite* is a kind of sugar of a weak saccharine taste, and is not changed to alcohol by fermentation. It is the chief ingredient of *manna,* a kind of sugar which exudes from the bark of a species of ash in Southern Europe, and is used in medicine.

385. *Lactic Acid,* $C_6 H_5 O_5 + H O$, so called because it occurs in sour milk (552), is a colorless, syrupy, very sour liquid, which combines with bases forming a class of salts, the lactates. It exists in sour-crout.

What is the viscous fermentation ? What is mannite ?
What is lactic acid ?

OF THE DERIVATIVES OF ALCOHOL.

386. *The Acetous Fermentation—Formation of Vinegar.*—
If the vinous fermentation is not checked, it passes into the
acetous fermentation; the alcohol is converted into acetic
acid, or vinegar. But this change is not direct An intermediate substance is formed, called aldehyde (from *al*-cohol
and *dehydr*ogenated—that is, deprived of hydrogen). Oxygen of the air unites with two atoms of hydrogen contained
in the alcohol, forming aldehyde, $C_4 H_4 O_2 + 2 H O$. By
absorbing two more atoms of oxygen, which it rapidly does,
the aldehyde is changed to acetic acid, $C_4 H_3 O_3 + H O$.
The formation of acetic acid is a process of oxidation, and
can only be carried on with access of air. Hence if liquors,
as wine or beer, are tightly corked, they may remain unchanged for years ; but if the air be admitted, they speedily
become sour (acetified) by the oxidation of their alcohol.

387. *Vinegar may be made quickly.*—A mixture of pure
alcohol and water will not absorb oxygen from the air ; some
vinegar or ferment must be added to begin the action, which
then proceeds until all the alcohol disappears. As oxygen
is the active agent in acetification, the rapidity of the process will obviously depend upon the abundance of its supply. If the liquid remains at rest, and the air comes in contact with but a small portion of it, many months may be
required to effect the change. In the *quick vinegar* process,
the liquor is made to trickle over beech-shavings, which have
been previously steeped in vinegar, and which fill a tall vessel made with holes in its sides, so as to admit a free circu-

In the acetous fermentation, what changes take place? Why is the presence
of air necessary? How may liquors and wines be kept for years ?
Upon what does the rapidity of acetification depend ? Describe the quick vinegar process.

lation of air. In this way a vast surface is exposed, the absorption of oxygen is very rapid, and the acetification completed by a few repetitions. of the process.

388. *Properties of Acetic Acid.*—Pure acetic acid is a colorless, intensely sour liquid, which blisters the skin. It combines with various bases, forming salts—the *acetates,* as acetate of alumina, acetate of copper (verdigris). It unites with various proportions of water, forming vinegar of different degrees of strength. Common table vinegar contains from three to five per cent. of acetic acid. Taken into the system in considerable quantity, it is said to cause leanness by producing languor of the digestive process. Cases are recorded in which its excessive use has proved fatal.

389. *Putrefaction of Vinegar.*—Vinegar which has been long exposed to the air, and particularly if it is not strong, is subject to a peculiar putrefaction, by which a thick slimy substance (vinegar mother) is produced ; also infusoria (vinegar eels) ; these may be destroyed and further change arrested for a time by boiling the vinegar. Exposed to the cold, water freezes sooner than acetic acid. This fact may be made use of to concentrate a weak vinegar. When the mixture is partially frozen, the acetic acid is drawn off.

390. *Adulteration of Vinegar.*—Vinegar is often adulterated with oil of vitriol. To detect it, evaporate a portion of the vinegar in a porcelain vessel ; if towards the end of the evaporation thick, suffocating fumes are given off, and a black charred residuum is left, sulphuric acid is indicated ; pure vinegar evolves only an agreeable vinegar odor, and leaves a brownish deposit, not charred. Pepper, mustard,

---

What are the properties of acetic acid ? How much is contained in common vinegar ? What is its effect upon the system ?

What is the result of putrefaction in vinegar? How may the change be arrested? How may a weak vinegar be concentrated ?

How may adulterations in vinegar be detected .

and other acrid substances are sometimes added to weak vir-
egar to give it strength.   The presence of these substances
may be ascertained by saturating the acid with an alkali ; the
acrid taste of the substances will then become sensible.

ETHER.

391. *Organic Radicals.*—When equal weights of oil of
vitriol and alcohol are heated in a retort, a vapor passes
over, which may be condensed into a colorless, limpid fluid,
known as ether, or *sulphuric ether*, because sulphuric acid is
employed to obtain it. The composition is $C_4 H_5 O$; differing
from alcohol in the absence of the elements of one atom of
water, which has been taken away by the sulphuric acid
(see Chart).   In a theoretical point of view, ether is looked
upon as the oxide of an *organic radical*, ethyle, which is
represented by the formula $C_4 H_5$.   Ether, according to this
view, would be oxide of ethyle, and alcohol a hydrated oxide
of ethyle.   The ethyle is looked upon as a radical, or root,
from which springs a series of compounds, just as potassium
may be regarded as the radical or root of potash, hydrate of
potash, sulphate of potash, &c.   Potassium is a simple radical, and as ethyle appears to comport itself in a similar manner, it is called a *compound* radical.

392. *Properties of Ether.*—Ether has a hot, pungent
taste, and a fragrant odor.   It is extremely volatile, disap-
pearing even when poured through the air from one vessel
into another.   It evaporates so rapidly that when poured
upon the hand it produces cold ; hence it is used in cooling
lotions in surgery.   It boils at 96°, or when exposed to the
sun in summer, and is very combustible, burning with more
light than alcohol, and some smoke.   It is used to relieve

How is sulphuric ether obtained ?   What is a compound radical ?
Enumerate the properties of ether.   For what is it used ?

and prevent spasms in asthma, in doses of half a tea-spoonful mixed with water. Vapor of ether, mixed with air and respired, produces an intoxicating effect like laughing-gas, and also insensibility to pain, like chloroform. It dissolves the fats and oils, and is hence of great importance in Organic Chemistry.

393. *Chloroform.*—This is made by distilling alcohol with chloride of lime in a capacious retort. Its composition is $C_2 H Cl_3$. It is a dense, limpid fluid, half as heavy again as water, and very volatile. Its vapor, when breathed, produces insensibility, so that severe surgical operations are experienced without pain.

CHEMISTRY OF BREAD-MAKING.

394. *Grain and Flour.*—The grain of which bread is made consists mostly of starch, gluten, and sugar: these are to be so changed from their raw state as to become agreeable to the taste and easily digested. The grain is pulverized, or *ground* in mills, and separated by *sifting*, or *bolting*, into different qualities of flour or meal. The ligneous husk of grain produces the bran, while the flour is formed by the interior white portions. The gluten is tougher and more difficult to grind than the starch, hence the finest and whitest flour, obtained by repeated siftings, contains a larger proportion of starch, the darker colored flour being richer in gluten; and as the nutritive properties of flour are in proportion to the quantity of the nitrogenized element (gluten), the latter kind will make the most nutritious bread.

How is chloroform made ? What effect does it produce when breathed ?

What are the chief substances in grain? What is the first process to which the grain is subjected? From what part of the grain is the bran derived? From what is the flour formed? What flour contains most starch ? What kinds are richest in gluten? Which will make the most nutritious bread?

395. *Adulterations of Wheaten Flour.*—The flour of wheat, which is most generally employed for bread, is sometimes adulterated with potato starch. It may be detected by adding nitric acid, which changes the flour to a fine orange yellow, whereas it does not affect the color of the starch.—(*Ure.*) It is also often mixed with chalk, lime, and gypsum, which is shown by the increased specific gravity of the flour, and by the excessive quantity of ashes left upon burning.

396. *Rising of the Dough.*—When flour is mixed with water, kneaded into a dough, and baked, if it be in a thick mass it will be tough and clammy; if spread out thin it will be hard and horny, and in both cases it will be very indigestible. To avoid these properties of bread, and form a light, spongy dough, various methods are employed. If a paste of flour and water be set aside for some days, in a warm place, it putrefies and turns sour; and if a portion of this be incorporated into fresh dough, it excites the vinous fermentation. The decomposing gluten acts upon the sugar (379) of the flour, resolving it into alcohol and carbonic acid. The carbonic acid is liberated, in the form of minute bubbles of gas, throughout the whole substance of the dough; and being caught, as it were, by the adhesive gluten, it causes the mass to swell and *rise*. These bubbles form the pores or vesicles, which, in the best bread, are small and uniform, but sometimes constitute large, irregular cavities, or holes, in the heart of the loaf. This is liable to take place if the dough is too watery, or not sufficiently kneaded, or if the flour is too finely ground, or the heat of the oven is insufficient.

How may the adulterations of flour be detected? How may the vinous fermentation be excited in bread? What is the effect of the liberation of carbonic acid? How do these vesicles appear in good bread? How in indifferent qualities? When will this be likely to occur?

397. *Ferment used in Bread-making.*—The putrefying dough used to excite fermentation is called *leaven*. Brewer's yeast, formed by the fermenting action of malt, in the process of making beer, is the most prompt and active of all the alcohol ferments; for making bread its use is regarded as much superior to common leaven. If the fermentation proceeds too far, the dough becomes sour; that is, the vinous passes into the acetous fermentation, the alcohol changes to vinegar. When this has occurred, the evil is readily corrected by the addition of a little carbonate of soda, or magnesia, which neutralizes the acid. The acetate of soda, or magnesia, thus formed, gives to the bread no disagreeable taste, and acts upon the system only as a mild aperient; it is therefore unobjectionable.

398. *Dough raised without Ferment.*—By fermentation the bread is raised at the expense of the sugar contained in the flour; but any method, by which a gas may be set free throughout the doughy mass, answers the same purpose. If bicarbonate of soda be mingled with the flour, and dilute muriatic acid afterwards added, the acid and soda combine, forming common salt, and carbonic acid is rapidly disengaged, forming a very light sponge. It must be kneaded immediately. Carbonate of ammonia (smelling-salts) is also used for the same purpose, particularly for making sponge-cake and light biscuit: the salt is volatilized by the heat of baking. Water, impregnated with carbonic acid, is sometimes used to raise bread.

399. *Effect of Baking upon Bread.*—In the process of baking, the elements of the dough are changed by heat.

What is the best leaven for bread-making? If the vinous fermentation passes into the acetous, how may the evil be remedied?

Is there any method of making bread light, except at the expense of the flour? What is it?

The alcohol formed by fermentation is expelled as vapor Attempts have been made in very large bakeries to condense and save it, and a weak spirit was obtained, but it seems not to have paid for the trouble of collecting it. The effect of heat upon the gluten and the starch is to destroy their distinctive characters ; they form a chemical compound, and cannot be separated, as before, by a stream of water. In consequence of this change, and also because of its lightness, bread is readily soluble in the juices of the stomach, or, in other words, is easy of digestion. We have seen that starch (363) by the action of heat is transformed into soluble dextrine, or gum ; a part of the starch also undergoes this change in the oven, especially on the surface of the baked bread, which receives the strongest heat from the roof of the oven. If the crust of the hot bread is rubbed over with water, and restored for a few minutes to the oven, some of the dextrine dissolves, forming that smooth, shining surface which we see on loaves of bread and rolls. The water added to the flour forms about one-third the weight of the bread. A small portion has evaporated by the heat of baking, but most of it becomes fixed, that is, enters into chemical union with the substance of the bread.

400 *Nutritive Value of Bread from Wheat.*—The experience of all civilized people agrees with the results of Chemistry in indicating wheat as the first of the bread-producing grains. The following comparison of its composition with that of *milk* and *blood* will show its high nutritive powers. It will be remembered that milk constitutes the sole food from which all the parts of the young animal are

What is the effect of baking upon bread ? How does the heat affect the gluten and starch ? How is the shining surface seen on the crust of bread and rolls formed ? How much water is contained in the bread ?
How is wheat classed among bread-producing grains?

formed; while blood, which supplies the whole body with its elements of nutrition, must necessarily represent the whole body in its chemical constitution.

Flour.	*Blood.*	*Milk.*
Fibrine,	Fibrine,	
Albumen,	Albumen,	Albumen.
Caseine,	Caseine,	Caseine.
Gluten,	Coloring matter,	
Oil and starch,	Fats and oils,	Butter.
Sugar,	Sugar,	Milk-sugar.
Chloride of potassium,		
Chloride of sodium,		
Phosphate of soda,	Ditto.	Ditto.
" " lime,		
" " magnesia,		
" " iron,		

The analogy in this case does not extend to the relative quantities of each element.

401. *Dyspepsia, or Graham Bread,* is formed from wheaten flour which retains its bran. With weak stomachs, it agrees better than the finer kinds, and is probably healthful for all. Rye forms a nutritive bread, although inferior in this respect to wheat. It is more retentive of water than wheat, and hence remains longer moist. Its effect upon the bowels is laxative. Rice has the opposite tendency. It is said that a mixture of 75 per cent. of rye with 25 of rice forms a good bread, free from the defects of both. Indian corn makes an excellent species of bread. It contains a much larger proportion of oil than the other grains. The proportion of the oily element varies from 8 to 10 per cent., the yellow variety containing more than the white. Corn-meal deteriorates in the air more quickly than wheat or other flour; this is caused by the rapid oxidation of

From what is Graham bread made? What is said of it? What is said of rye bread? What are the properties of bread made of Indian corn?

the oil (423), and does not take place when the grain is un-
ground. The oily matter which resides in a certain portion of
the seed-grain, by baking, is diffused throughout the starchy
and glutinous matter of the meal, communicating that peculiar taste and aroma which distinguishes corn-bread.

402. *Alum* is extensively used by bakers to improve the
appearance of bread. It augments its firmness and hardness, rendering it less liable to crumble when cut, and enabling the baker to separate the loaves more readily after
their removal from the oven. It also increases its whiteness,
so that inferior kinds of flour can be made into bread of the
best aspect. Several other saline substances are also sometimes introduced into baker's bread for dishonest purposes.
Their presence is easily detected. 2000 grains of pure bread
will not yield more than from 15 to 25 grains of ashes; if
more than this is found, they have been added fraudulently.

OLEAGINOUS PRODUCTS OF PLANTS.

FATS AND OILS.

403. *Identity of the Oils and Fats.*—The oils and fats
possess the same chemical qualities, the only difference being in their *consistency*, which depends upon the temperature. An oil may be called a liquid fat, or a fat, a solid oil.
The same body, as tallow or lard, by a slight alteration of
temperature, changes from a solid to a liquid, without altering its essential properties. What the Africans call palm-
oil, and know only as a liquid, we call palm-butter, because
in this country it is a solid. Oily substances are found in

For what purpose is alum used in bread ? *How may impurities in bread be detected ?*
What is the difference between an oil and a fat ? In what parts of plants does
oil occur ? What are the hard oils called ?

considerable quantities in plants. They occur in many seeds, as that of flax, also in nuts, as the walnut and almond, from which they are obtained by pressure. They are of various degrees of consistence, from thin almond or spermaceti oil, to solid tallow. The hard oils of vegetables are frequently termed vegetable butters, as nutmeg-butter, palm-butter. The animal fats, in strictness, require to be considered among animal products in the third division of the work; but in properties and composition they are identical with the vegetable oils, and therefore cannot be conveniently separated from them.

404. *Volatile and Fixed Oils.*—The oils are of two kinds, fixed and volatile. The fixed oils are highly inflammable, do not unite with or dissolve in water, are slippery and unctuous, and do not evaporate in the air; if placed upon paper, they communicate to it a permanent stain. They are usually bland and mild to the taste, and are decomposed by the action of heat. The *volatile* oils are also inflammable and nearly insoluble in water, but they are hot and pungent to the taste, and evaporate in the air. A drop left upon paper passes away, leaving no stain. They occasion the peculiar odor emitted by many plants.

405. *Amount of Oily Product from different Sources.*— The oily substances of vegetation are principally accumulated in the fruit, and particularly in the seed. In herbaceous plants they are less abundant, although existing in considerable proportion in the straw and stalks of grain. The proportion of oil in various substances, by the most recent determinations, is as follows: In Indian corn, 9 per cent., oats 3·3, fine wheat flour 1·4, bran from the same 4·65, rice

How are the oils divided? Give the properties of the fixed oils. What is the character of the volatile oils?

How is the oil from plants obtained?

1, dry hay 3 to 4, straw of wheat 3·2, oat-straw 5·1, olive seeds 54, linseed 22, white mustard 36, black mustard 18, almonds 46, cocoanut 47, walnuts 50, yolk of eggs 28·75, cow's milk 3·13 per cent. They are obtained by mechanical pressure, as linseed oil, by the agency of heat, as in the animal fats, by distillation, and by solution in ether.

406. *Proximate Principles of the Oils.*—Chemists have shown that fats and oils have a true saline composition; that is, they consist of acids in combination with a base. The proximate principle of the oils, which plays the part of a base, neutralizing acids, is called glycerine, so named from its sweetish taste. When pure it is a thick, syrupy, inodorous liquid, soluble in all proportions in water and alcohol, and has the composition $C_5 H_8 O_6$. It is expelled from its combination by the ordinary alkalies. Glycerine is united in the oils with three acid substances: Stearic acid ($C_{38} H_{38} O_4$), margaric acid ($C_{34} H_{34} O_4$), and oleic acid ($C_{36} H_{34} O_4$).—(*Silliman.*) With stearic acid it forms stearate of glycerine, or *stearine :* with margaric acid it forms margarate of glycerine, or *margarine ;* and with oleic acid it forms oleate of glycerine, or *oleine.* Stearine, margarine, and oleine are therefore distinct oily or proximate principles. They are each a combination of a fatty acid with a base. They have different properties, and may be readily separated from the oily bodies in which they are combined together.

407. *Oleine* is that portion of oil which causes its fluidity. The thinner and more liquid an oil or fat, the more oleine does it contain. Olive oil, and vegetable oils generally, contain a large portion of oleine. The hard fats contain less

What have chemists shown to be the composition of the oils ?   What is glycerine ?   With what is it united ?   What does it form ?   What are these three substances ?

What is oleine ?   In what substances is it found abundantly ?

of it in proportion to their hardness, hence it exists in greater quantity in the fat of the swine than in the harder tallow of the sheep or ox.   It is expressed on a great scale from lard, for burning in lamps, and for other uses.

408. *Stearine and Margarine.*—Stearine gives to certain fats and oils the opposite property of solidity.   It is most abundant in tallow and suet.   It is obtained by subjecting the solid fats to great pressure, in flannel or hair bags, between hot iron plates ; the oleine is separated, and flows away.   The solid stearine thus procured is used for the manufacture of *stearine candles,* which very much resemble those of wax.   Oils which are liquid at common temperatures contain a small proportion of stearine in solution, as may be shown by exposing them to the action of snow or ice, when the stearine is deposited and the oleine floats above · hence in winter olive and castor oils deposit solid stearine, and become thick.   A pound of tallow contains about three-fourths of a pound of stearine, of olive oil not more than one-fourth. Margarine resembles stearine in its property of hardness ; it exists in human fat, butter, goose-fat, and olive oil.

409. *Variation in the Proportion of these Elements.*— The solid and fluid parts are mixed together in different proportions in the oily substances of different plants and animals, and in different parts of the same animal.   They are also modified by feeding, and other circumstances.   Thus the tallow from animals fed upon dry, ripe fodder, is more solid than when they are fed upon grains.   The superior hardness of Russian tallow is due to this circumstance, their animals being fed upon dry fodder eight months in the year.

What property does stearine give to substances ?   Where is it most abundant ? How is it obtained ?   For what is it used ?   Why do olive and castor oils become thick in winter ?   What is said of margarine ?   Where is it found ?

What effect does the food of animals have upon their oily parts ?   How may fats and oils be bleached ?   Upon what does the odor of oils depend ?

Fats and oils are generally either colorless or slightly yellow, but may be bleached by the protracted action of light. The stearic, margaric, and oleic acids which they contain are without smell, but some of them have peculiar odors dependent upon the presence of certain *volatile acids;* thus, butter contains *butyric acid,* goats' fat *hircic acid,* whale oil *phocenic acid,* &c.

410. *Why Oily Bodies are Inflammable.*—By reference to the Chart, or the formula we have just given (406) for their proximate principles, it will be seen that the oil group consists almost entirely of carbon and hydrogen, with but a very small proportion of oxygen. They are thus composed of two elements, which have a most powerful affinity for oxygen ; we should, therefore, conclude that they must be exceedingly combustible, and such is the fact. Every one is aware of the violence with which they burn when set on fire ; and being rich in hydrogen, they produce a large flame. So strong is this attraction for oxygen, that when cotton, tow, straw, and cloth, which present an extended surface to the action of the atmosphere, are imbued with oil, they often take fire spontaneously (spontaneous combustion), and thus frequently occasion conflagrations. In consequence of their combustibility, and the large quantity of light which they emit in burning, oleaginous bodies are universally used as a source of illumination. Some of them are converted into gas (oil gas), several of them are consumed in lamps in the liquid state, while the solid fats are formed into candles.

411. *Way in which a Candle Burns.*—In burning gas no wicks are used, and yet their use in lamps and candles seems to be to bring their materials into a gaseous form In a burn-

How does the composition of the oils account for their exceeding combustibility ? For what are the oils universally employed ? In what forms ?

Fig. 20.

ing candle, the fat below is melted by the heat into the form of a hollow cup, $b\,d$, Fig. 20, which may be considered a reservoir of oil. The wick, consisting of parallel cotton fibres, acts as a system of capillary vessels, drawing or sucking up the liquid as fast as it is consumed above. The liquid oil is thus carried into the hollow interior of the flame (77), where it is exposed to a high temperature without being able to come in contact with air ; it is in the same position as if it were inclosed in an iron retort between red-hot coals. It is here immediately converted into gaseous and vaporous combustible products, which form the inner dark portion of the flame. The office of the wick is to maintain a steady supply of oil to be distilled or vaporized in the flame ; but as the candle burns down the wick of course extends upward in the centre of the flame, where it remains charred and unconsumed, the access of air being prevented by the surrounding cone of fire. As the charred wick increases in size, it impedes the activity of combustion, and consequently causes a deposit of unburnt carbon, in the form of a spongy, sooty snuff at the top, which darkens the flame.

412. *Plaited Wicks.*—In some of the finer candles, as wax, sperm, and stearine, this evil has been avoided by plaiting or twisting the wicks. By this means the free ends of the fibres constantly bend out of the flame, as at c, Fig. 20, and are reduced to ashes. The symmetry of the flame is injured by this arrangement, as it follows the direction of the inclining wick fibres. The rim of the cup is also apt to be melted down on one side, so that the liquid fat gutters

over the edge. This evil is so serious as to prevent the use of plaited wicks in common tallow candles, which suffer more than the harder and more infusible kinds. The power of the common wick to influence the quantity of light emitted by a candle flame, is thus shown by the experiments of *Peclet*. The intensity of the light from a freshly snuffed candle (six to the pound) being represented by 100, it becomes in 4 minutes 92, in 8 minutes 50, in 10 minutes 41, in 12 minutes 38, in 15 minutes 34, in 20 minutes 32, in 22 minutes 25, in 24 minutes 20, in 28 minutes 19, in 30 minutes 17, and in 40 minutes 14. Less than half an hour, therefore, is sufficient to reduce the light of an unsnuffed candle to one-seventh its original brilliancy.

413. *Different Candles Compared.*—It has been found that the quantity of material consumed per hour in burning, by different candles, is as follows : they were six to the pound, and occasionally snuffed, so as to maintain as nearly as possible an equable flame. Stearine consumed per hour 164 grains, spermaceti 143, wax 134, tallow (moulds) 128. The relative proportions of light produced were, for the spermaceti 10, the stearine 7·4, the wax 6·6, and the tallow 4·7. The consumption of sperm oil by a well-trimmed argand lamp of the ordinary dimensions (wick one inch in diameter) was about 800 grains per hour ; it gave a light equal to 10 or 11 spermaceti candles of six to the pound.

414. *Oil as a Preservative.*—Oily bodies are lighter than water, and will not mix with it ; they therefore float upon its surface, and are sometimes employed to protect substances from the action of the air. Thus fresh lemon-juice, if exposed

candles ? In what time is the light from a freshly snuffed candle diminished *wo-* half ?

Does a stearine or tallow candle consume most rapidly ?

How does oil protect substances from the action of air ? What is its effect upon our shoes ? Upon iron ? Upon wood ?

to the air, speedily moulds, but if covered with oil it does not. Preserved fruits also keep much longer when melted butter is poured over them. Having no affinity for water, substances which are imbued with it are impenetrable to that liquid ; hence by greasing our shoes they are protected from absorbing moisture. Oiled iron does not rust in damp air, while wood or fabrics which are charged with oil are preserved from decay by the exclusion of water, which is an active agent of decomposition.

DRYING OILS.

415. *Oily* bodies, if protected from the air, undergo little change ; if exposed to it, they absorb its oxygen, gradually thicken, and some finally become quite hard and solid. These are termed *drying oils*, and are used in paints and for the manufacture of varnishes.

416. *Linseed Oil.*—This is the most important of the drying oils, and is obtained by expression from the seeds of common flax, which yield from 20 to 25 per cent. of their weight. When the seeds are submitted to pressure at common temperatures (*cold drawing*, or *cold pressure*), the oil is of a pale-yellow color and of the greatest purity, but if at a steam heat a larger quantity may be obtained ; it is then of an amber color, and more liable to become rancid (423). It is slowly bleached by sunlight, and when long kept in a half-filled bottle it thickens, and does not dry well. It has a specific gravity of 0·93. The drying properties of linseed oil, which adapt it to the painter's use, are greatly increased by boiling for several hours with the addition of a little litharge (protoxide of lead)—two to four ounces of litharge

to every gallon of oil; a little acetate of lead and sulphate of zinc are also sometimes introduced with benefit. The product is known as boiled oil, purified oil, and drying oil. It acquires by boiling a brownish-red color, and hence when white-lead is to be made into a paint with linseed oil it is prepared in the unboiled state, in consequence of its paler color. The change wrought in the oil by boiling, consists in depriving it of certain gummy, mucilaginous matters which are dissolved in it, and greatly retard the drying. The compounds of lead combine with this mucilage, forming an insoluble body, which is precipitated as a white sediment. If, after boiling for a time, the oil is set fire to and permitted to burn for half an hour, and the flame then extinguished by placing a cover upon the vessel (burning oil or fat should never be quenched with water), it acquires a viscid, tenacious consistency, and forms *printers' ink* by the addition of a due quantity of lamp-black.

417. *Oil-silk* consists of silk cloth to which several coatings of purified linseed oil have been successively applied. *Oil-cloth* is cotton cloth which has been treated in a similar manner. Mixed or ground with various coloring matters, chiefly metallic oxides, linseed oil forms numerous paints, which are smeared upon wood to preserve it and give it color.

418. *Walnut Oil* is obtained by pressure from walnuts; it is of a pale yellowish-green color, and of a peculiar odor. When fresh it is sometimes used for culinary purposes, but when rancid it is purgative. It is more drying than linseed oil, and possesses less color, which renders it a valuable in-

properties increased? What is it then called? Why is it not boiled when white-lead is to be used with it? What is the effect of boiling? How is printers' ink made?

What is oil-silk? What is oil-cloth? What is said of walnut oil?

gredient of many paints. It is sometimes used for burning in lamps, and as a basis for varnish.

419. *Hemp-seed Oil* is of a greenish-yellow color, has a disagreeable smell, and a mawkish taste. It is extensively used for making paints, varnishes, and soft soaps.

420. *Poppy Oil*, expressed from the seed of the poppy, is of a pale-yellow color, inodorous, and of a slightly agreeable flavor, much resembling olive oil, which is sometimes adulterated with it. It makes a clear varnish, and is used at the table as a substitute for olive oil. It has none of the narcotic properties of the poppy-juice.

421. *Croton Oil* is expressed from the seeds of a plant which grows in India. It is a thick, brown oil, of a peculiar odor, and acrid taste. It is powerfully purgative.

422 *Castor Oil* is obtained from the seeds, or beans, of the castor-oil plant. It is of a pale straw color, and has a bland, but somewhat nauseous flavor. Its principal use is in medicine, as a mild laxative. It is also used for printing-ink, and in perfumery as an application to the hair.

THE UNCTUOUS OILS.

423. *The Unctuous Oils* are such as do not dry up when exposed to the air, but continue soft and sticky. This property renders them very valuable for diminishing the friction of rubbing surfaces, as the axles of carriages and other machines, a purpose to which the drying oils are not adapted. For the same reason, the unctuous oils are worked into leather to maintain it in a soft and pliable condition. The unctuous oils and fats are liable, by long exposure to the air, to turn *rancid;* that is, they absorb oxygen and generate

What is said of hemp-seed oil? Of poppy oil? Of croton oil? Of castor oil?

peculiar acids, which emit a disagreeable odor. This change appears to result principally from minute quantities of nitrogenized organic tissues, which remain diffused through the fats. The rancidity of oleaginous bodies may be in a great measure removed by boiling them with water and a little magnesia, until it has lost the property of reddening litmus.

424. *How Unctuous Oils are Purified.*—As the drying oils are purified by oxide of lead, so the same change is produced in unctuous oils by sulphuric acid. We have seen (189) that this acid possesses the property of charring organic substances, but it does not act with equal energy upon all. When added to oil, it first attacks its nitrogenized and mucilaginous impurities : these are decomposed and precipitated. When just sufficient acid is used to effect this object, the mucilage alone is charred ; if too much, the oil itself is decomposed.

425. *Olive Oil, or Sweet Oil.*—This oil is obtained by pressure from the fleshy or pulpy part of the fruit of the olive-tree. The finest kind is of a yellowish color, has a thin consistence, a slight odor, an agreeable taste, and when swallowed leaves a very slight sense of acrimony in the throat. When pure it has less tendency to change than almost any other of the fat oils, but the inferior qualities soon become *rancid.* It contains 72 per cent. of oleine and 28 of margarine, the latter of which congeals in cold weather. Being less apt than most other oils to thicken by exposure to air, it is preferred for greasing delicate machinery, especially watch and clock work. It is used at table as a condiment for salads, and is hence termed *salad oil.* In Spain it is used as

What are the unctuous oils? For what are they used? What is rancid oil? What causes the change? How may it be removed?

What is the effect of sulphuric acid upon the unctuous oils?

How is olive oil obtained? What are its properties? For what is it used?

a substitute for butter. Taken in large quantities, it acts as a mild laxative.

426. *Palm Oil* is a solid butter-like oil, of an orange-yellow color, obtained by pressure from the fruit of the palm-tree. It is readily blanched by heat, or the joint action of air, light, and moisture, and also by chlorine. It contains 70 per cent. of oleine and 30 of stearine, and is used in the manufacture of soap and candles. *Oil of almonds* is expressed from sweet almonds; also from bitter almonds by cold pressure, as if heat is employed the oil contains prussic acid. It is mainly used in liniments, ointments, and soap. Unctuous oils are also obtained from *rape-seed, beech-nuts, hazel-nuts,* and the stones of fruits.

ANIMAL FATS.

427. These are contained in the bodies of animals, in what is termed *cellular tissue* or *adipose membrane.* They are obtained by a heat sufficient to liquefy the fat, and burst the including cell, or sack. The more solid portion of the fat (stearine) forms a 'layer next to the inner surface of the cell-membrane, the softer part (oleine) being inclosed within. Fat forms about one-twentieth the weight of a healthy animal.

428. *Mutton Tallow.*—This is a very white and solid fat. It has little odor when fresh, but acquires a peculiar, rancid smell, when exposed for some time to air.

429. *Beef Tallow* is of a yellowish-white color, firm, and yields 75 per cent. of stearine to 25 of oleine.

430. *Neat's-foot Oil* is obtained from the feet of oxen, by

What is palm oil? What is said of the oil of almonds?
In what part of animals is the fat deposited? How is it obtained?
What is said of mutton tallow? Beef tallow?
19

first divesting them of the hoof and hair, and then boiling them with water. This oil remains liquid below 32°, and is not liable to change or rancidity. It is used for oiling leather and greasing machinery ; particularly steeple-clocks, which require, in consequence of the cold to which they are often exposed, an oil not liable to solidify.

431. *Hog's Lard* is a white, inodorous, soft fat, which, when long exposed to the air. grows yellow, rancid, and sour. It yields 38 per cent. of stearine, which has been used for the manufacture of candles, and 62 per cent. of oleine, which is considerably used for burning in lamps. *Goose-fat* consists of 68 oleine and 32 stearine

432. *Change of the Human Body into Adipocere.*—Human fat is soft, yellowish, without odor, varying little in different parts of the system. The bodies of persons that have been for years buried in church-yards are sometimes found to have been changed into a peculiar substance, resembling fat, and termed *adipocere.* The same kind of fatty matter is formed in the vats which collect the offal from dissecting-rooms and slaughter-houses ; it is also found when the bodies of animals are exposed to running water till the muscular and membranous parts have been washed away. It has been shown that this substance is the original fat of the body, which has resisted decomposition, and is partly in the state of a fatty acid, and partly saturated by ammonia, with traces of lime and magnesia.—(*Brande.*)

433. *Train Oil* (*Whale Oil*).—Oil is obtained from the fat of various fishes, as the whale, the dolphin, the seal. It is of a yellow color, and not of a disagreeable odor, unless the fish were putrid, or the oil was expressed by a strong

What is said of neat's-foot oil ?   Hog's lard ?   Goose-fat ?
What is adipocere ?   When is it formed ?
What is said of whale oil ?

heat. Whale oil is used for illumination, to grease leather, in medicine, and in soap-making.

434. *Spermaceti Oil* is extracted from cavities in the head of the sperm whale, and is superior to common whale oil for burning in lamps. When cooled, after the death of the animal, it deposits a white, sparkling, crystalline, fatty substance, so hard that, when rubbed, it crumbles to powder. When purified, it is used for candles.

WAX.

435. Some plants produce a considerable quantity of a substance resembling beeswax, and which, in some of its properties, approaches the fatty bodies. The glossy coating, or varnish, which is observed upon the surface of leaves, fruit, and bark, rendering them impermeable to water, consists of vegetable wax. It occurs in large quantities in the common cabbage.

436. *Beeswax*, a secretion of the honey-bee, is the most important of these bodies. In its ordinary state it is yellow, but is bleached white by exposing it for some time in thin ribands, to the joint action of air, light, and moisture. Commercial beeswax is very commonly adulterated with the flour of peas and beans, with starch, and even brick-dust. These may be readily detected by spirits of turpentine, which takes up the wax, but leaves the impurities undissolved. Resin, too, is often used: it may be separated by cold alcohol, which dissolves it. Wax is much used for candles, but is not adapted to be either dipped or moulded. The wax candles are made either by applying wax, softened in hot water,

Spermaceti oil? For what is it used?

Is wax a vegetable product? Upon what parts is it found?

How may impurities in beeswax be detected? How are wax candles made? What are the uses of beeswax?

little by little, to the wick, by the hand, or by pouring melted wax upon the suspended wick with a ladle. When the candles have thus grown sufficiently large, they are rolled upon a table to give them the exact form. Beeswax is used for smoothing sewing-thread, and when dissolved in potash-ley it forms a peculiar soap, used for polishing floors.

437. *Point at which Oils Solidify.*—The temperatures at which various oily substances pass from the liquid to the solid state are thus compared : Beef tallow about 100° F. ; mutton tallow 100° to 106°, stearine from tallow 131°, palm oil 85°, stearine from palm 120°, hog's lard 81°, stearine from hog's lard 110°, spermaceti 112°, beeswax 150°, almond oil 30° ; olive oil deposits 28 per cent. of stearine at 22°, margarine of butter 118°, oleine of butter 32°.

438. *Oily Bodies as Food.*—As the oily bodies are found diffused in considerable quantities in those vegetable substances which form the natural diet of man, there can be no doubt of their healthfulness as food. Yet it is equally certain that when separated and consumed as they often are in large quantities, they prove highly injurious. " Fixed oil or fat," says Dr. Pereira, " is more difficult of digestion, and more obnoxious to the stomach, than any other alimentary principle. Indeed, in some more or less obvious or concealed form, I believe it will be found the offending ingredient in nine-tenths of the dishes which disturb weak stomachs. Many dyspeptics who have most religiously avoided the use of oil or fat in its obvious or ordinary state (as *fat meat, marrow, butter,* and *oil*), unwittingly employ it in some more concealed form." Much of the bad effects of oily substances upon the stomach is probably caused by

Give the temperatures at which oily bodies solidify.

What is said of oily bodies as food ? Why is frying the most objectionable mode of preparing oil for food ? Will fatty bodies taken as food sustain life ?

the way in which they are frequently cooked. The fats, by heating, give off, with other voaltile oils and fatty acids, a peculiar acrid substance called *acroleine*. In the process of frying, which is carried on at a high temperature, they are liable to this decomposition, and when taken into the stomach turn sour and rancid, producing heartburn. For this reason, frying is the most objectionable of all the methods by which oily substances are prepared for the table. Fatty bodies are ranked among the heat-producing foods (574) or elements of respiration, for which they are remarkably adapted. They cannot support nutrition nor sustain life. Animals which have been fed entirely upon butter and lard, refuse to take it after some time, and ultimately die of inanition.

ACTION OF ALKALIES UPON THE FIXED OILS.

439. *Saponification, or Production of Soap.*—It was stated that the proximate principle of the oils and fats, stearine, margarine, and oleine, are saline bodies ; that is, they consist of fatty acids combined with a common base, *glycerine*. When other bases, as potash, soda, or ammonia, are made to act upon the fatty substances, they expel the glycerine from its combination, and take its place, uniting with the fatty acids, and forming soaps. Soaps are therefore regular salts, combinations of margaric, stearic, and oleic acids, with potash, soda, ammonia or lime. The change by which they are produced is called saponification. The capability of being saponified is one of the most important properties of the oil family, and they are hence divided into two classes, the saponifiable and the non-saponifiable oils. The *fixed* oils belong to the former class.

How are soaps formed ? What are they ? What is saponification ? How are the oils divided ?

440. *Process of Soap-making.*—The alkalies in general use for soap-making are potash and soda. They require to be in a cáustic state, which is produced by dissolving them, and passing the solution (ley) through newly slaked lime, which takes away their carbonic acid. In this caustic ley the fats are boiled, their glycerine is set free, and the fatty acids combining with the alkali form soap, which exists as a solution in the water. In order to obtain the soap in a solid form, the solution is boiled down to a certain degree of concentration, when the soap ceases to be soluble, and rises to the surface in a soft, half-melted state. This being drawn off into moulds, cools and forms hard soap. If soda ley is used, the soap may be separated from the water in which it is dissolved by adding common salt which forms a brine, and at once coagulates the soap ; if potash ley is used, the addition of salt decomposes the potash soap, and forms a soap of soda.

441. *Hard and Soft Soaps.*—The consistence of soaps depends chiefly upon its alkalies, soda giving rise to *hard soap*, and potash to *soft soap*, the latter alkali being the more deliquescent. The consistence of the oil also somewhat influences the quality of hardness. The stearate of soda, therefore, forms the most solid soap, and the oleate of potash the softest. Between these two extremes, any required degree of firmness can be obtained by selecting the proper materials, and stopping the evaporation at any desirable point.

442. *Composition of different Kinds of Soap.*—Common yellow hard soap consists of soda with oil or fat and resin.

Describe the process of soap-making.
Upon what does the consistence of soap depend?
Of what is common hard soap composed? White or curd soap? Castile soap? Windsor soap? Fine toilet soap?

The latter element will not form a good soap with alkali alone, but requires to be worked with at least an equal weight of oil. The acid powers of resin are very feeble; it neutralizes the soda less completely than oil, and the soap is therefore very alkaline, acting too powerfully upon woollen fabrics and all other animal fibres to which it is applied. Common *white soap* or *curd soap* consists of tallow and soda. *Castile soap* is composed of olive oil and soda colored with metallic oxides, chiefly oxides of iron, in such a way as to give it the desired mottled appearance. Green and black soap, employed in factories for cleansing colored cotton fabrics, is made of fish oil and potash. *Windsor soap* consists of tallow, a small proportion of olive oil and soda. Cocoanut oil gives to soap the property of forming a strong lather. *Fine soft* toilet soap is made with purified hog's lard and potash, colored and perfumed. Fancy soaps are essentially common soaps, mixed with different aromatic oils and coloring substances, and diversified in form so as to suit the fashion of the day.

443. *Value of Soaps.*—Soap has a powerful affinity for water, and may retain from 50 to 60 per cent. of it and still remain in the solid state. Even when dry and hard it holds from 25 to 30 per cent. of water. There is hence an advantage to the consumer in purchasing dry and old soap, while the vender is interested in selling it with as large an amount of combined water as possible. To effect this, it is often kept in damp cellars and an atmosphere saturated with moisture to prevent it from drying. The quantity of moisture is easily determined by cutting the soap into thin slices, weighing and drying at a temperature not exceeding 212°; the loss of weight shows the proportion of water. The

How and why is soap often saturated with moisture? How is a good soap known?

value of soap thus mainly depends upon its dryness, but it should also possess the proper degree of solubility. Some dissolve too freely in washing, and hence waste very rapidly when used, while others possess the opposite quality ; as, for example, " the small cubic mass of white, waxy, stubborn substance generally met with on the washing-stands of bed-rooms in hotels, and which for an indefinite period passes on from traveller to traveller, each in turn unsuccessfully attempting by various manœuvres and divers cunning immersions in water to coax it into a lather." A good soap should dissolve quite freely, feel very soft and pleasant upon the skin, and afford a thick, copious lather.

444. *Properties of Soap.*—Soap is soluble in fresh water, but remains insoluble in salt water, except that made from cocoanut oil, which dissolves in weak brine, and is therefore used for washing with sea-water. Acids, as acetic and sulphuric, decompose soap, uniting with its bases and setting free the fatty acids. Soaps of soda and potash are decomposed by the salts of lime, a lime-soap being formed which is insoluble in water ; hence waters which contain sulphate or carbonate of lime wash badly (96). *Hard* water, when an alkaline soap is added, decomposes it, forming a rough, sticky, disagreeable, earthy soap, having no detergent properties, and being therefore unfit for washing. Soaps of metallic oxides, as oxide of lead, are employed medicinally for *plasters.* Soap is soluble in alcohol, forming tincture of soap, which is an excellent liniment for bruises. Soap dissolved in spirits of camphor forms *opodeldoc.* Volatile liniment is an ammoniacal soap.

445. *Mode in which Soaps act in cleansing.*--As water

has no affinity for oily substances, and will not dissolve them, of course it cannot *alone* remove them from any surfaces to which they may adhere. The skin is perpetually bedewed with oily matters which exude from the glands, and, uniting with dust and dirt, form a film or coating all over the body. Soap being always alkaline, acts upon the oil during ablu·tion, partially saponifies it, and renders the unctuous com·pound freely miscible with water, so as to be easily removed. The cuticle or outer layer of the skin is composed of albu-men, which is soluble in the alkalies (373). A portion of the excess of alkali which exists in soap must soften and dis·solve a part of the cuticle, which, when rubbed off, carries with it the dirt. Thus every washing with soap removes the old face of the scarf-skin, and leaves a new one. If the hands are too long exposed to the action of a very alkaline soap, they become tender, that is, the cuticle is dissolved away, and becomes so thin as not to protect the inner or sensitive skin. On the contrary, where the scarf-skin and dirt are rarely disturbed by soap, the sensibility of the skin is necessarily benumbed. The action of soap in cleansing textile fabrics is of a similar nature ; the alkali not only acts upon greasy matter, but, as is well known, dissolves all or·ganic substances. Being partly neutralized, its solvent power is less active than if it were in a free condition. The oily nature of the soap also increases the pliancy of the articles with which it is washed. It is said that woollen fabrics, if washed with a weak solution of carbonate of soda, will not shrink as when washed with soap.

What is the action of soap in cleansing clothes ? What is its effect upon the skin ? If the skin is long exposed to the action of soap, what is the result ? If soap is seldom applied, what follows ? What is said of washing woollen fabrics ?

OF THE VOLATILE PRINCIPLES OF PLANTS.

VOLATILE OILS.

446. *Their Sources and Preparation.*—The volatile or ethereal oils take their name from the property of readily evaporating in the air. They dissolve in alcohol, and their solutions are called *essences.* From this circumstance they are also known as *essential oils.* They are met with in all parts of plants—in the leaves, bark, and root, but principally in the flower. Sometimes different parts of the same plant contain different oils, as, for instance, the orange-tree, which furnishes one from its leaves, another from its flower, and a third from the rind of its fruit. Essential oils are not so volatile as water; nevertheless, they rise with the vapor of water; and it is by this means that they are generally extracted. The plant is put into a still, or alembic, containing water, and heat is applied. The vapor rises, passes over, and condenses in the receiver, carrying with it the oil which is found swimming upon the surface of the distilled water. When flowers or leaves are used, they are suspended in a cage in the centre of the still, in order to be acted on by the vapor only, because if they come in contact with the sides of the vessel the heat would injure them.

447. *Properties and Uses of the Ethereal Oils.*—The volatile principles of plants are generally limpid and lighter than water, yet some are heavier, and others, as camphor, solid. They have not the greasy feel of the fat oils, but

What are volatile oils? Why are they called essential oils? Whence are they obtained? How are they separated from the plant?

Give the properties of the essential oils. What is stearopten? Elaopten? How are medicated waters formed? Perfumed waters? Perfumed vinegar? Pomatum?

are rather rough to the fingers, causing a cork moistened by them to squeak when twisted into a vial. They are inflammable at lower temperatures than the fixed oils, and burn with a smoky flame. The more solid portion of the essential oils is called *stearopten*, the liquid part *elaopten*. Exposed to the air, they imbibe oxygen, and are either converted into acids or dry up, and are changed to *resins* (453). A small portion of these oils is dissolved by water, sufficient to communicate to it their peculiar taste and smell. These solutions are sold by apothecaries under the name of medicated waters. Various oils, as bergamot, lavender, rosemary, &c., dissolved in alcohol, form perfumed waters, as *Cologne water (eau de Cologne)*. They dissolve in strong acetic acid, forming *perfumed vinegar*, and when mixed with lard and other fixed oils form *pomatum, hair-oil,* &c.

448. *Composition of the Volatile Oils.*—As respects composition, the volatile oils are of two kinds. The first class consists of but two elements, carbon and hydrogen; and a large number of them, as oil of turpentine, oil of lemons, oil of juniper, oil of black pepper, oil of citron, oil of parsley, are isomeric, all having the composition $C_5 H_4$, or $2 (C_5 H_4)$. These are, therefore, vegetable hydro-carbons. The second class contains, in addition to carbon and hydrogen, a small proportion of oxygen, and sometimes sulphur and nitrogen. These are distinguished by their pungent, acrid properties, irritating the eyes, provoking tears, and, when placed upon the skin, blistering it. The oils of mustard, onions, garlic, horse-radish, hops, and asafœtida, are the most common examples of this class.

How are the volatile oils divided? Of what does the first class consist? What are they called? What is the composition and properties of the second class?

ESSENTIAL OILS WHICH CONTAIN ONLY HYDROGEN AND CARBON.

449. *Oil of Turpentine,* commonly called spirits of turpentine, is obtained by distilling with water the thick semifluid turpentine, which flows from the wounded bark of certain species of the pine, and is the cheapest, most abundant, and most useful of all the volatile oils. It is a limpid, colorless liquid of a peculiar odor. It boils at 314°, and has a sp. gr. of 0·87. It burns with a very luminous flame, and is extensively used as a source of light; but in its common or crude state, it deposits a resinous substance, and soon clogs the lamp. To prevent this, it is redistilled, or *rectified,* and then goes under the name of camphene. The lamp must be so constructed as to furnish a copious supply of air, or the turpentine will smoke. Mixing with it a portion of alcohol also corrects this evil. A pint of good oil of turpentine burns in an argand lamp about ten hours, giving a light equal to about twelve spermaceti candles. It is largely employed in the manufacture of varnish to dissolve the resins, also in the preparation of paints, to remove greasespots from cloth, dissolve India-rubber, and in medicine.

450. *Oil of Lemons* is obtained from the rind of the lemon, both by expression and by distillation. It is very fluid, colorless, of an agreeable lemon odor, a pleasant, pungent flavor, and is often used by cooks as a substitute for lemonpeel. Oil of lemons is sold under the name of *scouring-drops,* and used to remove grease stains from silk, as the fixed oils all dissolve in the ethereal oils. *Oil of black pep-*

How is spirits of turpentine obtained ? What are its properties ? What is camphene ? With what should the lamps be furnished ? For what other purposes is spirits of turpentine employed ?
What is said of the oil of lemons ? Oil of black pepper ?

per is limpid and colorless, but by keeping, it becomes yellow. In odor it resembles pepper, but is devoid of its hot taste.

451. *Oil of Juniper* is obtained by distilling bruised juniper-berries with water. It is limpid, of a faint yellow color, and used for flavoring gin. *Oil of orange-peel* closely resembles the oil of lemons. *Oil of bergamot* is a thin yellow liquid from the rind of the bergamot orange. *Oil of roses*, attar or otto of roses $(C_4 H_4)$, condensed, is olefiant gas, obtained by distilling rose-flowers, or, in the East Indies, by stratifying them with a certain kind of seed which imbibes the oil, and then yields it by expression. The roses of this climate do not furnish sufficient oil to be worth procuring, and even in the East (Asia) the produce is very small, one hundred pounds of the roses yielding about three drams of oil. It is of a pale-yellow tint, and of a strong odor, resembling the fresh flower.

ESSENTIAL OILS CONTAINING THREE OR MORE ELEMENTS.

452. *Oil of Peppermint*, obtained from the peppermint plant by distillation, is of a pale-yellow color, which deepens by age. It has a strong odor of the herb, and a hot, aromatic flavor, succeeded by a sense of coldness upon the tongue. *Oil of lavender* is at first colorless, but acquires an amber tint. It is highly pungent, and is much employed as an article of perfumery. *Common camphor*, $C_{10} H_8 O$.— This concrete or solid essential oil is extracted from the roots and wood of the camphor-tree, which are chopped up and boiled with water in an iron vessel, with an earthen head containing straw, upon which the camphor condenses

What is said of oil of juniper? Oil of orange-peel? Oil of roses? Oil of peppermint? Oil of lavender? Camphor?

after sublimation. Camphor is a white, half-transparent crystalline substance, having a warm, pungent, and somewhat bitter taste. It evaporates in the air at ordinary temperatures, and sublimes in close vessels, attaching itself to the surface most exposed to light. It is soluble in alcohol, and is used in medicine both internally and externally.

THE RESINOUS PRODUCTS OF PLANTS.

453. *Source and Properties of the Resins.*—Resinous substances are very common in vegetables, and are found as proximate constituents of most plants; they are obtained from two sources. The *balsams* which exude from the bark of certain trees consist of resins dissolved in essential oils; when the oil has been dissipated by evaporation, the resin remains in the solid state. The volatile oils also, by sufficient exposure to the air, absorb oxygen, thicken, and are themselves converted into resin. The resins are, therefore, oxidized essential oils. This explains why volatile oils thicken and lose their odor and properties when kept and exposed to the air, and why old spirits of turpentine is not good for removing grease-spots from clothing, as it leaves a resinous stain. They are non-volatile solids, fusible, and highly inflammable. When pure, they are inodorous, and usually of a pale yellow or brown color; but as commonly met with, they are odorous from traces of essential oil, and variously colored by foreign substances. They are insoluble, or but partially soluble in water, but dissolve in alcohol, ether, and the essential oils, and form varnish. They are feebly acid, combining with alkalies, and forming resinous soaps, which are capable of producing lather, and possess a low detergent power (442).

How are resins obtained? What are they? Give their properties.

454. *Colophony* (*Common Resin*), $C_{40} H_{30} O_4$.—This is. the residue left after distilling turpentine from pine-trees to obtain its oil. 250 lbs. of turpentine yield about 30 lbs. of oil of turpentine and 220 of resin. Resin is a brittle, tasteless, almost inodorous substance, of a smooth, shining fracture, easily reduced to powder when cold, softening at 160°, and melting at 275° F. It produces a contrary effect to oil as regards friction, rendering a surface which is covered with it rough, uneven, and adhesive. It is hence applied to the bow of the violin, and the cords of clock-weights, and belts of machinery, to increase their adhesion and prevent them from slipping. If resin is set on fire in the open air, and after a sufficient time the flame is extinguished, a soft, black, pitchy substance remains, known as *shoemaker's wax*.

455. *Lac.*—This is a resinous substance flowing from several plants, in the East Indies, through punctures made in their branches by insects. The twig becomes incrusted with a reddish substance, which consists of the juice of the plant, hardened and imbued with coloring matter, derived from the insect. These twigs, broken off, constitute the *stick-lac* of commerce; when removed from the twigs it is *seed-lac;* when melted, strained, and poured upon a smooth surface, so as to spread out into thin plates, it forms *shellac*. The coloring matter of lac is used as a scarlet dyestuff, in two forms, under the names of *lac-lake* and *lac-dye*. The best shellac is of an orange color, the inferior kinds of a dark brown. Being hard and tough, it is used to make *sealing-wax*. For this purpose, turpentine is added to increase its inflammability, and various coloring matters to give it the

What is common resin? What are its properties? Why is it used on violin-bows and the belts of machinery? How is shoemaker's wax obtained?

How is lac obtained? What is stick-lac? Seed-lac? Shellac? Lac-lake? Lac-dye? How is sealing-wax made?

proper tint; vermilion to produce red, white-lead for white, and ivory-black for black sealing-wax.

456. *Amber* is a transparent fossil resin, of a light yellow, milk-white, and sometimes of a brown color. It is the hardest of all the resins, scratches gypsum, receives a fine polish, and is worked into ornaments in lathes, and by whetstones. It is chiefly procured from the southern coast of the Baltic Sea, where it is thrown out upon the shore. It also occurs in beds whose position is below several of the more recent geological formations. Amber is inferred to have originally existed as a soft balsam, as it is found to contain the remains of numerous varieties of insects beautifully preserved, and the leaves and stalks of vegetables. It is used in perfumery to make varnish, and as a medicine. When rubbed, amber exhibits highly electrical properties; this was known to the ancients, who ascribed to it a soul, and held it as sacred. The men who work it are often seized with nervous tremors in the hands and arms, in consequence of its electrical effects.

457. *Copal* is slightly yellow, and very hard. It dissolves in ether, and partially in pure alcohol, but it is insoluble in common alcohol. It is extensively used in varnish-making. *Mastic* is a yellowish resin, and occurs in rounded tears. *Sandarach* much resembles mastic : it is the product of an evergreen which grows in Africa. *Benzoin (frankincense)* is extracted by incision from a tree. Its color is a mixture of white, yellow, and red, with brown spots, or veins. The best quality, when broken, has the appearance of white marble. It is used in cosmetics. *Dragon's blood* is a resin of a brownish-red color. *Guaiacum* has a brownish-green, or olive color.

What is amber?   Whence is it obtained?   What are its properties?
For what is copal used ?   What is mastic ?   Sandarach ?   Frankincense ?   Dragon's blood ?

458. *Bitumen* (*Asphaltum*), *Mineral Pitch.*—This is a solid, brittle, glassy, bituminous, inflammable substance, found in great quantity upon the shores of the Dead Sea, which was hence called the *Asphaltic Lake*. It is also obtained from the West Indies. In the island of Trinidad there is a lake of asphaltum called Tar Lake. It lies on the highest land in the island, and emits a strong smell, sensible at ten miles distance. Its first appearance is that of a lake of water, but when viewed more nearly it resembles glass. In hot weather its surface liquefies to the depth of an inch, and it cannot then be walked upon. It is circular, about three miles in circumference, and of a depth not ascertained. *Petrolium* is a solution of asphaltum in a peculiar hydro-carbon liquid, called *naphtha*. In many localities, particularly in Asia, petrolium is found abundantly in wells a few feet deep, into which it flows. It is used by the natives as a source of light and fuel. It is probable that these substances have been produced by the action of subterranean fire upon beds of coal.

459. *Varnish* is a solution of resinous matter, which is spread over the surface of any body, in order to give it a shining, hard, transparent coat, capable of resisting, in a greater or less degree, the influence of air and moisture. The varnish-coat consists of the resinous part of the solution after the liquid solvent has either evaporated away or dried up. A good varnish should retain its brilliancy and lustre when exposed to light and air, and should adhere firmly to the surface, and neither crack nor scale off: it should also dry quickly. When the resinous substances are dissolved in alcohol, a *spirit-varnish* is formed; when linseed or nut oil is employed, *oil-varnish* is produced. The former are gen-

What is bitumen? Where is it found? What is said of Tar Lake? What is petrolium? How are these substances supposed to have been produced?
What is varnish? For what is it used? What are the properties of a good var-

erally the most brilliant, but also most brittle. *French pol-ish* is an alcoholic solution of shellac with a small quantity of oil. It is laid on by a ball of cotton, and then rapidly rubbed in the direction of the fibres of the wood. The finer articles of furniture are usually polished, the more ordinary ones varnished. Oil of turpentine is a leading solvent of varnish. *Japan*, or *black varnish*, contains asphaltum, and elastic varnish India-rubber.

460. *Gum-resins.*—Many plants, particularly in hot climates, produce compounds which contain both the resinous and gummy principles. Their gummy portion is soluble in water, and the resinous portion in alcohol. Opium, asafœtida, aloes, gamboge, myrrh, and frankincense are vegetable products of this nature.

461. *Caoutchouc (India-rubber, Gum Elastic).*—This well-known substance is obtained by making incisions through the bark of certain trees, of the fig or banian species, which grow in South America and the East Indies : a milky juice flows out, which, upon evaporation, yields about 32 per cent. of caoutchouc. The poppy, the lettuce, and other plants, having viscid, milky sap, seem also to contain it. Caoutchouc, when pure, is white and transparent; its dark color being due to the blackening effect of the smoke in drying. It is highly elastic, and the freshly cut surfaces adhere strongly, if pressed together. It is insoluble in water, alcohol, and acids; but dissolves in ether, naphtha, spirits of turpentine, and other essential oils. The solutions in ether and naphtha leave the caoutchouc in an elastic state. It is a simple hydro-carbon, containing no oxygen, and burning with a

---

nish ? How is a spirit varnish made ? What is oil varnish ? What is French polish ? How is it applied ?
Mention some of the gum-resins.
How is India-rubber obtained ? What are its properties ? What are its uses ?

luminous, sooty flame. Its uses are very various. Dissolved, and applied to fabrics, t forms water-proof cloth: it is also used for shoes; and when cut into thin shreds, and boiled with linseed oil (4 oz. caoutchouc to 2 lbs. of oil), it forms a mixture used for making boots water-tight. It forms gas-bags, flexible tubes, and connectors for the laboratory. India-rubber is *vulcanized* by impregnating it intimately with sulphur, whereby its elasticity is increased at low temperatures, and other useful properties added to it.

462. *Gutta Percha* is obtained from the milky juice of certain East Indian trees, in the same way as caoutchouc. When pure it is of a dirty-white color, of a greasy feel, and has a peculiar leathery smell. At ordinary temperatures it is non-elastic, tough, and as hard as wood; but when immersed in hot water it softens, so as to admit of being moulded into any shape, and again hardens when cooled. It melts at 250°, is highly inflammable, and burns in a manner similar to sealing-wax. It dissolves in boiling spirits of turpentine, but not in alcohol or the fixed oils. It is applied to many uses in the arts.

THE ACID PRODUCTS OF PLANTS.

463. *The Organic or Vegetable Acids.*—These substances are numerous in the vegetable kingdom, occurring largely in fruits, and sometimes in the leaves and roots. They exist in a free state, and combined with bases, forming acid salts both soluble and insoluble. They are composed of carbon, hydrogen, and oxygen, with the exception of oxalic acid, which contains only carbon and oxygen. In general, the oxygen is greatly in excess; in acetic acid only is it in the

proportion with hydrogen to form water. The hydrogen and oxygen, shown upon the Chart at the left of the organic acids, represent the basic water with which the acid is combined, and which cannot be separated from it without destroying also the organic acid.

464. *Tartaric Acid,* $C_8 H_4 O_{10} + 2 H O$—(*Brande*).— This acid is found abundantly in grapes and tamarinds. It exists also in rhubarb, the potato, and in the roots of wheat, madder, and the dandelion. When new wine is decanted from the lees, and set aside in vats or casks, it gradually deposits a hard crust or *tartar* on the sides of the vessel. This is a compound of tartaric acid with potash, familiarly known as *cream of tartar.* From this tartaric acid is produced, by the action of chalk and sulphuric acid. It is used in calico-printing and in medicine. It has an agreeable acid taste, dissolves readily in water, and causes a violent effervescence when mixed with a solution of carbonate of potash or of soda. It is extensively used in artificial soda-powders and effervescing draughts.

465. *Citric Acid (Acid of Lemons),* $C_{12} H_5 O_{11} + 3 H O$. —This acid gives their sourness to the lemon, the orange, the cranberry. It also exists, mixed with much malic acid, in the currant, cherry, gooseberry, raspberry, strawberry, and whortleberry. It is obtained chiefly from the juice of the lemon, and is used, like tartaric acid, for effervescing draughts. *Malic Acid,* $C_8 H_4 O_8 + 2 H O$—(*Brande*).— This is the principal acid of unripe apples (hence its name, from *malus,* apple). It also exists in the free state in pears, peaches, quinces, plums, apricots, cherries, gooseberries, raspberries, strawberries, grapes, blackberries, currants, elder-

---

Where is tartaric acid found? What is cream of tartar? What are the uses of tartaric acid?

What is said of citric acid? Whence does malic acid derive its name? Where is it found?

berries, and several other fruits. It has a very sour taste, but is not used in a separate state.

466.ᴧ *Tannic Acid* (*Tannin*), $C_{18} H_5 O_9 + 3 H O$—(*Liebig*).—This substance is found in the leaves and bark of certain trees, and imparts to them a puckering taste. It is nearly colorless, soluble in water, and has a powerfully astringent taste. Nut-galls contain of tannic acid 27·4 per cent.; oak bark, 6·3; chestnut bark, 4·3; elm bark, 2·7; sumach, 16·2; green tea, 8·5; Souchong tea, 10. The astringent quality of tea is due to the tannin it contains. Tannic acid combines with the peroxide of iron, forming a blue-black precipitate (pertannate of iron), which is used for coloring gray and black, and also for making *writing-ink*. Gum is added to the ink to retain the coloring matter in suspension, and to prevent excessive fluidity.

467. Tannic acid also possesses the peculiar property of combining with gelatine, and forming a compound insoluble in water. Upon this property depends its extensive application in the manufacture of leather, by uniting with the gelatine of which the skins of animals are chiefly composed (535). The skins are packed in vats with layers of ground bark, and the whole is immersed in water. The tannin dissolved out of the bark gradually unites with the skin. The process is quickened if conducted under pressure (quick tanning), by which the solution is made to penetrate the tissue more rapidly.

468. *Gallic Acid*, $C_7 H O_3 + 2 H O$—(*Liebig*).—This acid is found associated with tannin in bark, and is formed from tannic acid, by exposing a solution of it to the air for

---

What are the properties of tannic acid? Where is it found? How is writing-ink made from it?

What effect does it produce upon the skins of animals? How are the skins tanned?

What is said of gallic acid?

some time. Like tannic acid, it yields a precipitate with protosalts of iron, but a deep blue-black with a persalt. It does not precipitate gelatine.

469. *Pectic Acid* (*Pectine, vegetable jelly*), $C_{12} H_8 O_{10}$— (*Mulder*).—Pectic acid exists in the juice of most pulpy fruits, and is extracted, for dietetical purposes, chiefly from currants, apples, quinces, strawberries, and raspberries. Pectic acid and pectine have the same composition. They have an insipid taste when pure, and are somewhat allied in properties to the gums. Fruit jellies prepared with sugar form agreeable cooling articles of food in febrile and inflammatory complaints. It is but slightly nutritive.

470. *Oxalic Acid*, $C_2 O_3 + H O$.—This acid imparts the sour taste to common sorrel and the rhubarb plant, in which it exists combined with potash and lime. It is obtained in crystals, which are intensely sour and poisonous, chalk or magnesia being the antidote. It may be made artificially by the action of nitric acid upon sugar or starch, which yield about half their weight of the oxalic acid. Oxalic acid is the test for lime, and forms with it an insoluble salt, oxalate of lime. It removes ink and iron stains from linen.

BASIC PRODUCTS OF PLANTS.

471. *Vegetable Alkalies.*—Most plants give rise to peculiar substances, usually in very small quantity, which exhibit alkaline properties ; they are much less abundant than the vegetable acids, and are generally sparingly soluble in water, of a bitter taste, and always contain nitrogen. They form the active medicinal agents of the plants in which they occur, and are generally very poisonous. These bodies are of in-

terest only to physicians and chemists, and therefore cannot be described in this place.

COLORING MATTERS PRODUCED BY PLANTS.

472. *Different Kinds of Coloring Matter.*—As a class, vegetable coloring matters do not possess many chemical characters in common, and are associated together on account of their common application in the arts. Most of them are acids, but some are neutral: some are ternary and others quaternary. The most vivid and brilliant of vegetable colors, those of flowers, are fugitive, small in quantity, and very difficult to separate. The coloring matters in the interior of plants, where they are not exposed to light, are less brilliant but more durable. The most common color of the vegetable kingdom is green, but the substance which gives rise to this color (chlorophyl) is of an oily nature, and cannot be easily applied to cloth. Nearly all the coloring matters of plants which are capable of being separated are blue, yellow, and red. No genuine black coloring substance has ever been obtained from plants. Acids and alkalies act so remarkably upon vegetable coloring matters, that the latter are employed as tests for these substances (45, 47).

BLUE COLORING MATTERS.

473. *Indigo.*—This well-known dye-stuff is obtained from the juice of several plants which grow in hot climates. The juice is colorless, but when exposed to the air it absorbs oxygen and deposits a blue sediment, which is thrown into market, in the form of a powder, often cohering in cakes, as

---

How do the vegetable coloring matters differ in character? What is said of the most brilliant colors? What color is most abundant in vegetables? Why can it not be separated? What coloring matters can be separated from plants?

commercial indigo. It is tasteless, without odor, insoluble in water, and nearly so in all other liquids except sulphuric acid. When placed in situations which deprive it of oxygen indigo loses its blue tint, becomes colorless, and soluble in water. On exposure to the air, the deoxidized indigo absorbs oxygen again, and acquires its deep blue color and insolubility. Fabrics may, therefore, be steeped in a solution of colorless or *white indigo*, as it is called, and by subsequent exposure to the air the color is developed. Indigo affords a bright tint, and adheres to textile fibres with great permanence.

474. *Litmus.*—This coloring substance is extracted from certain species of moss which grow upon rocks. They yield at first a purple or red coloring matter, which is changed to blue by the action of the alkalies. The cubes of litmus used for making test-paper are thus prepared.

RED COLORING MATTERS.

475. *Madder.*—The roots of the madder-plant, ground to powder, furnish this valuable dye-stuff. The powder is at first yellow, but reddens by exposure to air and absorption of oxygen. · Besides red, madder furnishes a purple, a yellow, an orange, and a brown.

476. *Brazil-wood* and *sandal-wood*, the former yielding a coloring substance soluble in water and the latter a resinous body insoluble in water, are used for dyeing red. *Carmine* is of animal origin, being derived from the cochineal, a dried insect of Mexico. . It affords an intense red. *Lac-dye* is also of animal origin.

Whence is indigo obtained? What are its properties? To what is its blue color owing? What is said of its permanence?

How is litmus obtained? For what is it used?

What colors are obtained from madder?

What is Brazil-wood? Sandal-wood? Carmine?

YELLOW COLORING MATTERS.

477. These are obtained from the bark of the black oak (durecitron), from the wood of the West Indian mulberry (fustic), and from the green berries of the buckthorn. *Anatto*, extracted from the pulp of certain seeds grown in South America, is much used to color butter and cheese. It is also employed to give an orange color to milk. *Turmeric* is derived from the roots of an East Indian plant, and *saffron* from the flowers of an herb growing in the temperate climates.

GREEN COLORING MATTERS.

478. *Chlorophyl (Leaf-green)* —This is the substance to which the vegetable world owes its uniform green color. It is of a waxy nature, soluble in alcohol and acids, but insoluble in water, as is shown by the fact that rain falling over leaves is not turned green. Berzelius asserts that chlorophyl exists only in very small quantity in plants, the leaves of a large tree not containing perhaps more than 100 grains. This substance appears to be a direct, and perhaps the first product, of the action of light upon vegetation, as it never appears except in those parts exposed to the luminous agent. Thus plants removed from a dark cellar into the sunlight turn rapidly of a green color, and every one may have remarked in spring, when the foliage begins to start, how quickly, after a few days of cloudy weather, the color of the leaves is changed to a deep green by the rays of the sun. A writer mentions a forest upon which the sun had not shone for twenty days. "The leaves during this period were ex-

From what are yellow coloring matters obtained? What are the uses of anatto? Whence is turmeric obtained? Saffron?
What is chlorophyl? How is it shown to be insoluble? Is it ever formed in

panded to their full size, but were *almost white*. One fore-
noon the sun began to shine in full brightness; the color of
the forest absolutely changed so fast that we could perceive
its progress. By the middle of the afternoon the whole of
this extensive forest, many miles in length, presented its
usual summer dress." The vegetable green is changed to
yellow in autumn, probably by oxidation. It has been remarked that all trees and shrubs the leaves of which redden
in autumn bear red fruit or berries; the nature of this red
coloring matter is not known. *Sap-green* is an extract prepared from the juice of the buckthorn berries.

479. *Principles involved in Dyeing* —The art of the dyer
consists in impregnating textile fabrics with the various coloring matters in such a manner that they will remain permanent or *fast*, and not change by wear or washing. Some
coloring substances, as indigo, for example, unite directly
with the fibres, forming fixed colors. Others, those chiefly
that are soluble in water, if applied to the goods do not of
themselves adhere, but are discharged by washing. These
require some intermediate substance which has an affinity
both for the coloring matter and the fibre, and will link them
together in one insoluble compound; such a substance is
called a *mordant* (from *mordeo, I bite*), because it is said to
bite the color into the cloth. The principal mordants are
salts of tin, iron, and alumina (218). In *calico-printing* the
mordants are first fixed upon the cloth, either uniformly or
in spots, and the color subsequently applied by means of
blocks or revolving cylinders. The cylinder machines communicate colors very rapidly, the cloth passing through them
at the rate of a hundred feet per minute, or a mile in the

the dark ?   What striking occurrence is mentioned illustrating this point?   What
is sap-green ?

In what does the art of the dyer consist?   In what respect do colors differ ?
What is a mordant?   How are mordants used ?

hour. The textile fibres consist of hollow tubes (Figs. 21, 22), which the mordants are supposed to enter, filling them like bags, and remaining there to receive the coloring matter.

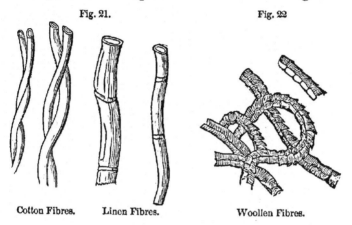

Fig. 21. Fig. 22

Cotton Fibres. Linen Fibres. Woollen Fibres.

EXTRACTIVE MATTER.

480. This term has been applied to numerous substances which have been extracted by chemists, chiefly from vegetables, by the action of various solvents, and which have not yet been accurately examined. The number of known plants exceeds a hundred thousand, and each possesses peculiar principles in small quantity, to which its flavor and medicinal properties are due. Of this vast number, but few comparatively have been studied by the chemists, and whatever they meet with of this kind that is unknown is designated as extractive matter.

CULTIVATION OF PLANTS.

481. *Its Relations to the Air.*—When a vegetable substance is burned, the mass of it disappears, taking the form

of gases and escaping into the air, and a small residue re·
mains, termed *ashes*. Now when plants grow, they draw
back again from the atmosphere all those gases which escape
into it by combustion, and obtain from the soil only those
mineral solids which form its ashes. Thus the great bulk of
vegetable matter is derived from the air, and as the atmosphere is uniform in composition, that portion of the nutrition·
of plants which depends upon this source may go forward in
all places with nearly equal facility. The air contains an
exhaustless store of elements for the use of vegetation, and
so far as *it* is concerned, all plants may be grown with equal
success in all places.

482. *Relations to Heat and Light.*—But it is not so with
the agencies of heat and light which radiate from the sun.
In consequence of the globular figure of the earth, these fall
unequally upon its different parts. At the equator, where
the rays are perpendicular, the heat and light are most intense, while as we pass towards the poles, the rays strike the
surface more obliquely, and the effect is diminished in intensity. Now to these variations plants are adapted. Equatorial vegetation, requiring large quantities of heat and light,
cannot flourish in temperate climates, for although the atmosphere and soil may contain all the chemical elements neces
sary to its composition and nourishment, one of the condi
tions essential to its growth is wanting.

483. *Relations to the Composition of Soils.*—In addition
to the part played by the atmosphere and climate, which
may be regarded as independent of human control, there is
a third condition of the growth of plants which relates to the

How does the burning of a vegetable substance divide its elements? What
becomes of the part that escapes into the air? Are these matters abundant in
he air?

Are the agencies of heat and light equally distributed over the earth? Why can
not equatorial plants be grown in temperate regions?

composition of soils. If there is a want of elements derived from this source, growth is impossible; but if they are abundantly supplied, nutrition is rapid, and growth luxuriant. To ascertain and regulate the adaptations of soils to plants, to find out what elements are necessary for their development, and the most economical method of supplying them, is the great problem of Agriculture.

484. *Effect of Organic Manures.*—It has been stated (139) that the source of the organic elements of vegetation—carbon, hydrogen, oxygen, and nitrogen—is the air. This is proved by the slow and gradual accumulation of organic substances in the soil of forests and of meadows, where it could not have been added artificially. But in growing cultivated plants, we do not depend entirely upon this source. A plant supplied with all the necessary inorganic substances, and *allowed sufficient time*, will extract the necessary gases from the air and attain a vigorous development. But if it is desired to hasten the maturity of a plant, as is frequently necessary in certain climates, or to stimulate it to excessive development, then organized substances, vegetable or animal, are added to the soil, which by decay and putrefaction generate large quantities of carbonic acid and ammonia in the immediate neighborhood of the roots, by which they are taken up, dissolved in water.

485. *Inorganic Elements of Soils.*—The inorganic elements of plants (ashes), though small in quantity, are nevertheless of the highest importance. Unlike the organic elements, which are the same in all plants, these vary in different varieties of vegetation. Consequently, as one kind of plant takes

---

What condition besides the climate and atmosphere is necessary for the growth of plants? What is the great problem of Agriculture?

If we wish to stimulate the growth of plants, what plan is to be adopted?

Why do farmers change the kind of crop upon a soil instead of growing one

one mineral from the soil, and others take other kinds, the farmer finds it advantageous to cultivate in succession different varieties of plants upon the same ground (rotation of crops). If a soil yields good crops of one vegetable and not of another, it must be wanting in the characteristic mineral elements of the latter, which should then be supplied. And if any particular plant, cultivated or wild, flourishes in any given spot, an examination of its ashes indicates at once the capabilities of the soil, by showing what soluble salts it furnishes.

486. *Substitution of Elements.*—Although the ashes of certain plants are distinguished by the prevalence of certain bases, as those of potatoes and turnips by potash, and those of peas and beans by lime, yet to a certain extent one base may be substituted for another, as soda for potash, or magnesia for lime. This can only be done, however, by forcing nature, as it were, out of her regular course.

487. *The best Manure for a Plant.*—Decaying vegetable and animal substances applied to crops, act not only by supplying carbonic acid and ammonia, but also by furnishing such inorganic salts as the decomposing substance may happen to contain; hence, for any particular crop, as hay, grain, or potatoes, there is no manure so good as the same kind of vegetable in a state of decay, or its ashes, or the manure of animals fed upon it; but in the latter case, it is of the first importance to make use of the *whole* manure of the animal, as its liquid excretions, the part most liable to be lost, are by far the richest in soluble salts.

488. *The Golden Rule of Agriculture.*—The great rule

---

kind constantly ? If a plant flourish upon a soil, what information do we gain by examining its ashes ?

What is said of the substitution of one element for another ?

What is the best manure for a plant ?

ro be followed in this branch of agriculture, is to *restore to the soil, in the shape of manure, exactly what it has lost in the crop;* as by this means alone the fertility of the soil can be maintained, and the vocation of the farmer be sustained upon a remunerative basis. By failing to heed this rule, millions of acres of the finest land in this country have been already so exhausted as not to be worth cultivating, and millions more are now undergoing the same ruinous process. No one who contemplates for a moment the deplorable waste of manure (especially human excreta, the richest of all) which is so prevalent both in our cities and large towns, and also among the generality of farmers, can be at a loss to account for this gradual decline in the fruitfulness of land. Manure is the raw material which is to be worked up into sustenance for human beings; but in our seaboard cities it is thrown into the ocean, and in other cities it is cast into rivers and borne seaward, as if it possessed no value whatever. Every consideration, therefore, as well of public beneficence as of private thrift, demands that all fertilizers, every kind of manure, both liquid and solid, shall be saved with the most rigid economy. It is the farmer's motive power: with it he can do every thing, without it, nothing.

What is the golden rule of agriculture? What is the result of neglecting this rule? What, then, should demand the first consideration of the farmer?

ORGANIC CHEMISTRY.

ANIMAL CHEMISTRY.

GENERAL NATURE OF THE ANIMAL FUNCTIONS.

489. ANIMAL CHEMISTRY instructs us in the composition and chemical properties of the several parts of the animal body, and throws light upon many of the changes to which they are constantly subjected in the living being. Very much, however, that transpires within the vital mechanism is still wrapped in mystery which Chemistry at present is unable to penetrate. Physiology has but recently consented to avail herself of the assistance of this science in solving her problems, and already many beautiful and highly important results have been obtained. The rapid advance lately made in this interesting and most useful department of knowledge, justifies the expectation that the animal system will continue still further to surrender its secrets, until the whole field of legitimate investigation shall have been explored.

490. *The Exercise of Power produces Waste of Matter.*— It is an established law of nature, that the exercise of all force is attended by a waste of matter. No action, however trifling, can take place but at the expense of the material engaged in its performance. Every breeze that sweeps

What does Animal Chemistry teach ? Does it explain all the chemical changes that occur in animals ? What has recently been done ?
What law is here given ? In obedience to this law, what course is pursued by mechanics ?

over the ground alters somewhat its surface.   The rain that falls upon a naked rock bears away some portion of it to the sea.   So well is it understood that motion can only occur at the cost of material, that mechanics resort to every contri-vance which can diminish the amount of this loss ; they con-struct machines of the hardest and most lasting substances, they execute the nicest adjustments, apply oil or other lubri-cating bodies to all rubbing surfaces, yet, notwithstanding these precautions, the mechanism finally falls a prey to its own activity, or in other words, it becomes worn out.

491. *Waste of Matter in Organized Structures.* — But it is not alone in the department of mechanics or the inor-ganic world that we observe the operation of this law ; it is displayed on a vastly more imposing scale in the organic kingdom of nature.   The vital actions of plants, their growth, and the development of their various parts and products, can only take place by means of an enormous waste of matter, as we have seen when speaking of evapo-ration from the surface of the leaves (324).   In the animal system, every motion which it performs, voluntary or invol-untary, every movement of a limb, and indeed every exer-tion of the mind, is accompanied by a destruction or waste of the material of which the animal fabric is composed Through the lungs, the kidneys, the bowels, and the whole surface of the body, the worn-out, and, as it were, used-up atoms, are rejected from the system to the extent of several pounds each day.   It is an error to suppose that decay and decomposition begin only after the death of the body.   They proceed during every moment of life, from the first kindling of the vital spark to its extinction in death.

What examples of the operation of this law are seen in the vegetable and ani-mal kingdoms?   Upon what does the maintenance of life depend?   What is the distinction between living and dead matter?

Indeed, the maintenance of animal life is only possible by the perpetual waste and destruction of the organism by which it is manifested. In the passage of constituent particles from the living to the dead state, consists the life and power of the individual. Were this process of dying by atoms, in a measured and regulated way, suddenly to cease, the death of the whole system would be the consequence. It is usually said that dead animal matter is marked by its necessary tendency to decay, while the living body is distinguished by its power of *resisting* decay. But so far is this from being true, that the very opposite is the fact. The fixed condition of the continuance of life in an animal is the decomposition which all its parts constantly suffer, while dead animal matter may be preserved, it is well known, for almost any length of time unchanged. Meat, by partially cooking and sealing up free from air, may be kept sweet even in the moist state for years. Cold also arrests decay. In Russia, animals are long kept in the market in a frozen state, and their flesh, when thawed, is as good as ever.

492. *Reparative Power of the Living Being.*—But in one very important respect the living mechanism differs from the inanimate machine; the latter has no ability to repair the destruction it suffers by use. There is no inherent power in a watch or a steam-engine to restore its wasted parts; action goes forward until checked by loss of substance and consequent derangement, when the combination is handed over to the mechanic for reconstruction. The living body, on the contrary, is endowed with a capacity of self-renovation. It can repair its failing tissues, and counteract its own constant tendency to ruin. The process by which this renewal takes place is called *nutrition,* and the substances employed to carry it on constitute *food* or *nutriment,*

By means of food, therefore, the living organism can com-pensate the rapid expenditure of its own substance, restore its losses, and maintain its power.

493. *Supply of Matter to the Plant.*—This process of nutrition is accomplished by different methods in the two great departments of organic life. The plant is fixed to one spot, and has no power of changing its locality. Its roots penetrate the soil to a limited distance, and its leaves are spread through the air. Within this narrow space it finds the elements necessary to its growth. Water, with mineral salts, and gases extracted from the earth and atmosphere, constitute its food. If these happen to abound, the plant exhibits a condition of high activity, a rapid and luxuriant growth ; if this supply is deficient, development is corre-spondingly feeble and imperfect. The simple object of the plant is to *grow*, and form various proximate substances. It is hence found in immediate connection with the sources of its nourishment, and there remains throughout the whole term of its life.

494. *Mode in which Animals are supplied with Matter.*— The case is different with animals, especially the higher classes. They are organized for the accomplishment of other purposes besides bare vegetative development, and the nutritive operations are so carried on as not to interfere with the higher functions. Having the power of locomotion, by which it is capable of moving from place to place, the ani-mal is supplied with a cavity (stomach), into which it receives a store of food sufficient to last it for a considerable time, in-dependent of a supply from any external sources. From this cavity the system is gradually supplied with nutritive mat-

To what conditions is the plant confined ?
How do the conditions of nutrition in animals differ from those of plants ?
What constitutes a fundamental distinction between animals and plants ?

ter until its contents are exhausted, when the store is again renewed as occasion may require. The presence of this digestive cavity or stomach, for the reception of a stock of nourishment, is peculiar to animals, and it may be looked upon as a fundamental feature of distinction between the animal and vegetable races.

495. *Office of Water in the Animal Economy.* — The constant and rapid changes of which the living body is the theatre, require that it should be so organized as to permit the greatest possible freedom of motion among its elements. This could only be done by making use of a perfect liquid as a medium and vehicle of that incessant transportation of particles which takes place within the organism. Water is the instrument chosen for this purpose. Its complete liquidity within a considerable range of temperature, together with its numerous other properties (91), adapt it in a won derful degree to this office, and it is therefore found to be the leading and fundamental constituent of all organized fabrics, existing to the extent of 75 per cent. throughout the animal system. Whatever is to take part in the processes of the living body must first be reduced to a state of solubility, so as to be carried to its appointed stations by the liquid currents which are constantly flowing to all parts of the organization. To effect this purpose is one of the chief objects of *digestion.*

496. *Operations to which Food is subjected in the Body.* — In a comprehensive sense, *digestion* may be regarded as the conversion of food into blood. But this act consists of several steps or stages which are commonly distinguished as, 1st, *mastication and insalivation,* or chewing the food and

Why must a large portion of the animal system be in a liquid condition ? How is water adapted for this purpose ?
What is digestion ? What are the several stages of digestion ?

mixing it with the saliva of the mouth ; 2d, *chymification,* or digestion proper, solution in the stomach ; 3d, *chylification,* or the production of chyle by further digestion in the intestines ; and 4th, *sanguification,* or the conversion of chyle into blood. We shall gain the clearest idea of the subject, in the hasty glance to which we are confined, by following this natural order, and tracing the food through the series of interesting and remarkable changes which are successively impressed upon it, until it becomes part of the fabric of the animal system, and by then inquiring in what manner and for what purposes it is separated and thrown back again to the inorganic world, from whence it was first derived by plants.

CULINARY PREPARATION OF FOOD.

497. The changes which food undergoes by the various operations of cooking may be considered as preparatory to digestion ; and as they greatly influence this process by either aiding or obstructing it, it is proper at this point briefly to notice them.

498 *Effect of Cooking upon Vegetables.*—The general effect of cooking upon vegetable substances is more or less completely to destroy their organization by means of the decomposing agency of heat. By boiling, the grains of starch which constitute a large portion of most vegetable foods are ruptured or disorganized, and partially dissolved. Vegetable albumen is coagulated or solidified by boiling (373). When potatoes are boiled, the starch of which they mainly consist does not form a mucilage or jelly, such as is produced by boiling pure starch. This is probably due to the

What is the general effect of cooking upon vegetables ? What is the effect of boiling upon starch ? Upon albumen ? Why does not the starch of potatoes form mucilage upon boiling ? What other results are produced by boiling vegetables ? What is said of roasting and baking ?

22

effect of the albumen which exists in the tuber in the form of a filmy envelope around the starch grains, and thus partially cuts them off from the solvent action of the water. The hard parts of vegetables become softened, and the tissues, which are more or less tough, as the leafy portions of greens, &c., by sufficient boiling become tender, and are easily dissolved in the stomach. Sugar, gum, and various other substances are dissolved, and volatile oils dissipated by boiling. A quite similar effect is also produced upon the starch and albumen of vegetables by the processes of roasting and baking.

499. *Animal Food.*—The changes produced upon animal food differ in some respects from those upon vegetable substances, the nutritive value of flesh depending greatly upon the manner in which the cooking operations are conducted. The flesh of the lower animals which is used as food possesses the same constituents and properties as that of man, and therefore the fewer changes it undergoes by culinary preparation, the easier and more complete will be its transformation in the system. If flesh employed as food is again to become flesh in the body, it is clear that none of its elements should be withdrawn from it by any preliminary operations to which it may be submitted.

500. *Effect of Boiling upon Flesh.*—The muscular fibre of meat, in the natural state, is everywhere surrounded by liquid albumen, and when this is removed, the fibre which remains is the same in all animals. The effect of boiling upon free muscular fibre, which constitutes the basis of lean meat, is to render it hard and tough in proportion to the briskness and duration of the process. But this effect is, to a certain

---

Upon what does the nutritive value of flesh depend? Why should flesh be changed as little as possible in cooking?

What is said of muscular fibre? What is the effect of boiling upon it? Why is the flesh of young animals more tender than that of old ones?

extent, prevented by the coagulation of the albumen, which envelops the fibres, and protects them from the full effect of ebullition. Hence the flesh of young animals, which is richer in albumen, is more tender than that of old ones, which contains much less. The albumen, by protracted boiling, becomes hard, but not tough.

501. *Nutritious Juices of Flesh.*—The juices of flesh contain not only its dissolved albumen, but also other soluble substances to which the agreeable taste and flavor of meat, as well as its nutritive effect, are due. Hence, if flesh is chopped fine and soaked in cold water, these substances will be all dissolved out, so that the fibrinous residue, when boiled, proves perfectly tasteless. If the watery solution is concentrated by evaporation, and poured over the meat from which it was removed, it restores the natural flavor. All sorts of flesh are alike in this respect, their peculiar odorous and sapid principles existing in the soluble state. Hence, if a cold aqueous solution of venison or fowl is added to boiled beef and the whole warmed together, the beef acquires the taste of the venison or fowl. The common practice of boiling meat and vegetables in large quantities of water, which is thrown away and with it nearly the whole of the soluble matter, is thus seen to be wasteful and injurious in a high degree. We also see that the plan of stewing, in which all the soluble matter is retained in the sauce or juice and served with the meat, has decided advantage over boiling. Liebig, who has lately investigated this subject, suggests the following application of these principles:

502. *Best Method of boiling Meat.*—" If the flesh intended to be eaten be introduced into the boiler *when the water is in*

a state of brisk ebullition, and if the boiling be kept up for some minutes, then so much cold water added as to reduce the temperature to 165° F., or 158°, and the whole kept at this temperature for some hours, all the conditions are united which give to the flesh the quality best adapted to its use as food. When it is introduced into boiling water, the albumen immediately coagulates from the surface inwards, and in this state forms a crust or shell, which no longer permits the external water to penetrate into the interior mass of flesh. But the temperature is gradually transmitted to the interior, and there effects the conversion of the raw flesh into the state of boiled or roasted meat. The flesh retains its juices, and is quite as agreeable to the taste as it can be made by roasting; for the chief part of the sapid constituents of the mass is retained under these circumstances in the flesh."

503. *Best Method of preparing Soup.*—" Soups which are to contain the soluble portions of meat are not best obtained by long boiling the flesh. The boiling water coagulates and renders insoluble that which should be dissolved in the soup, and which may be extracted by cold water. When one pound of lean beef, free of fat, and separated from the bones, in the finely divided state in which it is used for beef-sausages or mince-meat, is uniformly mixed with its own weight of cold water, slowly heated to boiling, and the liquid, after boiling briskly for a minute or two, is strained through a towel from the coagulated albumen and fibrine, now become hard and horny, we obtain an equal weight of the most aromatic soup, of such strength as cannot be obtained, even by boiling for hours, from a piece of flesh. When mixed with salt and the other usual additions by which soup is seasoned, and tinged somewhat darker by means of roast-

---

Why should not the flesh be long boiled, in making soup? What process is recommended?

ed onions and burnt sugar, it forms the very best soup which can in any way be prepared from one pound of flesh."

504. *Effect of Salting upon Meat.*—"It is universally known that, in the salting of meat, the flesh is rubbed and sprinkled with dry salt, and that where the salt and meat are in contact, a brine is formed, amounting in bulk to one-third of the fluid contained in the raw flesh. I have ascertained that this brine contains the chief constituents of a concentrated soup or infusion of meat, and that, therefore, in the process of salting, the composition of the flesh is changed, and this, too, in a much greater degree than occurs in boiling. In boiling, the highly nutritious albumen remains in the coagulated state in the mass of the flesh; but in salting, the albumen is separated from the flesh; for when the brine from salted meat is heated to boiling, a large quantity of albumen separates as a coagulum. It is now easy to understand that in the salting of meat, where this is pushed so far as to produce the brine above mentioned, a number of substances are withdrawn from the flesh which are essential to its constitution, and that it therefore loses in nutritive qualities in proportion to this abstraction."—(*Liebig.*)

505. *Other Methods of preparing Meat.*—In *roasting*, meat parts with a considerable portion of its water by evaporation; the albumen it contains is coagulated; the muscular fibre is hardened, especially upon the outside, where it is often partially carbonized before the interior is sufficiently done. Broiling and baking produce similar effects to roasting. Frying is the most injurious method of cooking meat, as the heat is applied by means of boiling oil or fat. By the high temperature these are so changed as to

What is the effect of salting upon meat? How is it shown that the albumen is separated from the flesh?
How is meat affected by roasting? Broiling? Baking? Frying?

22*

become very indigestible, and this property is also, in a degree, communicated to the meat. The flesh of animals is rendered harder and more indigestible by drying, smoking, pickling, as well as by salting.

MASTICATION.

506. *Instruments of Mastication in Man.*—The instruments of mastication, by which the food is crushed and reduced to fineness, are chiefly the teeth. The form of the teeth varies in different animals, according to the nature of their food. Thus in the carnivora (*flesh-eaters*) they have cutting-edges, and work against each other like the blades of a pair of scissors. In the graminivora (*grain-eaters*) they are terminated by large, flat, rough surfaces, adapted for grinding. The roughness of these surfaces is preserved by the unequal wear of the teeth, as they are composed of alternate vertical plates of substances having unequal degrees of hardness. Human teeth are of both these forms; they are 32 in number. The four front teeth in each jaw are termed incisors (*cutting-teeth*), the next tooth on each side the cuspid (*canine* or *eye tooth*), the next two bicuspids (*small grinders*), the next three molars (*mill-like*, or *grinders*).

507. *Mode of reducing Food by Birds.*—In birds, the office of reducing food is performed by the *gizzard*, a hollow muscle, furnished with a hard, tendinous lining, which in the grain-eating birds is strong and thick. The mechanical powers of the gizzard have been tested by causing the birds to swallow with their food balls of glass, which were soon ground to powder; and the points of needles and of lancets,

What is the form of the teeth in the carnivora? In the graminivora? How are they kept rough? What is said of human teeth? How many are there of each kind, and what are they termed?

What is the office of the gizzard in birds? What instances are mentioned

fixed in a ball of lead, were blunted and broken off, whilst its own coat was not injured. In some of the lowest species of animals, the place of the gizzard is occupied by a curious pair of jaws, armed with teeth, by the working of which the food is effectually crushed.

508. *Structure and Decay of the Teeth.*—The teeth of man and the higher animals are composed of three very different substances—the *enamel* (a), (Fig. 23), which covers the whole crown of the tooth; the *cement* (d), which covers the fangs; and the *ivory*, or *dentine* (b), which constitutes the body of the tooth. The enamel is formed of fibres, or tubes, laid parallel to each other. It is composed almost entirely of mineral matter (phosphate of lime and fluoride of calcium), and contains not above two per cent. of animal matter, and is generally so hard as to strike fire with steel. The cement resembles bone (539), containing about 40 per cent. of animal matter. The body of the tooth contains about 25 per cent. of animal matter, its mineral matter being phosphate and carbonate of lime, in the form of very minute tubes. When teeth decay, the enamel is first worn off so as to expose the ivory, which is gradually dissolved by the acid of the unhealthy mucous membrane and saliva. The decay is thus deepened, until it reaches the nerve (c), when toothache occurs. The teeth are not supplied with nourishment, and hence have little or no power of restoring lost portions.

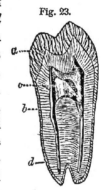

Fig. 23.

---

showing the mechanical powers of this organ? What is found in some of the lower animals?

Describe the teeth of man. What are the composition and properties of enamel? Cement? Dentine? How does the process of decay proceed in teeth?

509. *Tartar of the Teeth.*—This term is applied to a deposit formed upon those parts of the teeth which are not protected from the cleansing action of the tongue. It is most abundant in the mouths of persons who speak much, and keep the mouth open, so as to allow the evaporation of the saliva. It consists of the earthy phosphates contained in the saliva, together with about 20 per cent. of animal matter.

510. *Importance of complete Mastication of Food.*—It is the office of the teeth to destroy the cohesion and mechanical texture of food, and separate its particles, so as to expose the largest possible surface to the chemical solvents in the digestive process. The chemist well understands the importance of thorough mechanical pulverization as a preliminary to solvent action. It is important, for the same reason, and to the same extent, that food should be well masticated before swallowing. The necessity of finely dividing food, in order to extract from it the fullest nutritive effect, has been shown by experiment. Cows fed upon ground barley yielded a larger product of milk than when fed upon an equal quantity of whole grain.—(*R. D. Thompson.*)

INSALIVATION.

511. *Properties of the Saliva.*—Saliva, or spittle, is the fluid which moistens the mouth. It is separated from the blood by three pairs of glands, two beneath the tongue, and one in the cheeks, each pouring out its secretion by a separate canal. It is a transparent, viscid fluid, containing about one per cent. of earthy and alkaline salts, with a little mucus, and 99 per cent. of water. It has the property of entangling a large quantity of air, the oxygen of which, being swallowed

What is said of the tartar of the teeth?
Why is thorough mastication necessary? What example illustrates its advantage?
What is saliva? What organs supply it? What are its properties?

with the food, is probably essential to digestion. The secretion of saliva is commonly just sufficient to lubricate the mouth, but during chewing it is poured out copiously. The amount has been estimated at from 15 to 30 ounces per day in a healthy adult. According to Mitscherlich, the saliva is commonly acid, but is alkaline during a meal. In some diseases, as intermittent fever, it is very sour.

512. *Use of the Saliva.*—The principal purpose of the saliva appears to be, when mixed with the food during mastication, to begin the chemical work of digestion. It has the power of converting starch into sugar, and sugar into lactic acid, and, when acidulated, of dissolving flesh and albuminous substances. "In general, the benefit derived from this process of insalivation is just that which is obtained by the chemist when he bruises in a mortar with a small quantity of fluid the substances which he is about to dissolve in a large amount. If the preliminary operations of mastication and insalivation be neglected, the stomach has to do the whole of the work of preparation, as well as to accomplish the digestion; thus more is thrown upon it than it is adapted to bear; it becomes overworked, and manifests its fatigue by not being able to discharge its own proper duty."

CHYMIFICATION—DIGESTION.

513. *The Stomach: its Form and Size.*—The masticated food is carried by the act of swallowing (*deglutition*) into the œsophagus (*gullet*), which conducts it downward into the stomach. This organ is a large membranous bag, placed across the upper part of the abdomen. Its form is exhib-

Where does the process of digestion commence ? What changes are effected by the saliva ? If the process of insalivation is neglected, what effect follows ?
What is the course of the food when swallowed? Describe the stomach. In what animals is it largest ? In what is it smallest ? What is the size of the human stomach ?

ited in Fig. 24, the large end being situated on the left side
of the body, as is there seen.   In different animals the size
of the stomach varies exceedingly, according to the *concentration* of the food upon which they live. · Thus in the flesh-
eating animals it is very small, only a slight enlargement of
the œsophagus; while in those which feed upon herbage,
it is distended into an enormous cavity, or rather into several, as in the cow and sheep.   The capacity of the human
stomach is about three pints.   As a general rule, it is larger
among those that live upon coarse, bulky diet.

514. *Structure of the Stomach.*—It consists of three membranous layers or coats, traversed by numerous blood-vessels
and nerves.   The outer layer is a smooth, glistening, whitish
membrane, such as lines the abdomen, and covers all the internal organs. Its use is to strengthen these organs, and by its
smoothness and constant moisture, to permit them to move
upon each other without irritation.   The middle coat consists
of two layers of muscular fibres, one of which runs length-
ways and the other crossways, or around the stomach.   By
means of these muscles, it is enabled to contract its dimensions
in all directions, so as to adapt its capacity to the amount of
its contents ; they also play an important part in giving motion to the organ. The third layer of the stomach lines its internal surface.   It is a soft, velvet-like membrane, of a pale pink
color in health, and of much greater extent than the outer coats,
by which it is thrown into numerous folds or wrinkles.   It is
constantly covered with a thin, transparent, viscid mucus.

515. *Properties of the Gastric Juice of the Stomach.*—
From the blood-vessels, which are distributed thickly over
the stomach, there is separated, or poured out upon its in-

What is the appearance and use of the outer coat of the stomach ?   The middle
layer?   The inner coat?
What are the properties of the gastric juice ?

ner surface, a pure, limpid, colorless, inodorous, slightly viscid, and always distinctly acid fluid, known as the *gastric juice*. It is readily diffusible in water or spirits, and effer-vesces slightly with alkalies. It is never obtained pure, but always mixed with another secretion of the stomach—a vis-cid, semi-opaque substance, salt to the taste, and without acid properties. The gastric juice, when taken from the stomach, may be kept for many months, if excluded from the air, without becoming foetid. It is powerfully antisep-tic, checking the progress of putrefaction in meat.

516. *Composition of the Gastric Juice, and Mode of its Ac-tion.*—The acid properties of the gastric juice are due to free hydrochloric, acetic, and lactic acids, which have been discov-ered in it by different chemists. Its solvent power over food depends upon the action of these acids (some suppose chiefly the hydrochloric), and also upon a peculiar animal principle, called *pepsin*, which is probably derived from the coats of the stomach, and is supposed by Liebig to act in the same way as ferment (379). It seems to affect nitrogenous aliments in the same way that diastase does starch (363), converting them into a state of solubility. The gastric juice also contains salts, muriates, and acetates of potash, soda, magnesia, and lime, although it may be observed that its composition varies in different animals, and seems adapted to different kinds of food.

517. *The Power of Digestion is limited.*—The gastric juice is not secreted constantly or regularly by the walls of the stomach, so as to accumulate and be in readiness for the food when it is introduced. It is poured out only when

What acids are found in the gastric juice ? To what does it owe its solvent power ? How is it supposed to act upon the food ? What salts are found in it ? Is it alike in all animals ?

What causes the flow of the gastric juice ? How is the amount produced regu-lated ? Why should not the food taken exceed a fixed amount ? If food is taken in excess, what is the consequence ?

food or some other substance is brought in contact with its interior surface, by which its secreting vessels are stimulated or aroused to action. When the stomach is empty, any solid substance taken into it will start the flow of the juice; but if the substance be not of a nutritive character, the secreting vessels speedily discover the cheat, and withhold the secretion. It is an important fact, also, that the amount of gastric juice which the stomach is capable of producing is *not in proportion to the quantity of food taken into it, but in proportion to the amount of food that the system requires for healthful nutrition. A definite proportion* of food only can be digested in a given quantity of the fluid, as its action, like that of other chemical solvents, ceases after having been exercised on a fixed amount of matter. When the juice has become saturated, it will dissolve no more, and if an excess of food has been taken it rests as a burden upon the stomach, or passes half digested into the bowels, producing irritation, pain, and disease.

518. *Effect of the Motions of the Stomach.*—The food, as it enters the stomach through the cardiac orifice (Fig. 24), is immediately subjected to a peculiar movement by which it is thoroughly intermixed with the gastric fluid. This motion is produced by the alternate contraction and relaxation of the muscular bands (514), which produce a constant agitation or churning of the alimentary mass. The muscular contractions appear to take place in a kind of succession, by which the contents of the stomach are made to revolve or pass around the interior of the stomach in a circuit. This route is traversed by the food in from one to three minutes, but as chymification advances, the rapidity of the motions increases. The combined effect of this agitation and of the

mingled solvent is to reduce the solid food to a uniform, pulpy, semi-fluid condition, in which it is known as *chyme.* It is of a grayish color and creamy aspect when the aliment used is rich ; and when otherwise, of a gruelly appearance.

519. *Results of Dr. Beaumont's Experiments.*—We are indebted for many interesting particulars concerning digestion to the observations of Dr. Beaumont, made upon the stomach of a young man named Alexis St. Martin, who had a hole perforated in his stomach by a gun-shot wound. It healed, leaving a permanent orifice of such size that the finger could be readily introduced, substances transferred, and various observations made upon the nature of the processes which went forward within. Dr. Beaumont availed himself of the opportunity thus afforded to study the operations of digestion, and the results he obtained have added greatly to our knowledge of the subject. Among the conclusions to which he arrived are the following : That the presence in the stomach of any substance which is difficult of digestion interferes with the solution of food that would otherwise soon be reduced ; that *bulk* is as necessary for healthy digestion as nutritious matter itself, a fact which explains the custom of the Kamschatkans, of mixing earth or sawdust with the train-oil ; that soup and fluid diet are not, alone, fit for the support of the system, and are not more easily digested than solid aliment ; that moderate exercise facilitates digestion (except, perhaps, immediately after a full meal) ; and that temperature controls digestion. This was shown by adding the gastric juice to finely divided food in vials, and frequently agitating it. At 100°, which is about that of the stomach, the solution proceeded with considerable rapidity ; while in

To what circumstance are we indebted for the experiments of Dr. Beaumont? What is the first of his conclusions? The second? What custom does this explain? What is his next conclusion? How was this shown? What substances did he find to require most time for digestion? What the least?

the cold air the food was scarcely affected. A gill of water at 50°, injected into the stomach, lowered its temperature upwards of 30° ; the natural heat was not fully restored again for more than half an hour; the habit of drinking ice-water freely during or after a meal must therefore retard digestion. Dr. Beaumont also made numerous experiments to determine the time required for different articles of diet to digest in the stomach, a summary of which is given in the following table :

Articles	Preparation	Time. h. m.	Articles.	Preparation.	Time. h. m.
Rice	Boiled	1 —	Pork, recently salted	Raw	3 —
Pig's feet, soused	Boiled	1 —	Soup, chicken	Boiled	3 —
Tripe, soused	Boiled	1 —	Oysters, fresh	Roasted	3 15
Trout, salmon, fresh	Boiled	1 30	Pork, recently salted	Broiled	3 15
" " "	Fried	1 30	Pork steak	Broiled	3 15
Apples, sweet, mellow	Raw	1 30	Corn bread	Baked	3 15
Venison, steak	Broiled	1 35	Mutton, fresh	Roasted	3 15
Sago	Boiled	1 45	Carrot, orange	Boiled	3 15
Apples, sour, mellow	Raw	2 —	Sausage, fresh	Broiled	3 20
Cabbage, with vinegar	Raw	2 —	Beef, fresh, lean, dry	Roasted	3 30
Codfish, cured, dry	Boiled	2 —	Bread, wheat, fresh	Baked	3 30
Eggs, fresh	Raw	2 —	Butter	Melted	3 30
Liver, beef's, fresh	Broiled	2 —	Cheese, old, strong	Raw	3 30
Milk	Boiled	2 —	Eggs, fresh	Hard boil'd	3 30
Tapioca	Boiled	2 —	" "	Fried	3 30
Milk	Raw	2 15	Flounder, fresh	Fried	3 30
Turkey, wild	Roasted	2 18	Oysters, fresh	Stewed	3 30
" "	Boiled	2 25	Potatoes, Irish	Boiled	3 30
" domesticated	Roasted	2 30	Soup, mutton	Boiled	3 30
Potatoes, Irish	Baked	2 30	" oyster	Boiled	3 39
Parsnips	Boiled	2 30	Turnip, flat	Boiled	3 30
Pig, sucking	Roasted	2 30	Beets	Boiled	3 45
Meat hashed with vegetables	Warmed	2 30	Corn, green, & beans	Boiled	3 45
Lamb, fresh	Broiled	2 30	Beef, fresh, lean	Fried	4 —
Goose	Roasted	2 30	Fowls, domestic	Boiled	4 —
Cake, sponge	Baked	2 30	" "	Roasted	4 —
Cabbage-head	Raw	2 30	Veal, fresh	Broiled	4 —
Beans, pod	Boiled	2 30	Soup, beef, vegetables, and bread	Boiled	4 —
Custard	Baked	2 45	Salmon, salted	Boiled	4 —
Chicken, full-grown	Fricasseed	2 45	Heart, animal	Fried	4 —
Apples, sour, hard	Raw	2 50	Beef, old, hard, salted	Boiled	4 15
Oysters, fresh	Raw	2 55	Pork, recently salted	Fried	4 15
Bass, striped, fresh	Broiled	3 —	Cabbage, with vinegar	Boiled	4 30
Beef, fresh, lean, rare	Roasted	3 —	Ducks, wild	Roasted	4 30
" steak	Broiled	3 —	Pork, recently salted	Boiled	4 30
Corn, cake	Baked	3 —	Suet, mutton	Boiled	4 30
Dumpling, apple	Boiled	3 —	Veal, fresh	Fried	4 30
Eggs, fresh	Boiled soft	3 —	Pork, fat and lean	Roasted	5 15
Mutton, fresh	Broiled	3 —	Suet, beef, fresh	Boiled	5 30
" "	Boiled	3 —	Tendon	Boiled	5 30

520. *A part of the food only is dissolved in the stomach.*—
The act of digestion is but partially performed in the stomach. The gastric juice possesses the power of dissolving
only the nitrogenized elements of foods (372)—albumen,
fibrine, gluten, caseine. The ternary compounds, starch,
sugar, and the oily bodies, are unaltered. Indeed, the incipient changes begun in the starchy principles by intermixture
with the saliva are arrested in the stomach. Chyme, therefore, is food out of which the nitrogenized principles have
been dissolved by the gastric fluid, leaving its remaining
proximate elements, starch, sugar, and oily matters, without
essential change. A portion of the nitrogenized substances
dissolved is supposed to be absorbed directly into the blood,
by the veins which are distributed throughout the coats of
the stomach. A portion of the water, also, which is taken
into the stomach to allay thirst is taken up in the same manner by the coats of the stomach, and carried by the veins
into the general circulation. As this stage of digestion is
completed, the chyme gradually passes out of the stomach,
through the pyloric orifice (situated at its small extremity,
see Fig. 24), into the intestines.

521. *The intestinal tube or alimentary canal,* into which
the chyme flows from the stomach, is divided into two parts—
the small intestine, and the large intestine, or *colon.* In man
the former is estimated to be about twenty-six feet in length,
and the latter about six feet.—(*Bell.*) The small intestine
is disposed in a convoluted or twisted manner, so that a
great extent of it may be packed within a small compass:
the larger portion is arranged very much as is represented

Does the gastric juice dissolve all the food? How does it affect the ternary
group of bodies? What becomes of the dissolved albuminous substance?
Into what does the chyme pass from the stomach? What is the duodenum?
What substances flow into the duodenum near the pyloric orifice?

in Fig. 24. The first portion of the small intestine connected with the stomach is slightly larger than the rest, and
is called the duodenum. A few inches from the pyloric

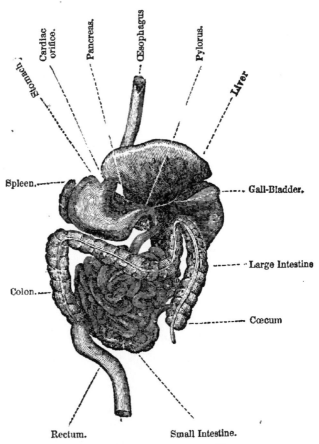

Fig. 24.—DIGESTIVE APPARATUS OF MAN.

orifice there opens into the intestine two passages or ducts,
through which the bile from the liver, and the pancreatic
juice from the pancreas, are emptied into the duodenum.

522. *The Pancreatic Juice.*—Through the pancreatic duct a liquid is poured which is secreted by the *pancreas*, and known as the *pancreatic juice*. In its properties it closely resembles the saliva, but contains from 8 to 9 per cent. of solid matter. It is generally considered to be alkaline, but when rendered acid it possesses the properties of gastric juice, and is more powerful (524).

523. *The Bile.*—This liquid is separated from the venous blood by the liver, and flows into the gall-bladder, whence it is poured into the duodenum at a point a little below the entrance of the pancreatic duct. It is a viscid, oily substance, of a greenish-yellow color, a nauseously bitter taste, and mixes in all proportions with water. Bile is alkaline, from the presence of soda. It gives 12 per cent. of ash, 11 of which are carbonate of soda. It also contains a peculiar substance of feebly acid properties called *choleic acid*, or *bilic acid*. This acid neutralizes a portion of the soda in the same manner as the fatty or resinous acids, forming choleate of soda. In consequence of this soapy property, it is used, as in the case of ox-gall, to remove greasy spots from cloth, and the bile of the sea-wolf is ordinarily employed as a soap by the Icelanders. Although the bile is looked upon as an excretion from the blood (581), yet it performs an important office in digestion.

CHYLIFICATION.

524. *Duodenal Digestion.*—The chyme is mingled with the biliary and pancreatic secretions as it passes into the duodenum. Their intermixture is effected, as in the case of

What are the composition and properties of the pancreatic juice? Where is the bile produced? What are its properties? For what is it sometimes used?
With what is the chyle mixed in the duodenum? By what means are they

the stomach, by the contraction of the muscular walls of the intestine (*peristaltic motion*), which serves at the same time to propel the mass along the alimentary tube. The chemical action begun by the saliva during mastication, and suspended in the stomach, is here resumed. The starch is converted into dextrine and sugar, and a part of the sugar still further changed to lactic acid. It is probable, however, that a portion of the sugar is converted into fat, as the recent experiments of Meckel appear to show that bile possesses the power of effecting this transformation. He found that when bile was mingled with grape-sugar, and allowed to remain in contact with it for some time, a much larger quantity of fatty matter existed in the mixture than could have been present in the bile. The oily substances of the chyme are dissolved, or reduced to the state of an emulsion, so as to be readily absorbed. This change was formerly supposed to be produced exclusively by the bile. The late researches of Bernard, however, have proved that this is the function of the pancreatic juice. When this secretion is mixed with oily or fatty matters out of the body, it effects this change on them at once, although neither saliva, gastric juice, nor bile are able to perform it. The product of these changes is a whitish, opaque, milky-looking liquid, termed *chyle*. Its appearance is due to innumerable oily globules which are diffused through it.

525. *Effect of the Different Juices.*—The gastric juice of the stomach is charged with the office of bringing the nitrogenized elements of food into a state of solution, while the saliva of the mouth, the bile, and pancreatic juice effect the

mingled together? What chemical changes now occur? What appears from the experiments of Meckel? What is the office of the pancreatic juice? What is chyle?

By what are the nitrogenized elements dissolved? The non-nitrogenized? If

same change upon the non-nitrogenized principles. If the acid of the gastric juice is neutralized, as by the introduction of bile into the stomach, it loses its power of dissolving albuminous substances, and attacks oily bodies; on the other hand, if the bile and pancreatic fluid are rendered acid, they cease to affect the ternary compounds, but act upon those which are nitrogenized. The methods thus employed to bring the food into a state of solution are purely of a chemical nature, in all respects analogous to those adopted by the chemist in attaining a similar object. The analogy is complete in the following particulars: first, in both cases the solids are brought to a state of fine division; second, they are agitated and completely intermixed with the solvents; third, a fixed quantity of liquid can act only upon a definite proportion of solid matter; fourth, heat influences the process; fifth, the same solvent acts differently upon different solid substances.

SANGUIFICATION.

526. *Mode in which the Chyle is removed from the Intestines.*—So long as the alimentary matter remains in the intestinal cavity, it can no more minister to the wants of the system than if it were in contact with the external surface of the body; indeed, strictly speaking, it has not yet been taken into the system. It is absorbed by a peculiar set of vessels called the *lacteals*, which commence in the intestinal tube by a multitude of little rootlets that unite at first into minute trunks, then into larger ones, and at length deliver

---

the gastric juice is made alkaline, what follows? If the bile be made acid, what is the result? In what respect do these processes resemble the operations of the chemist?

What is the office of the lacteals? What do they consist of? Where do they

their contents into a kind of common reservoir, the *thoracic duct*, which empties into a large vein near the shoulder. In their course the lacteal tubes are convoluted, or twisted together, into peculiar knot-like bodies, by which they are greatly prolonged ; these knotty masses, or ganglia, are called *mesenteric glands*, because they are inclosed between two layers of a membrane or fold called the *mesentery* (Fig.

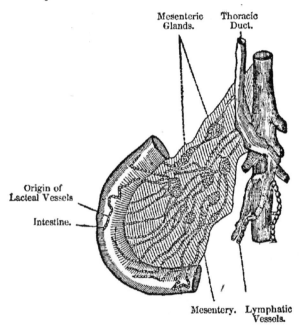

25). The lacteals do not open by distinct apertures into the intestinal tube, but terminate in numberless minute projections, called *villi*, which form a loose tissue upon the mucous membrane of the intestinal wall. It has been found that the act of lacteal absorption is carried on by means of vast numbers of exceedingly minute *cells* or *sacs*, which are formed within the villous tissue.   In the intervals, when there is no chyle to be absorbed, these cells cannot be seen; but every time digestion takes place, a new crop springs up. Their growth is very rapid and their life transitory.   In growing, they absorb into themselves part of the fluid that surrounds them ; and it is probable that when they are ma ture, they either burst or dissolve and deliver the fluid to the absorbent vessels.   That it is the special office of the lacteals to absorb the chyle, is shown by the fact that they are not distributed upon the stomach, or upon that portion of the intestinal tube above the point where the bile and pancreatic juice enter the duodenum.   They are abundant upon the small intestine, but less numerous upon the large one.

527. *Selecting Power of the Lacteals.*—The lacteals pos- sess the power of absorbing only that portion of the contents of the intestinal canal which is capable of being used by the system ; and as the food which is eaten contains other sub- stances, these, of course, are left as a residue in the intes- tines.   This solid residue (excreta), which remains to be ex- cluded from the alimentary passage, must be looked upon, not as having taken any part in the grand processes of the system, but as mainly composed of matters incapable of any such service.   It however contains a small proportion of the waste matters of the system, as the brown coloring mat- ter of the bile, mucus, and some salts, chiefly insoluble phos- phates of lime and magnesia.

528. *Changes which occur in the Lacteals.*—In its course through the lacteals, the chyle undergoes a change, by which

What is said of their growth ?   Of their disappearance ?   From what do we infer that the lacteals absorb chyle ?

Do the lacteals take up all the contents of the alimentary canal ?   What is said of the residue ?

What change takes place in the chyle during its passage through the lacteals ?

it is brought into a closer relationship with blood. If exam‧ ined at its first entrance into these vessels, before it has pass‧ ed through the glands, it is entirely destitute of that power of spontaneously coagulating, or *clotting*, which is so remarka‧ ble in blood. It consists, in 100 parts, of 90 water, $3\frac{1}{2}$ albu men, the same of oils, and about 3 parts of other animal and saline matter. But the chyle drawn from the lacteals, after it has passed through the mesenteric glands, possesses the power of coagulating slightly; this is caused by the trans‧ formation of a portion of the albumen into fibrine, by which the fluid begins to assume the properties of blood. When the chyle has reached the thoracic receptacle, its proportion of albumen is still further diminished, while the fibrine is correspondingly increased; and it now separates promptly, like blood, into *clot* and *serum*, in which state it is mingled with the venous current of the great circulation. Thus the prominent chemical change occurring in the lacteal vessels consists in the conversion of albumen into fibrine. Other transformations take place, but they are not so well under‧ stood, and cannot be detailed here.

THE BLOOD.

529. The series of changes which have just been described have for their object to prepare from the food a nutritious fluid which shall supply materials of renovation and growth to all parts of the body. This fluid is called *blood*, and the apparatus of tubes and channels (blood-vessels) by which it is conveyed into all parts of the body is termed the circulatory system.

530. *Properties of the Blood.*—In man and the higher

What is the object of the changes just described? What is the circulatory sys‧ tem?

What are the properties of blood? Of what two parts does it consist? What is the form of blood-disks in man? What do they consist of?

orders of animals, the blood is of a red color; florid and approaching to scarlet when drawn from the arteries, and of a deep purple when taken from the veins. It has an unctuous or soapy feel, a slightly nauseous odor, a saline taste, and an alkaline reaction. When first removed from the body, the blood appears to the naked eye a uniform red liquid; but when examined by a microscope, it is seen to consist of two distinct parts—a clear and nearly colorless fluid, called the *plasma* or *liquor sanguinis*, and of an immense number of minute, rounded, red particles floating in this fluid, which are known as *blood-globules*, *blood-disks*, or *blood-corpuscles*. They vary greatly in size and form in different animals. In man they are flat disks resembling pieces of money, but usually exhibiting a slight depression towards the centre, and having a diameter from about the $\frac{1}{2800}$ to $\frac{1}{4000}$ of an inch. The corpuscles consist of a thin membrane or sac (*globuline*), a nitrogenized substance, filled with a red coloring matter (*hematine*), in which iron is a large element.

531. *Coagulation.*—After the blood has been removed from the body for a short time, it spontaneously *coagulates*, or separates into a dark-red jelly, or clot (*crassamentum*), and a pale-colored, slimy liquid (*serum*). Coagulation is caused by the change of soluble fibrine contained in blood to the insoluble state. It was formerly supposed that the blood was alive, and that this change consisted in its death; but the same event is constantly taking place within the body, as the liquid fibrine of the blood is deposited to form solid flesh. As the fibrine coagulates, it forms a fine net-work or jelly throughout the liquid, which entangles and incloses the red corpuscles. It also contains a portion of the serum, which

may be removed by pressure. The serum consists of water, albumen, fatty matter, and various salts. Gregory states that the healthy proportions of serum and clot are 87 per cent. of the former, to 13 of the latter; but it is obvious that these proportions must vary in the healthy individual, from a great variety of causes. Thus the mere swallowing of a draught of water must alter the composition of blood, and thus effect its analysis. The general constitution of the blood is here given, from Lecanu:

Water,	780·145	Crystalline fatty matter,	2·430
Fibrine,	2·100	Oily matter,	1·310
Coloring matter,	133·000	Extractive matter,	1·790
Albumen,	65·090	Salts and bases,	14·185
			1000·000

NUTRITION

532. The formation of the various parts of a living body from a single homogeneous liquid—the blood—the nourishment and growth of a young animal upon milk, and the development of a chicken from the liquid contents of an egg, are phenomena alike wonderful and mysterious. Of the vital force, by which these changes are guided, we comprehend nothing; something is however known of the transformations which occur, and more of the chemical nature of the products which are formed. The process by which the various organs and tissues of the system are elaborated from the blood is called *nutrition*.

533. *Source of the Animal Tissues.*—We have observed that woody fibre, of which the fabric of plants is almost entirely constructed, is composed only of three elements—car-

bon, hydrogen, and oxygen. The fundamental tissue
animal fabric is equally uniform in its chemical constit,
containing the same elements as woody fibre, with the addition of a large proportion of nitrogen. Vegetable tissue is
thus totally incapable of conversion into animal tissue; but
the nitrogenized products of plants are adapted to this purpose, and it is from these that they are wholly constructed.
The *areolar tissue*, which is composed of membranous cells,
diffused throughout all parts of the body, the muscular
fibres which constitute flesh, together with the various blood-
vessels and membranes which form the groundwork of the
animal system and the chief portion of its solids, all have
the same chemical composition as the nitrogenized compounds of plants,—gluten, vegetable albumen, and caseine.
They all contain nitrogen to the extent of 17 per cent.

534 *Nutrition of the Tissues.*—The nutrition of the animal tissues is therefore, in a chemical point of view, a very
simple process; consisting essentially in the coagulation
or solidification of fibrine, which has its origin in plants.
When albumen is changed from the liquid to the solid state,
it exhibits no traces of organization; that is, the particles
arrange themselves into a brittle mass, instead of tough,
thready fibres, and it has not the qualities which would
adapt it for muscular tissue. fibrine, on the contrary, presents
these qualities in an eminent degree, coagulating into fibres
or filaments, so that blood in which fibrine is dissolved has
been very properly termed liquid flesh. The relations of
albumen, fibrine, and flesh have been very justly compared
to those of raw cotton, the spun yarn, and the woven fabric.
The conversion of albumen into fibrine which has been noticed

What is the difference between coagulated albumen and coagulated fibrine? To
what are the relations of albumen, fibrine, and flesh compared? What is said to
be the result of late researches? How does the nutrition of carnivorous and her
bivorous animals differ?

as occurring in the lacteals (528), and which is also constant‹
ly taking place in the blood, is therefore a simple flesh‐
forming process, the product necessarily remaining in a
liquid state, that it may be distributed by the circulation
into all parts of the system, while it gradually coagulates
into fibrous and muscular tissue, Late microscopical dis‐
coveries render it probable that .he process of nutrition is
carried on by means of the growth of innumerable cells,
which are developed and extended upon the solid surfaces.
The nutrition of the grain and herb-eating animals is of the
same nature as in those which subsist upon flesh, the con‐
stituents of their blood being in both cases of vegetable
origin.   The only difference is, that carnivorous animals ap‐
propriate those elements of nutrition (blood and flesh), which
have already served a similar purpose in animals which live
upon vegetation.

535. *Consumption.*—If the conversion of albumen into
fibrine is incomplete, the tissues are imperfectly nourished,
and the strength and vigor of the body are impaired.   The
formation of *tubercles* in the lungs, which give rise to con‐
sumption, is due to this cause—the imperfect elaboration
of the fibrine.   Tubercular matter consists of half-formed
cells, fibres, &c., and coagulated albumen, deposited in the
tissue of the lungs, which consequently impairs respiration,
and produces irritation and inflammation, like any other for‐
eign matter.   The only manner in which any curative means
can be brought to bear upon this terrible scourge is by at‐
tention to the constitutional states from which it results.
This is sometimes hereditary, and sometimes induced by in‐
sufficient nutrition, habitual exposure to cold and damp,

What is the cause of tubercles in the lungs?   Of what does tubercular matter
consist?   What effect does it produce?   What circumstances will induce tuber‐
cular disease?   What treatment is recommended?

long-continued mental depression, &c. The treatment must be directed to the invigoration of the system, by good food, active exercise, pure air, warm clothing, and cheerful occupations; and by a due employment of these means, at a sufficiently early period, many lives might be saved, which would otherwise fall a sacrifice to tubercular disease.—(*Carpenter.*)

PRODUCTS OF NUTRITION.

536. *Gelatine.*—When the tendons, ligaments, cartilages, skin and bones of animals are for some time boiled in water, a substance is extracted, which *gelatinizes*, or forms a jelly, on cooling. It is a nitrogenized compound, having the formula $C_{13} H_{10} O_5 N_2$ (*Mulder*); but, unlike the albuminous substances, it is not formed by plants, nor is it found in the blood: it must, therefore, be looked upon as a secretion, although some chemists maintain that it is formed by the process which is employed to obtain it, and has no real existence in the animal organism. The gelatine from cartilage is termed *chondrine.* Pure gelatine is colorless, transparent, inodorous, and insipid. In cold water it gradually softens and swells, but does not dissolve until heated. The cooled solution remains as a more or less firm jelly. Gelatine is insoluble in alcohol, ether, and the fixed and volatile oils. *Isinglass* is the name given to a commercial form of gelatine, which is obtained chiefly from the air-bladder of fish, as the sturgeon and cod. When the membranes are cleansed, dried, and scraped, they form *leaf* isinglass; when folded into packages they constitute *book* isinglass. It is ex-

From what substances is gelatine obtained? How does it differ from the albuminous substances? How do some chemists regard it? What is chondrine? What are the properties of pure gelatine? What is isinglass? Leaf isinglass? Book isinglass? For what is it used? How may it be preserved?

tensively employed as an article of diet, in the form of jelly: one part of isinglass dissolves ,in 100 of hot water, forming a thick, tremulous jelly, when cooled. Jelly may be kept in close vessels for some days without change, but in open vessels it soon becomes mouldy, especially in the vicinity of blossoming plants (*Brande*): it then putrefies, although this change, it is said, may be arrested by a little acetic acid, without much affecting the jelly.

537. *Glue* is a form of gelatine extracted from bones, the parings of hides, and the hoofs and ears of cattle, by boiling in water, or by steam pressure. The solution obtained cools into a stiff jelly, which is cut by wires into thin slices, and dried upon netting, to which its peculiar grooved appearance is due. Good glue is hard, brittle, translucent, and of a brownish color. By immersion in cold water, it absorbs three or four times its weight without dissolving. Where less water is absorbed, or where the glue loses its viscid aspect in cold water, it is unfit for use. The employment of glue, in uniting or binding substances together, is well known. Its adhesive power is increased by adding to it white-lead or borax—an ounce of the salt to a pound of glue.

538. *Court-plaster* is silk cloth, varnished over with a solution of gelatine. Transparent wafers are also made of gelatine; common wafers being made from flour-paste, colored with various substances.

539. *Bones, their composition.*—Bones consist of gelatinous tissue, into which mineral matter has been deposited, until it possesses a stony hardness. The mineral substances are phosphate and carbonate of lime. The phosphate predominates in the higher animals; in the lower, the carbonate. The amount

What is glue? What are the qualities of good glue? How is poor glue known? How may the adhesive power of glue be increased?
What is court-plaster? Of what are wafers made?
What do bones consist of? What is said of the mineral matter of bones?

of mineral matter in bones increases with age: thus in the child it forms about half the weight of the bone, in the adult four-fifths, and in the old person seven-eighths.

540. *Mineral and Organic Elements of Bones.*—If a bone is soaked in diluted muriatic acid, the mineral salts are dissolved out, the animal matter remaining as tough, flexible, nearly transparent gelatine, having the same form as the bone. If, on the other hand, we submit a bone to strong heat, the animal portion is burned out, and the earthy part remains. The bone is then brittle, and falls to pieces at the slightest touch. Hence bony structures owe their *tenacity* to the organic element, and their hardness and stiffness to the mineral substances of which they consist. In the disease called *rickets* there is a deficiency of the inorganic constituents, and the bones, therefore, become twisted and distorted. A solution of phosphate of lime, in phosphoric acid, has been prescribed as a remedy. There is also a malady of an opposite nature, in which there is less than a healthy supply of animal matter. In this case the bones are exceedingly liable to fracture. The nails, claws, and horns of animals, are analogous in composition to the bones.

541. *Mode in which the Shells of Crustacea are produced.* —In some of the lower species of animals, as crabs and lobsters (*crustacea*), the bony skeleton, instead of traversing the interior of the body, exists in the form of an external covering, or shell. This shell is periodically thrown off, and renewed again in a very speedy and curious manner. There is, laid up in the walls of their stomach, a supply of carbonate of lime, in the form of little concretions, known as "crab's

How may we separate the animal from the earthy portion of bones? To what is the tenacity of bones due? To what do they owe their hardness? What is the cause of rickets? The remedy? What other disease of the bones is mentioned? In the crustacea, where is the bony skeleton found? When this shell is cast off by the animal, how is a new one formed?

eyes." When the shell is cast off this matter is taken up by the blood-vessels, and carried out to the surface of her body, where a new shell is formed in a day or two

542. *Hair, its Composition.*—The basis of hair is a nitrogenized animal tissue, containing deposits of lime, magnesia, and salts of iron, together with a considerable quantity of sulphur, to which much of its disagreeable odor in burning is due. The various colors of hair are due to the differences in its chemical composition. Thus, according to Wilson, red hair contains a reddish-colored oil, a large proportion of sulphur, and a small quantity of iron; fair hair a white oil, with phosphate of lime, and the white hair of the aged a considerable quantity of the phosphate.

543. *Fat.*—The properties of fat have been already described (427). It is separated from the blood, and deposited in the adipose tissue, throughout all parts of the body, in the shape of small globules, from the $\frac{1}{300}$ to $\frac{1}{600}$ of an inch in diameter. This deposit forms a layer, of various degrees of thickness, which gives roundness and symmetry to the animal form, and at the same time furnishes a kind of pad, or cushion, for the support of movable parts. It has been an earnest question among chemists whether the fat of animals is exclusively derived from vegetables, or in part generated within the organism from the non-nitrogenized elements of food. It is at present thought that the animal does possess such a power, while it is known that fat exists in plants to a much larger extent than was formerly supposed.

544. *Nervous Matter.*—The nerves are minute threads or cords, which in man extend into all parts of the body, and

---

Of what is hair composed? To what are its various colors owing? What does red hair contain? Fair hair? Gray hair?

From what is the fat of the system derived? What are some of its uses? What question concerning its production has been discussed by chemists?

which perform a twofold object: one class or set transmits sensations to the brain, the seat of the mind, while another set conveys the mandate of the will from the brain to the muscles, by which it is executed.

545 *Composition of the Nerves.*—The chemical composition of the nerves is the same as that of the brain. The nervous matter of an adult gives, upon analysis in 100 parts:

Of Water,..72·51
Albumen,........ .... 9·40
Fat, ,............................. .... 6·10
Osmazome and Salts,............ ....10·19
Phosphorus, ... 1·80
                                                                    ————
                                                                    100·00

The structure of the nerves is tubular, the wall being composed of albumen; within it is contained minute fat globules, and with these the phosphorus is associated. This element, as will be shown in another place (592), is essentially connected with the operations of the mind. The amount of phosphorus in the nervous matter of infants was found upon analysis to be 0·80, in aged persons 1·00, in adults 1 80, and in idiots 0·85 per cent.—but half that which is found at the adult period, or condition of greatest mental vigor. *Osmazome* is an ill-defined compound, to which the aromatic flavor of soup has been attributed. It is lately shown to be a mixture of several substances.

SECRETIONS.

546. Those substances which are separated from the blood, not for the purpose of purifying it, but to answer some pur-

pose in the animal economy, are termed *secretions* The saliva, gastric juice, and pancreatic juice, already described, are examples. To these may be added *mucus*, which is secreted from the surface of membranes (*mucous membranes*), and *lymph*, which is poured out from the lymphatic vessels; neither of which have been satisfactorily examined. The *tears* (*lachrymal secretion*) consist of water, rendered slightly saline by common salt, and containing also a little albumen, combined with soda.

MILK

547. *Its Source and Composition*—This fluid is secreted from the blood of females, of the class *mammalia*, for the nourishment of their young. It is the only substance completely prepared by nature as an article of food; and it is so constituted as to furnish materials for the development of all the various organs and compounds of the young animal: its composition must, therefore, be a matter of interest. It is a white liquid, of a sweetish taste, a peculiar odor, and contains, dissolved, sugar, caseine, and salts; also a fatty substance, butter, which is diffused throughout it in the form of minute globules, that are visible with the microscope, while at the same time the liquid appears transparent. The composition of fresh cow's milk is as follows:

Water,	88·30
Caseine,	4·82
Milk-sugar,	3·89
Butter,	3·00
Salts,	0·49
	100 00
Solid matter,	11·07

What are secretions? Give examples What do tears consist of?
What is said of milk as food? State its properties. What is its composition?

548. *The Lactometer, or Milk-measurer.*—When freshly drawn milk is permitted to stand, the butter-globules rise to the surface and form *cream*. The proportion of cream in milk may be determined by means of an instrument called the lactometer, which consists simply of a glass tube, six or seven inches long, which is marked off into a hundred equal divisions. It is filled with a sample of milk and allowed to stand, when the per cent. of cream which forms upon the surface is read off upon the scale.

549. *Production of Butter.*—Butter is obtained either from cream or from milk, by agitating it in various ways (churning). This is necessary, because the oil-globules are invested by a delicate membrane, which requires to be ruptured before the butter will cohere into a solid mass. *Heat* also bursts the globules and causes them to unite, but the butter thus produced is of a poorer quality. The best temperature for churning is, for cream, 55° to 58°, and for milk 65°.—(*Johnston.*) During the process the temperature rises from 4° to 10°, and the milk or cream, if sweet, turns sour, oxygen is absorbed, and acid formed, which seems to aid in the coalescence of the oil-globules. From a great variety of causes, butter is liable to changes by which its quality is impaired; among these may be mentioned the absorption of bad odors by cream, if not kept in a perfectly clean place with a frequent renewal of fresh air; washing with water containing much lime or organic matter, and packing with impure salt. But the chief source of injurious changes in butter is the putrefaction of cheesy matter, caseine (375), of which it always contains a small portion.

What is cream? What is the lactometer? How is it used?

How is butter obtained? Why is churning necessary? What is said of butter produced by heat? What is the best for churning? What changes occur during the process? How does butter sometimes become deteriorated in quality?

The caseine converts the sugar of milk into lactic acid, and that into butyric acid, to which the disagreeable smell of rancid butter is mainly due.

550. *Milk-sugar* (*Lactine*), $C_{12} H_{10} O_{10} + 2 H O$.—This is the substance which gives to milk its slightly sweet taste. It is obtained by evaporating clarified whey until it crystallizes. It is much less soluble than cane or grape sugar, and therefore much less sweet: it is also hard and gritty.

551. *Caseine*, or the curd of milk, has the same composition and properties as vegetable caseine (375): it exists in milk in a state of solution, but is very insoluble in water, one pound of caseine requiring 400 pounds of that liquid to dissolve it. Caseine is held in solution in milk by means of a small quantity of soda; if this is neutralized by an acid the caseine is at once precipitated, as insoluble curd, and an addition of a little carbonate of soda or potash, so as to form a weak alkaline solution, redissolves it.

552. *Natural Curdling of Milk.*—When milk is exposed to the air for a certain length of time, it becomes sour and curdles, that is, its caseine is precipitated. The curd, however, does not readily separate from the liquid part (whey), unless a gentle heat be applied, when it contracts in bulk and rises to the surface. The souring and curdling process proceeds slowly in the cold, but quickens as the temperature is elevated; and is observed to take place first at the surface of the milk, where it is in contact with the air. The changes that here occur are begun by the oxygen of the air, which induces decomposition in the nitrogenized caseine; this decomposition is propagated to the sugar of milk, which is

What is said of milk-sugar?
What is said of caseine? How is it held in solution? What precipitates it How may it be redissolved?
How is milk curdled? How is the curd separated from the whey? When does

changed to *lactic acid*, probably by being first converted into grape-sugar; but this is not precisely known. The lactic acid gives to milk its sourness, and by neutralizing its soda precipitates the caseine.

553. *Artificial Curdling of Milk.*—It seems to matter nothing whether the acid is generated spontaneously by the elements of milk, or is added artificially, the effect being the same. Almost any acid substance possesses the power of curdling milk. In Holland, muriatic acid is said to be extensively employed for this purpose in the cheese manufacture. In Switzerland they add a little sour milk to produce the curd; while in other countries vinegar, tartaric acid, lemon-juice, cream of tartar, and salt of sorrel, are also employed. But the substance most generally used for this purpose usually consists of the lining membrane of the stomach of a calf, prepared by salting and drying. The rennet is soaked in water or whey, which being added to the milk, and the temperature raised to 95°, coagulates it promptly. It has been hitherto considered that the coagulating action of rennet is due to a portion of gastric juice which it retains; but late researches show that it acts in the same manner as caseine (552), by changing milk-sugar into lactic acid, through its decomposition. Gastric juice, it is true, curdles milk rapidly; but the thorough and repeated washings and dryings to which rennet may be subjected without destroying its efficacy, renders it impossible to ascribe its action to that solvent, while it is well known that other membranes besides that of the stomach, in a state of decomposition, convert sugar of milk into lactic acid.

---

it curdle most rapidly? Where does the process begin? State the changes that occur.

How may milk be artificially curdled? What substances are employed for this purpose? How does rennet act in the curdling of milk? How does it appear that gastric juice is not the agent in producing the change?

554. *Experiment of Berzelius.*—The small quantity of rennet which takes part in the process is well illustrated by an experiment of Berzelius. He took a bit of the lining of a calf's stomach, washed it completely, dried and weighed it carefully, and put it into 1800 times its weight of milk. He then heated it 120°, and when coagulation was complete withdrew the membrane, washed, dried, and again weighed it: the loss was $\frac{1}{17}$ of its entire weight. But one part of the membrane, therefore, was used in coagulating thirty thousand of milk.

555. *Preservation of Milk.*—Milk or cream may be preserved, or restored to a state of sweetness when it has begun to sour, by adding to it a small quantity of soda, pearlash, or magnesia, which neutralizes the lactic acid: the lactates thus formed are not unwholesome. The action of curd, in decomposing sugar of milk, is arrested or prevented by heating it to the boiling temperature. Hence if milk be introduced into bottles, well corked, put into a pan with cold water and gradually raised to the boiling point, and after cooling be taken out and set away in a cool place, the milk may be preserved perfectly sweet for half a year.—(*Johnston.*) If the bottle in this case be uncorked, and the milk exposed to the air, the caseine, after a few days, resumes its property of decomposing milk-sugar and forming lactic acid. By evaporating milk at a moderate heat, with constant stirring, its solid constituents are left as a dry mass, which may be kept for any length of time, and which, when dissolved in water, is said to possess all the properties of the most excellent milk.

556. *Adaptation for Food.*—Milk contains all the saline substances which are found in the blood (400), or which the

---

Describe the experiment of Berzelius.

How may sour milk be restored to sweetness? How may milk be prepared so as to remain sweet for months? What is the effect of uncorking the bottle?

growing animal requires, phosphate of lime in large quantity (40 gallons contain 1 lb.) for the development of bones, common salt to furnish by its decomposition the hydrochloric acid of the gastric juice and the soda of the bile, and also a trace of iron, which reappears in the coloring matter of the blood. The other constituents of milk perform equally important offices in nutrition; the butter yields fat, the sugar is burned for the production of heat, the caseine forms flesh, and the large proportion of water supplies this necessary element to the system.

RESPIRATION.

557. *Destructive Force in the System.*—Thus far the changes that have been noticed as occurring in the animal body are of a formative nature, their object being to build up the system by constant additions of matter to all its parts. The amount of food taken for this purpose of course varies very much in different individuals and different circumstances, but it may be stated as an average that an adult man consumes each day two pounds and a half of solid food, and from four to five pounds of liquid, besides taking into his system two pounds of oxygen gas from the air. And yet his body does not increase in its weight, but in health remains of a uniform bulk and weight from year to year. A destructive process must therefore be constantly going on in the system, sufficiently active to use up and carry away the same amount of matter that is supplied

---

How does the composition of milk compare with that of blood? What offices do its different constituents perform in nutrition?

How much food does an adult consume daily? How much oxygen? Why does not his body increase in weight? What is the channel of this waste?

through the channels of nutrition. The source of this perpetual waste and destruction is the act of respiration, by
which common air is brought into contact with every portion of the animal organization.

558. *Nature of Respiration always the same, its Modes
different.*—The relation of animals to the atmosphere is of
a most direct and vital nature. All the peculiar actions
which take place in the animal structure, and which taken
collectively we call life, are set in motion and kept in motion
by atmospheric oxygen. Its effect is exerted upon the body
through the medium of the *respiratory organs.* The action
of oxygen is exactly of the same nature in all animals, but
the structure and arrangement of the respiratory mechanism differ according as they are destined to be acted upon
by oxygen in the condition of a gas, or in a state of solution
in water. Animals low in the scale of nature, whose structure is simple, and the composition of their bodies porous,
have no separate breathing apparatus; their respiration is
what is called *cutaneous,* that is, air contained in the water
in which they live penetrates all parts of their body, and
acts upon the blood. Those animals which inhabit the
water have special organs for breathing, termed *branchia,* or
gills, which are composed of feathery filaments, or tufts of
blood-vessels, situated externally upon the body, and designed to be acted upon by the air which is contained in
water. The higher animals respire by lungs, which consist
of membranous bags lodged within the body, and which are
directly acted upon by the air.

559. *Respiration of Fishes.*—The *branchia,* or *gills* of

Does oxygen act in the same manner upon all animals? Is the respiratory apparatus of all animals alike? How is the respiration of the lowest animals performed? What is the breathing apparatus of fish called? What organs have the
higher animals for this purpose?

fish consist of a mass of blood-vessels in the form of delicate comb-like fringes, arranged in rows on each side of the
throat. The branchia are hence situated on the outside of
the body, but they are overlaid by a large valve-like flap,
which is termed the gill-cover, and which is seen in constant
motion when the fish is in its native element. A continual
current of water is made to pass over the gills by the action
of the mouth, which takes in a large quantity, and com-
pressing it by muscular contraction, the gill-cover opens, the
fibrils spread, and the water is forced out through openings
between the rows of fringes. Each fibril consists of two vessels, a vein and artery, one of which brings the blood, while the
other returns it again to the system. As the water flows over
the surface of these vessels an interchange takes place, the
carbonic acid of the impure blood escapes outwardly, while
the oxygen of the water-atmosphere (93) is absorbed into the
blood, which is thus purified.

560. The art of drowning fishes under water, which is
practised by anglers, consists in keeping their mouths open
by means of the hook, which makes it impossible for the
animal to breathe, and thus produces suffocation.

561. *Why Fish die when removed from the Water.* —
When a fish is withdrawn from the water, the fringes of its
gills speedily mat or clog together and dry up, so that the
air cannot exert any action upon them, and respiration therefore ceases; but if the gills are kept constantly moist, they
will continue to perform their office of absorbing oxygen,
and thus maintain life. There are certain fishes which possess the means of securing this condition. The gill-filaments

Describe the breathing organs of fishes? How are the gills supplied with oxygen? Of what does each fibril consist? What chemical change takes place?
By what means are fish drowned in water?
How may fishes be kept alive when out of water? What contrivances have some
fish, enabling them to live for some time upon land?

are so arranged that they do not clog together, and by means of little reservoirs of water, which are provided for the purpose, they may be kept moist for some time. These contrivances are said to enable some species of fish to remain sufficiently long upon land to migrate from lake to lake.

562. *Respiration of Whales.*—Many marine animals, as whales, seals, porpoises, &c., breathe atmospheric air, and are therefore compelled frequently to rise to the surface. Some possess the means of carrying with them a temporary supply of air; others, as the whale, have reservoirs in which the arterial blood can be accumulated: as it is rendered impure in the body, it passes into another reservoir connected with the veins, and the animal is thus enabled to remain for a considerable time beneath the surface.

563. *Respiration of Insects.*—The organs of respiration in insects are internal—within the system. The air is admitted through minute orifices called *spiracles*, arranged along the side of the body, which open into a system of tubes (trachea). These air-tubes ramify and extend into all parts of the body.

564 *Respiration of Reptiles.*—The low form of respiration which takes place in reptiles is carried on by means of air-sacs contained within the body, and which may be regarded as the rudest form of lungs. The air enters through the mouth; but reptiles have no power of filling their lungs by a process resembling our *inspiration*, or drawing in of air · they are obliged to swallow it by mouthfuls, as we do

Why are some marine animals often compelled to rise to the surface of the water? What arrangement has the whale which enables it to stay some time under the water?

Describe the respiratory organs of insects?

By what means is the respiration of reptiles carried on? How is air taken into their bodies? How may they be strangled?

food, forcing or pushing it down by muscular contraction
Reptiles, as well as fishes, may therefore be suffocated or
strangled by keeping their mouths constantly open.

565. *Respiration by Lungs.*—The higher animals breathe
by means of true lungs.   In man, these consist of a pair of
large, pouch-shaped organs, situated in the upper cavity of
the body (thorax), one on each side of the heart.   The
windpipe (trachea), which passes from the mouth to the
chest, there separates into two *bronchia*, one of which enters
each lung.   These divide into smaller bronchial tubes,
which again subdivide, and finally terminate in minute cavities called *air-cells*.   The whole arrangement has been compared to an inverted tree, the
trunk representing the windpipe, the branches and twigs
the subdivisions of the bronchia, and the expanding buds
the air-cells.   The air-cells are
about $\frac{1}{100}$ of an inch in diameter, and their number in a
person of average size has
been estimated by Weber at
600,000,000.   They are all
composed of one continuous
membrane, which is computed
to have a surface thirty times
greater than the exterior of
the body.   Fig. 26 represents
one side of the lung presenting its natural appearance, and

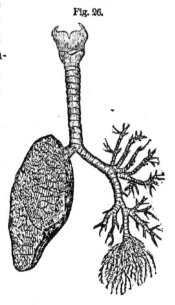

Fig. 26.

the other the branchings of the air-passages, or bronchial tubes, by which the air is conveyed to every part of the lungs. The lungs completely fill the cavity of the chest, so that by the alternate expansion and contraction of the surrounding walls and floor, they are correspondingly enlargéd and diminished in size; the contractile pressure of the chest driving the air out (expiration), and the the external pressure of the atmosphere forcing it back again (inspiration). By this means the constant renewal of the air in the lungs is secured.

566. *Circulatory Apparatus in Man.*—As the perpetual renovation of the vital fluid of the body takes place within the lungs alone, there must obviously be a provision for its constant passage through these organs; they are therefore included in the route of the general circulation of the blood. The higher animals possess two hearts, which, although located together (double heart), have yet no direct communication with each other. Each heart has two openings or cavities: the upper one being termed the *auricle*, or receiving cavity, and the lower one the *ventricle*, or propelling cavity, which connect with each other by means of orifices guarded by valves. In man, the blood which has been used in his system, and can be of no further service until purified, is all gathered into a large vein (*vena cava*), and poured into the auricle of his right-side heart. From this it passes to the ventricle, and is there driven through another large vessel (pulmonary artery) to the lungs. Having been properly changed here, it passes by another vessel (pulmonary vein) to the left-heart auricle, thence to the left ventricle, from which it is distributed through the aorta all over the body. The large trunks, both arteries and veins, as they pass from

---

Describe the heart of the higher animals? At what point is all the impure blood collected? Where does it then pass? After its purification in the lungs where is it again collected? By what vessels is it then distributed through the body? What

the central heart, divide into smaller branches, and these are still further divided until they become no larger than a hair, and are hence called capillaries (from *capillus*, a hair). The

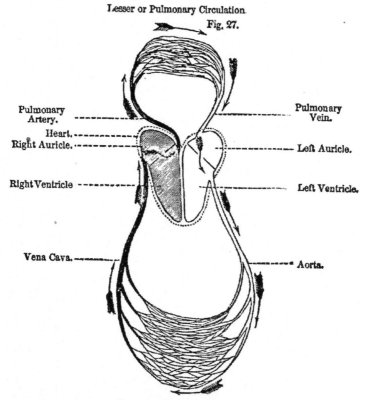

Lesser or Pulmonary Circulation.

Fig. 27.

Pulmonary Artery.

Pulmonary Vein.

Heart.

Right Auricle.

Left Auricle.

Right Ventricle

Left Ventricle.

Vena Cava.

Aorta.

Greater or Systemic Circulation.

air-cells of the lungs are covered with these minute vessels, called *pulmonary* capillaries, and it is through these that the blood flows from the right to the left heart in the lesser

---

are the minute divisions of the arteries and veins called? What are pulmonary capillaries? What are systemic capillaries?

or pulmonary circulation. Besides these, other minute blood-vessels are distributed throughout all parts of the system; they are therefore termed *systemic capillaries.* It is through these that the blood flows from the left to the right heart (systemic or greater circulation), the capillary arteries being continuous with the capillary veins. An ideal representation of the circulation in man is given in Fig. 27.

567. *Changes which take place in the Lungs.*—The blood which has been passed through the systemic capillaries and been returned by the veins to the heart is called *venous* blood. It is of a dark purple color; but when it reaches the lungs, and is submitted to the action of the air, it changes to a bright crimson, and is then known as *arterial* blood. Accompanying this alteration of color there is also a chemical change. Oxygen, from the air contained in the lungs, passes inward, or is absorbed through the cell-membrane, and combines with the blood; while at the same time carbonic acid and water from the venous blood escape through the membrane in the opposite direction, mingle with the air, and are thrown from the lungs by expiration. The power of membranes to condense and transmit gases has been noticed before (137).

568. *Oxidation occurs chiefly in the Systemic Capillaries.*— It was formerly supposed that the carbonic acid and water were formed in the lungs by the direct union of the oxygen with the carbon and hydrogen of the blood. But this idea has been abandoned, as it is shown that animals respiring pure hydrogen or nitrogen continue for some time to exhale carbonic acid, which would not be the case if it were only formed immediately by oxidation in the lungs. On the con-

What is venous blood? What is its color? What color does it acquire in the lungs? What is it then called? What chemical change also occurs?
How is it shown that the carbonic acid and water are not formed in the lungs?

trary, it is at the opposite extremity of the circulation, in the systemic capillaries, where the arterial system passes into the venous, that the oxidation of carbon and hydrogen takes place. It is here that the blood loses its florid arterial aspect and acquires a dark or venous tint, parts with its oxygen, and becomes charged with carbonic acid. These capillaries, therefore, which are diffused throughout all the body, perform exactly the opposite office to those of the lungs.

569. *Supposed Use of Iron in the Blood-Disks.*—The oxygen, when absorbed, combines not with the mass of the blood, but with its red disks only, and its union with them seems to be of a peculiarly loose nature, as it is surrendered up at all points of the organism to enter into other combinations. Liebig has thrown out a suggestion that the iron which exists in the coloring matter of the disks, and which is found nowhere else in the human body, has for its special office to carry oxygen and carbonic acid. He supposes the iron when it arrives at the lungs to be in the condition of a protoxide, but to be rapidly converted into a peroxide by the absorbed oxygen. In this state it is distributed to the capillaries of the system, where, coming in contact with the tissues which have a higher affinity for its oxygen, it yields it up, and is reduced to the condition of a protoxide. It then unites with carbonic acid, forming the protocarbonate of iron, and returns through the venous channels to the lungs, where its carbonic acid is discharged into the air, when it is again freighted with oxygen, to continue the round perpetually. This hypothesis is plausible, but is not yet accepted as a physiological fact.

In what part of the body are these substances formed? What is said of the systemic capillaries?

With what does the absorbed oxygen combine? What offices does Liebig attribute to the iron of the blood?

570. *The Change of the Blood is Chemical.*—That the change of the venous blood effected in the lungs is of a purely chemical nature, is shown by the fact that the same changes will take place when it is exposed to the air out of the body, even through the medium of a thick membrane, such as a bladder. In this experiment, the surface of the blood only is changed, as the air has no access to the interior of the mass; but in the lungs, as it flows through a multitude of little vessels so minute as to admit but one tier of disks, and as these vessels are scattered over a vast surface, a large quantity of blood is readily and completely acted upon.

571. Again, that the changes of the blood are entirely of a chemical nature and dependent upon chemical causes, is shown by the effect of excessive chemical action. When an animal which has been killed by the respiration of pure oxygen (81) is examined after death, the blood in the veins is found to have the same florid color as in the arteries.

572. *Rate of this Chemical Action.*—The activity with which the respiratory process in man is carried forward, and the changes impressed both upon the air and the blood, is very surprising. In a healthy adult man the pulsations number, upon an average, 75 in a minute, and physiologists are very generally agreed that two ounces of blood are driven by each contraction (pulsation) from the heart to the lungs, or 9 lbs. 6 oz. in a minute. The quantity of blood in the entire system is estimated by the best authorities to be about one-fifth the weight of the entire body, or 28 pounds in a person weighing 140 pounds. All the blood in the body will, therefore, flow through the lungs in the short period of

What are the proofs that the changes occurring in the blood are purely chemical? What is the number of pulsations in a minute in a healthy adult man? How much blood is driven from the heart to the lungs in the same time. What is the

three minutes, or the prodigious amount of 13,500 pounds every 24 hours. As to the quantity of air taken into the . lungs by respiration experimenters are less perfectly agreed, probably on account of the extreme variation to which it is liable in different circumstances. Coathupe fixes the average number of inspirations at 20 in the minute, and the average bulk of each inspiration at 16 cubic inches, which gives 266 cubic feet in 24 hours, but this is considered too low. Valentin estimates it at $398\frac{1}{2}$ cubic feet per day (about 2500 gallons), and Agassiz as high as 700 cubic feet.

573. *The Great Event of the Animal Economy.*—From what has been seen of the properties of oxygen, we shall be prepared to conclude that the introduction of this remarkable body into the animal system by means of special contrivances, which serve to diffuse it in the most rapid manner to all parts of the organization, is an affair of the utmost import in its connection with the phenomena of animal life. The elements of which the organism is chiefly composed are those for which this gas has the most powerful affinity. It enters the system in a free state, it leaves it in a state of combination; oxidation has therefore occurred within, and we are to find that this is the fundamental and characteristic process in the animal economy.

SOURCE OF ANIMAL HEAT.

574. The stiffening, benumbing, stupefying, and fatal effects of cold upon the living body, are well known. The performance of the vital functions requires a certain degree

estimated amount of blood in the entire system? According to this estimate what amount of blood passes through the lungs in 24 hours? What estimates of the amount of air inspired are given?

What is said of the introduction of oxygen into the system?

of heat, and this amount, which varies in different animals, is generated within the system. The temperature of the human body in a state of health, and in all climates, is constantly maintained at 98°. The extreme variations from this point are in scarlet fever and locked-jaw, when it has been known to run up to $110\frac{3}{4}°$, and Asiatic cholera and asthma, in which it has sunk to 20° below the healthy standard. The source of this heat is the chemical union of carbon and hydrogen with oxygen, a true combustion which goes on in the capillary system, and which is supplied on the one hand with fuel from the food which is eaten, and on the other with oxygen which is furnished by respiration. The use of the non-nitrogenized principles of food may now be perfectly understood; they are destined to be consumed by respiration—to be burnt in the capillary furnace of the system for the production of animal heat. The starch, sugar, gum, and oily substances contained in food, whatever intermediate changes they may undergo, are finally converted into carbonic acid and water by oxidation; and in whatever manner the combination takes place, heat must be developed.

575 *Conditions of its Development.*—The heat of the animal body being due to the chemical union of oxygen with the elements of food, it follows that the amount of heat produced must be in proportion to the amount of chemical action, and this depends upon two conditions: first, the quantity of oxygen supplied by respiration; and second, the quantity of carbon and hydrogen furnished in the food. In other words, the heat of the human body having the same

What is the constant, healthy temperature of the human body? What extreme variations are mentioned? What is the source of this heat? What purpose do the non-nitrogenized principles of food serve in the system? What are they all ultimately converted into?

Upon what two conditions does the heat of the animal body depend? How then may it be regulated?

source as that of a furnace, may be regulated in two ways—either by controlling the draught of air or the supply of fuel.

576. *Effect of the Rate of Respiration.*—The amount of heat generated in an animal is strictly related to its rate of respiration, and the amount of oxygen it absorbs. In reptiles and fishes, the structure of the respiratory organs (559, 564) is such that but a small proportion of oxygen is taken into the system; the quantity of heat which this produces is therefore small; their temperature rises and falls with that of the surrounding medium, and is never but a little above it; they are hence called *cold-blooded* animals. On the contrary, the respiratory mechanism of birds is on a most perfect plan: it works rapidly, and their temperature is consequently maintained at a high point, 100° to 112°. Infants breathe more rapidly than adults, and the temperature of their bodies is several degrees higher. But the most striking illustration of the control of the respiration over the bodily heat is seen in the case of those animals which pass the winter season in a state of profound sleep or torpor (*hybernation*). In this condition the breathing becomes very slow, the imperfectly oxygenated blood flows sluggishly through the heart, and the heat of the animal falls, it may be, almost to the freezing point. The animal becomes motionless, cold, and senseless, and "its entry into Death's chamber is prevented only by its being brought to his very door." The marmot in summer is a warm-blooded animal, but as it passes into hybernation the number of respirations falls from 500 to 14 in an hour, the pulse at the same time sinking from 150 to 15 per minute. Small as is the amount of oxygen which thus enters the sys-

What is said of the respiration of reptiles and fishes? Why are they cold blooded? How does the respiration and temperature of birds differ from these? Why is the temperature of infants above that of adults? What is the condition of animals in a state of hybernation? Give an account of the marmot.

tem, it must be neutralized, and the animal accordingly, be·
fore entering into winter-quarters, lays up a copious supply
of respiratory food in its tissues in the form of fat, which
slowly combines with the oxygen, producing a small amount
of heat, and protecting the vital structure from being destroyed.   These animals are consequently observed to come
forth in the spring in a very lean condition.

577. *Influence of different Kinds of Food in producing
Heat.*—The influence of food (fuel) in modifying animal
temperature is admirably exhibited in the provision made
by nature for obtaining a uniform degree of heat in men of
all climates.   In tropical countries, where the temperature
of the surrounding air rises nearly, or quite to blood-heat
(98°), it is obvious that the body will receive caloric, or be
heated from without to nearly the full extent of its require-
ment, and therefore have little need for generating it within.
But in the polar regions, where the prevailing temperature is
100°, or often 150° lower, a powerful demand is necessarily
made upon the heat-producing process.   Accordingly, we
find that the food, under these circumstances, is adapted to
the wants of the case.   Where little heat is to be disengaged, the amount of carbon and hydrogen in the food is in
a correspondingly small proportion; when the calorifying
energy of the system is to be powerfully taxed, they constitute the chief element of diet.   The inhabitant of the
tropic, with a high external temperature, finds ample sustenance in fresh vegetables and fruits, which contain, according
to Liebig, no more than 12 per cent. of carbon; while, on
the other hand, the residents of the arctic regions, subjected
to intense cold, live habitually upon train-oil and other fatty
substances, which consist almost entirely of hydrogen and

Why is there little need for generating heat within the body in tropical climates?
Why is it highly necessary in the polar regions?   How does the food of the Lap·

carbon. The West Indian disrelishes food which is rich in *grease;* and while the Laplander would dine comfortably upon tallow candles, he would be but ill satisfied with a meal of oranges or pineapples. To burn so large a proportion of combustible material, more oxygen is introduced into the lungs in frigid climates, in consequence of the greater condensation of the air by cold, while, at the same time, the respiration is greatly quickened by the greater amount of muscular exercise (584) which must be put forth to secure a supply of food.

578. *Quantity of Carbon consumed.*—The quantity of carbon burned in the system of an adult man daily, in a temperate climate, has been variously estimated, but is probably about 10 oz.; seven of which are supposed to escape as carbonic acid, through the lungs, and three through the skin, which is also charged in a limited degree with the function of excreting carbon from the system. According to the experiments which have been made, the heat produced by the oxidation of this amount of carbon is less than the quantity generated within the body. But it must be remarked that much hydrogen, as well as sulphur and phosphorus, are also oxidized with the evolution of heat, while the results of experiments upon the living body to determine this point, from their extreme liability to error, must be received with caution.

579. *Nervous Agency.*—It has been assumed that vital heat is to be ascribed not to chemical, but to nervous agency; but this idea seems to be clearly set aside by observing what takes place in plants. There are two marked periods in the

lander differ from that of the West Indian? Why is it that the arctic inhabitant ·
consumes more oxygen than those living in milder climates?

What quantity of carbon is estimated to be burned daily in the system of an adult man? Through what organs does its products pass from the system? What other substances are also burned to produce heat?

To what other cause has the production of animal heat been ascribed? How is

life of a plant, in which it exercises the heat-evolving function, and becomes independent of surrounding temperature. In the germination of seeds, as we have seen (320), there is a development of heat, and the same thing occurs during the act of flowering. Thus a thermometer, placed in a bunch of flowers of the *Arum*, rose to 121°, when the temperature of the air was but 66°. Now in both these cases there is an absorption of oxygen, which unites with the sugar of the flower and the oil of the seed, and a liberation of carbonic acid in exact proportion; and that the heat is simply due to oxidation, is proved by the fact that, if the presence of oxygen is prevented, no heat is evolved; whereas if pure oxygen gas is employed, the liberation of heat is more rapid than usual. The effect, in this case, cannot be due to nervous action, for plants have no nervous system. The production of heat in the animal body is *under the control* of the nervous system, probably in the same manner that the fire which drives a steam-engine is under the control of the stoker or fireman; but he certainly cannot be considered as the source of the fire—as producing the heat—but only as its regulator; he may extinguish the fire, or increase it, and in the same manner the nervous system influences animal heat.

580. *Animal Temperature regulated by Evaporation.*—It has been stated that the temperature in man, except in cases of disease, never rises higher than about 98° F. It is kept down to this point by the cooling effect of evaporation, which takes place from the surface of the skin. This organ is penetrated by a vast number of minute tubes (about 700 inches of tubing to each square inch of skin-surface), by which wa-

---

this shown to be erroneous? At what two periods is heat evolved by plants? What chemical changes occur? How is it proved that the heat is due to oxidation? Why can it not be ascribed to nervous agency? In what sense may the production of heat in the body be controlled by the nervous system?

By what means is the heat of the system kept down to 98°? How is the skin

ter (perspiration) is poured out and evaporated, thus carrying away the surplus heat from the body. The amount of fluid which escapes from the skin, as *insensible perspiration*, is estimated at 11 grains, and that from the lungs seven grains per minute. The power which men have exhibited of enduring excessive heat, for a short time, is due to the increased activity of surface-evaporation.

581. *Office of the Liver.*—If more respiratory food is taken into the system than is consumed by respiration or deposited as fat, it is separated from the blood by the liver. A special channel (*portal circulation*) carries the venous blood through this organ, where its surplus hydro-carbon (*fatty matter, bile*) is strained out. If too much work is thrown upon the liver it becomes disordered, and the substances which it should draw off accumulate in the blood, producing various symptoms, generally known as *bilious*. This is quite liable to happen in warm climates, when the elevation of the external temperature, combined with the want of sufficient exercise to stimulate respiration, leaves the non-nitrogenized elements of food unconsumed in the system. A similar disordered condition of the liver sometimes results from a diseased state of the lungs, by which they are rendered incapable of furnishing the due amount of oxygen for the combustion of the respiratory food. The office of both lungs and liver is to relieve the blood of excessive carbon: their functions are thus complementary; that is, when the action of one increases, the other diminishes. It is observed that, throughout the whole animal series, the development and activity of the respiratory organs stands in an inverse proportion to that of the

adapted for this process ? What is the amount of insensible perspiration ? How have men been enabled to endure excessive heat for a short time ?

What is the office of the liver ? How are bilious symptoms produced ? Where are they the most frequent ? What other cause sometimes produces disease of

26*

liver. Thus the respiratory system of insects is very extensive, while the liver is so small that for a long time it was
not recognized as such. In birds and mammalia also, which
breathe by lungs, the size of the liver is much less in proportion to that of the body than in reptiles and fishes, whose
respiration is feeble. In the lower aquatic animals, in which
respiration is least perfect, the liver is developed to an enormous size, often making up a large part of the bulk of the
body.

SOURCE OF ANIMAL POWER.

582. *It depends upon Oxidation.*—As the existence of
heat in animals has been shown to depend upon respiration,
and its quantity upon the activity of that process; so we are
now to find that *animal power* or *muscular force* has precisely
the same source, and that the degree of its manifestation
depends also upon the rate at which oxygen is introduced
into the system. It is now, however, the solid muscular
tissues which are oxidized, instead of the respiratory food.
The body can exert no power, perform no act, produce no
motion, but at the cost of a portion of the muscular system
by which these efforts are manifested. The power of a muscle to contract, and thus exercise force, originates only in the
process of its own destruction, in the separation and loss of
its constituent particles, which pass from the organized to
the inorganic state by the act of oxidation. This combination
of oxygen with the muscular tissues, for the production of
force, we shall also find to be an additional source of animal
heat.

583. *Power of Exertion sustained by the Respiration of*

the liver? In what relation do the lungs and liver stand in regard to each other?
State some examples of this.
In what does muscular power originate?

Oxygen.—Every one must have observed that active exercise produces rapid breathing. When the body is in a state of complete repose, as in sound sleep, the respirations are slowest; by moderate exertion they become more frequent, and violent effort, as in running, produces panting, or a quick succession of inspirations and expirations. That it is the oxygen in this case, which, by acting upon the system, sustains its power of exertion, is proved by the experience of those who have ascended high mountains. When they have attained such a height that the atmosphere becomes considerably rarefied, there is less oxygen taken into the system by the same number of inspirations than under ordinary circumstances. The result is, that they are fatigued by the slightest effort.

584. *Examples.*—The amount of oxygen which different classes of animals respire determines their energy or activity. We find, for example, that in birds and insects whose respiration is the highest, the muscular power is greater in proportion to their size than in any other animals, while in cold-blooded reptiles and fishes it is in a very great degree inferior: thus it has been ascertained that a butterfly, notwithstanding its comparatively diminutive size, consumes more oxygen than a toad. In those birds which are ever upon the wing, as swallows and eagles, the respiration is most active, their temperature rising to 112° F.; while in those birds which rarely fly it stands at 100° F. Insects, when in a state of rest, are cold-blooded; their respiration being feeble, and their temperature rising and falling with that of the surrounding air: but when in motion they are very active, consume much

Upon what does the rapidity of breathing depend? How is it shown to be the action of oxygen which enables the system to sustain exertion?

What is said of birds? Of reptiles? How does the consumption of oxygen in a butterfly compare with that in a toad? How does the temperature of insects vary? Give the example of the humble-bee. Of the nursing-bees.

oxygen, and generate a proportionate amount of heat. Thus a humble-bee was found to consume more oxygen, and pro· duce more carbonic acid in a single hour after its capture, during which its body was in constant action, than in the whole succeeding twenty-four hours, when it was at rest. Another, in a state of violent excitement, communicated to three cubic inches of air 4° of heat in five minutes, its own temperature being raised 7° in the same time. The "nursing-bees" of the hive maintain the temperature neces- sary for hatching the larvæ by means of an incessant motion of their limbs, by which quickened respiration is induced, and consequently heat; while they are seen crowding upon the cells, and clinging to them, for the purpose of communi- cating to them their warmth.

585. *Case of Carnivorous Animals.*—Animals which feed upon vegetation constantly consume the respiratory elements of their food, and lay up chiefly the nitrogenized portions in their tissues. In consuming their flesh, therefore, the car- nivorous animals find a deficiency of respiratory food, and must depend for the maintenance of their heat upon the car- bon and hydrogen set free from their muscular system by exercise. This necessity compels them to increasing activity, as is well illustrated by the restlessness of the tigers and hy- enas seen at menageries, which keep moving instinctively from side to side of their narrow cages. By this means there is a constant and sufficient waste of the muscular tissue to support the respiratory process.

586. *Necessity of Sleep.*—As the waste or oxidation of the tissues corresponds with their exercise, so, if they are kept in a healthy or natural state, their nutrition or renova-

---

'Why have carnivorous animals a deficiency of respiratory food ? How is their vital heat sustained ? What example have we of their constant activity ?
If the tissues of the animal are to be kept in a healthy state, what condition is

tion must in like manner correspond to their waste, or, in other words, the quantity of food eaten must, as everybody knows, be in proportion to the amount of exertion performed or of force expended. In the *involuntary* muscles, as those of the heart, which are constantly in play, the repair is as constant as the waste, and they are perpetually preserved in working order. But in the voluntary muscles, those which are controlled by the will and exercised in all kinds of labor, the exact balance between the nutritive and destructive operations is not maintained ; waste exceeds supply, the muscular parts fail in power, and they must periodically cease their activity, that the waste matters may be replaced, and the nutritive operations recover their equilibrium. This periodical rest is afforded by sleep.

587. *Why the Demand for Sleep is not Uniform.*—In infancy, the nutritive process is more active than that of waste, and the body increases in mass, or grows. Accordingly, infants sleep much the largest share of the time. In adult manhood, waste and supply are equal, the sleep being just sufficient to recruit the loss of strength. But in old age the destructive process predominates over that of nutrition, the body wastes away, and but a small amount of sleep is required to effect the imperfect renewal, of which the failing tissues are only capable. The decay and decline of the aged results from unchecked oxidation going on throughout the system, the activity of the nutritive process not being sufficient to counteract the destructive agency of oxygen.

588. *Estimate of Human Force.*—The muscular force which may be exerted by a healthy adult man is estimated,

necessary ? How is it with the involuntary muscles ? With the voluntary muscles ? How is the equilibrium restored ?

Why do infants sleep more than adults ? Why does the time required for sleep by adults and aged people differ ? What causes the decline of the aged ?

in mechanics, as equal to moving one-fifth of his own weight with a velocity of $2\frac{1}{2}$ feet per second, during eight hours of the day. Thus, if the weight of a man be 150 lbs., he is capable of carrying 30 lbs. a distance of 72,000 feet in eight hours, or of exerting a force equal to this in other directions. For the pioduction of this force, there is consumed by oxidation a certain definite amount of muscular tissue, and this must be restored again if the same effect is to be produced on the succeeding day. Liebig states that this restoration is accomplished and the waste matter renewed in seven hours' sleep.

589. *The Art of Fattening Animals* consists in placing them in certain conditions in which the power of nutrition, or the formative process, most completely prevails in the system. All causes which tend to depress the action of the destructive force, and exalt the nutritive or constructive force, favor the increase of the bulk of the animal. Animals, to fatten most rapidly, should be kept at an elevated temperature, so as to consume as little food as possible in the production of internal heat. They should also be maintained in complete repose, and not disturbed or excited in any way, in order to prevent the waste consequent upon muscular action. This state is most favored by darkness. Oily or starchy foods contribute to the formation of fat, and nitrogenized substances to the development of muscle or lean meat.

What is the estimated force of a healthy adult man ? Example. How much sleep is required to restore the waste produced by this expenditure ?

In what does the art of fattening animals consist ? What course should be pursued with such animals ? What foods form fat ? What foods produce muscle ?

WASTE OF MATTER A CONDITION OF MENTAL EXERCISE.

590. The nervous system, through which mental manifestations take place, participates with the muscular, in the property of being wasted or disintegrated by exercise. As all *movement* in the body occurs through the death of living muscular matter, so it seems to be established that *mental operations* can take place only by means of like changes impressed upon nervous substance. By this it is not meant that intellectual operations *arise* in material changes, but only that the material instruments which the mind employs for its manifestation are governed by the same general law of waste and supply, which controls the other parts of the organization.

591. *This Waste depends upon Oxidation.*—These changes depend upon the respiratory process, and consist in the oxidation of the nervous tissue. The amount of oxygenated blood which flows to the nerves is very large. The brain, although of but one-fortieth the weight of the body, is nevertheless estimated to receive one-sixth of all the blood which flows from the heart, the arteries being, in proportion to its bulk, more numerous and larger than those of any other organ. That the nervous energy, which is sustained by this excessive supply of blood, depends upon a process of destruction, rather than one of nutrition, appears from the fact that the state of activity cannot be long maintained in certain parts of it without an interval of repose, which we know is favorable to the reparative processes. When the mind has been long acting through its instrument, the brain, whether by continued and severe exercise of the intellect, or

What is said of the wear of the nervous system ?
What proportion of the blood of the body flows to the brain ? How does it appear that nervous energy is due to waste, and not to nutrition ?

by the excitement of the emotions, there is a corresponding degree of waste; and a prolonged season of rest and uninterrupted nutrition is required for the complete restoration of its powers.

EXCRETION BY THE KIDNEYS.

592. *Products of Nervous Waste.*—The separation from the blood, and expulsion from the system of those substances which cannot remain without detriment, and which serve no purpose in the animal economy, is termed the process of *excretion.* The peculiar products of muscular and nervous decompositions are to be found in the renal excretions (urine), which pass from the system by the channel of the kidneys. The nervous substance contains a large proportion of uncombined phosphorus (545), a substance which is not found in any considerable quantity in the other tissues. By oxidation, this is converted into phosphoric acid, which unites with the alkalies, soda, and ammonia, and in this form passes out of the system in the liquid excretions. Now, it has been found that the amount of the alkaline phosphates contained in these excretions bears an immediate relation to the intensity and duration of mental exertion or emotive excitement. Any unusual strain or wear of mind is sure to be followed by an increase in the proportion of phosphates voided by the kidneys.

593. *Products of Muscular Waste.*—When the muscular tissues are broken up by oxidation, the large share of nitrogen which they contain combines with hydrogen, giving rise to ammonia. But as ammonia is a very caustic substance, and if set free would irritate and inflame the delicate structures through which it is required to pass, it is united

What is to be understood by the process of excretion? What relation is said to exist between mental exertion and secretion by the kidneys?

What provision of nature exists for the removal of ammonia from the system?

with carbonic acid, which is formed at the same time, but not in such a way as to produce carbonate of ammonia, which would also be injuriously corrosive. Instead of this acrid salt, nature with admirable care produces an inert and perfectly harmless compound, known as *urea*. The composition of this substance is $C_2 H_4 O_2 N_2$, which, it is seen, would form carbonate of ammonia by the addition of two atoms of water. The same process of oxidation which gives birth to the elements of urea, also forms sulphuric acid (from the sulphur contained in the muscular tissues), which is neutralized by alkalies, and separated, together with urea, from the arterial blood by the kidneys. The amount of sulphates thus formed may be taken as a measure of the waste of the muscular tissues, and consequently of the degree to which they have been exercised.

594. *Nature of the Renal Excretion* —The kidneys are devoted to the excretion of all those waste matters of the system which are soluble in water ; eleven-twelfths of the nitrogen is estimated to pass out by this route in the form of urea, together with most of the salts, both earthy and alkaline, which have taken part in the vital processes. When more nitrogenized food is consumed than is required to supply the waste of the tissues, the surplus is carried off by the kidneys, which are thus made to perform more than their proper duty, and often become diseased. About 7 per cent. of solid matters may be separated from the urine, 3 of which are urea. A very small proportion of an albuminous substance is also present, which, when exposed to the air, speedily ferments and communicates its action to urea, which is changed to carbonate of ammonia by the addition of two atoms of water, giving rise to two atoms of the carbonate from one of urea. The liquid excretions of animals,

Of what do the renal excretions consist ? Why are their products supposed to be very serviceable in the growth of plants ?

unlike the solid (527), contain those substances which have actually served for the nutrition of the body ; they therefore represent the purely nutritive portions of food, and almost the whole of it that does not escape into the air in the form of gases. It might therefore be supposed that they would be eminently serviceable in promoting the growth of plants, by furnishing them in a soluble form the most important elements of their nutrition, and such is the fact. It is the interest of the farmer to prevent this source of fertility from running to wáste by every possible means, collecting it in tanks, and preventing the escape of its ammonia (127).

EXCRETION BY THE LUNGS

595. The lungs serve not only to introduce oxygen into the body, but what is of no less importance, to convey out of it carbonic acid, which is generated in proportion to the activity of respiration. The retention of any substances within the system which have fulfilled their purpose, and are ready to be rejected from it, is highly injurious, and a prompt source of disease. But so fatal is the influence of carbonic acid, and so rapid its formation, that if suffered to accumulate, even for a few minutes, it puts a stop to all the vital processes. In cases of suspended respiration (as phyxia), death is undoubtedly produced by the joint effect of want of oxygen and accumulation of carbonic acid ; but so potent are these combined causes that all muscular movement ceases in from three to five minutes, while the circulation stops entirely within ten minutes.

596. *Natural Decay a Source of Carbonic Acid.*—In addition to the sources of carbonic acid already mentioned,

---

What is the effect of the retention of worn-out substances in the system ? What is the cause of death in asphyxia?

namely, the direct combustion of respiratory food (574) and the waste of the tissues by exercise (584), another exists in that natural decay which is common to all organized substances, living and dead. This source is especially active in many diseases; as in putrid fevers, for example, which are accompanied by an increased tendency to decomposition, although the body remains completely at rest. In such cases carbonic acid is generated faster than it is set free by the lungs, and communicates to the blood a dark hue. To secure the excretion of this large amount of gaseous matter formed in the body, the lungs act upon simple physical principles (567), and are thus liable to less derangement than if their operations were purely vital. Their action is, however, liable to be impeded by certain conditions of the atmosphere, which will be hereafter noticed (607).

NECESSITY OF VENTILATION.

597. We are now prepared to comprehend with some degree of clearness the vital nature of the relationship which animals sustain to the atmosphere. The temperature at which the living organization must be continually maintained, the physical power which enables a man to execute the decisions of his will, and the intellectual force by which he explores and controls the natural world, are all dependent upon the chemical action of oxygen, and in that exact proportion in which it is supplied by perfectly pure air. Of the two conditions of animal life, the supply of nutriment, and of oxygen to decompose it, the latter is rendered in the plan of nature by far the most immediately and directly im-

---

What other source of carbonic acid is mentioned? In what cases is this source peculiarly active?

What is said of the relation between the powers of the system and the supply

portant. A person requires food but once in several hours, and may do without it for days, but if deprived of air for as many minutes he perishes. Accordingly, while the supply of food is to be had only by forethought and with active industry, and fails if these fail, on the other hand the supply of air is as boundless and omnipresent as its connection with life is intimate and indissoluble.

598. *The Supply of Air.*—We dwell at the bottom of an immense ocean of air, which presses upon all sides of us with the weight of tons. It accompanies us into all places, unless by special arrangements we contrive to bar it out. All that the infinitely wise Creator can do he has done to supply us with this first and highest of earthly necessities. The birds of the air, the beasts of the field, and even the savages of the forest in their open wigwams, enjoy the blessing in all its bounty and fulness. *Civilized man* alone cuts himself off from the beneficent, all-invigorating atmosphere, by retiring into air-tight chambers and using the same gases over and over again, as if they were a taxed commodity and he a miser. It is because the air is so abundant and all-pervading, and therefore costs no exertion to obtain it, and also because it is an invisible and ethereal medium, and therefore not fitted to strike the senses like most other forms of matter, that its relations to animal life have been so recently determined, and that so little attention is generally paid to a copious and healthful supply of it in the arrangement of dwellings.

599. *Effects of breathing Air artificially Condensed.*— The foregoing views of the connection established by the

of pure air? Which is the first condition of animal life, the supply of nutriment or air? What is said of the means of supplying these wants?

What is remarked concerning the abundance of the supply of air? What causes are assigned for the general neglect of this subject?

Creator between the atmosphere and animal life have been admirably illustrated and confirmed by experiments, in which the amount of oxygen introduced into the lungs varied from the normal quantity. They deserve to be attentively considered at this point of the subject. By means of a suitable apparatus, M. Junot subjected different persons to the effects of a considerable variation of atmospheric pressure. "When a person is placed," says he, "in condensed air, he breathes with a new facility; he feels as if the capacity of his lungs was enlarged; his respirations become deeper and less frequent; he experiences in the course of a short time an agreeable glow in the chest, as if the pulmonary cells were being dilated with an elastic spirit, while the whole frame receives at each inspiration fresh vital impulsion. The functions of the brain get excited, the imagination becomes vivid, and the ideas flow with a delightful facility; digestion is rendered more active, as after gentle exercise in the air, because the secretory organs participate immediately in the increased energy of the arterial system, and there is therefore no thirst."

600. *An Interesting Experiment.*—Similar effects have been produced in a novel way, and on a much more extended scale, upon workmen employed in a coal mine in France. The seams of coal are situated under a stratum of quicksand, some twenty yards in thickness, which lay below the bed of the river Loire, and was connected with its waters; they were therefore inaccessible by all the ordinary modes of mining previously practised. So insurmountable was this obstacle regarded, that the coal bed, although known for centuries, had remained untouched. M. Triger, an able engineer, at length grappled with the difficulty by sinking a

What effects are produced upon the system by breathing condensed air?
Why could not the coal bed under the river Loire be worked? How was the

shaft encased with sheet-iron cylinders or tubing riveted tightly together. The openings in the top to admit the miners were so contrived as to be closed perfectly air-tight, and into the cylinder air was driven, and sufficiently condensed by a steam-engine and forcing-pumps to repel the water and quicksand at the bottom, and thus permit the miners, who were immersed in the condensed air, to proceed with the excavation. The pressure employed was that of three atmospheres, that is, the air was made three times as dense as common air, and "it infused such energy into the miners that they could easily execute double the work without fatigue that they could do in the open air. Upon many of them the first sensations were painful, especially upon the ears and eyes, but ere long they got quite reconciled to the bracing element. Old asthmatic men became here effective operatives. Deaf persons recovered their hearing, whilst others were sensible to the slightest whisper—an effect due to the stronger pulses of the dense air upon the membrane of the drum of the ear. Much annoyance was at first experienced from the rapid combustion of the candles, but this was obviated by substituting flax for cotton thread in the wicks."—(*Supplement to Ure's Dictionary.*) The same increase of muscular energy is experienced by those who descend to considerable depths in diving-bells.

601. *Physiological Effects of breathing Rarefied Air.*—Now when the quantity of air received into the lungs is unduly diminished—when a rarefied atmosphere is breathed, either in a direct experiment or by those who have ascended in balloons to the higher regions of the atmosphere—we have an exactly op-

---

difficulty met? What was the condition of the air breathed by the miners? What effects did it produce upon them? How were the asthmatic affected? The deaf? Why were the candles consumed more rapidly?

What symptoms are produced upon those who breathe a rarefied air?

posite train of symptoms to those described in the former cases. The breathing is difficult, feeble, frequent, and terminates in asthmatic paroxysms. There is headache, depression of the mind, confusion of ideas, drowsiness, want of muscular power, pains in the chest, and a tendency to fainting. The secretions are scanty, or totally suppressed, and all the powers of the individual become prostrated. Thus the bodily energies of man rise and fall in quick response to all the variations which take place in the vital medium of respiration.

602. *Natural Variations in the Density of the Air.*—It is convenient to divide the variations to which the breathing quality of the air is liable into two kinds, those which are *beyond* and those which are *within* man's immediate control. The natural causes which affect the density of the air, and consequently its physiological relations, are fluctuations of temperature and atmospheric pressure. Air is rarefied by heat, and condensed by cold; we therefore take more oxygen into the lungs by the same number of respirations (full $\frac{1}{8}$ more, according to Liebig) in winter than in summer. This accounts in part for the lassitude experienced in hot weather, and in hot, close rooms, and the bracing influence of cold. In like manner, the slight rarefication of the atmosphere indicated by a low state of the barometer is sufficient to occasion languor and uneasiness in persons of delicate nerves, while the opposite condition of increased pressure, corresponding to a high state of the barometer, has an invigorating effect upon both body and mind. These changes, although palpable in their consequences, yet take place within very

How may the variations in the breathing qualities of air be divided? What are the natural causes which effect the density of the air? How much more oxygen is breathed in winter than in summer? What connection has this with the state of the body? What relation exists between the height of the barometer and the condition of body and mind?

narrow limits, and as far as they extend, are by no means of the worst character, as we shall presently ascertain.

603. *The Air without and within Doors.*—The volume of the atmosphere is so vast that its composition is not sensibly disturbed by the breathing of animals; the proportion of oxygen remains unchanged if respiration is performed in the open air, while the carbonic acid expired, instead of accumulating about the individual, is dissolved away by the great law of gaseous diffusion (136). But when a person enters a house or an apartment, surrounded on all sides by solid walls, impenetrable to air, the case is totally changed; the immense expanse of the atmosphere is suddenly reduced to the dimensions of a few hundred cubic feet: the alterations now produced by breathing are rapidly communicated to the whole mass of air, and the person occupies towards it an entirely new relation; one, however, over which he has absolute control.

604. *Oxygen removed from the Air by Breathing.*—The first effect of respiration upon the air is the withdrawal of its oxygen; and as the proportion of this life-sustaining element decreases, the bodily powers become less and less active, simply from want of their proper stimulus. The natural proportion of oxygen in pure air being adapted to the most perfect performance of the animal machinery, a reduction in this amount, however slight, must be attended by a corresponding depression of the vital energies. We have seen enough of what takes place within the bodily organism to understand that the condition of *health* depends upon the harmonious and balanced play of opposing forces. If the equilibrium of these forces is disturbed, the vital machine

---

What effect does the breathing of animals produce upon the air out of doors? How is the case changed upon entering an apartment?
What is the first effect of respiration upon the air? Upon what does health

goes wrong: it is in an unnatural—a diseased state. A slight diminution in the proportion of respired oxygen does not produce any immediate or palpable malady, but it certainly disorders the natural, healthful operations of the system, to a greater or less extent, and thus lays it open to the assaults of disease. It undoubtedly prepares the soil, and sows the seed, which, in due time, springs up into that luxuriant harvest of ailments and complaints which is reaped by the *victims* of modern refinement and civilization.

605. *Breathing charges the Air with Carbonic Acid.*—But it is not alone deficiency of oxygen which renders air irrespirable, the presence of an undue quantity of carbonic acid (172) is a still more potent cause of mischief. It has been shown by experiment that an animal may be kept alive in a limited quantity of air, until a very considerable exhaustion of oxygen takes place, provided the carbonic acid be removed as fast as it is formed; but if it is suffered to accumulate, death ensues much more speedily. In confirmation of the general statement, made in the preceding paragraph, it has been found that the baneful effects of carbonic acid upon the system increase with the deficiency of oxygen. From experiments upon inferior animals, it has been concluded that three per cent. of carbonic acid, if formed from the oxygen of the air, would prove fatal to man, while, with the natural quantity of oxygen, twice, or even thrice the proportion of carbonic acid might not produce death. The proportion of carbonic acid in expired air is from four to eight per cent.; and it is assumed by different experimenters, that this, together with

---

depend? What is said of the effect of breathing a slightly diminished proportion of oxygen?

What circumstance has a still more pernicious effect than a diminished quantity of oxygen? What has been learned from experiments upon inferior animals? At what rate does the carbonic acid, from breathing, contaminate the air?

the other exhalations of the body, contaminate from seven to 10 cubic feet of air per minute.

606. *Experiments.*—Air that has been once breathed will not sustain combustion. To illustrate this, take a stoppered bell-jar or bottle with an orifice in its bottom; place the empty bottle in a shallow pan of water, empty the lungs by a deep expiration, apply the mouth closely to the top of the bottle or jar, and draw the air which it contains into the lungs, the water will rise and fill the bottle. After a moment or two, breathe the air back again into the bottle, and close it with a stopper as soon as the lips leave it. If now a lighted taper or candle is introduced into the bottle by removing the stopper, it will go out as quickly as if immersed in water.

607. *Other Evils of Impure Air.*—The excretion of carbonic acid from the lungs is less complete in proportion as the external air is already charged with this gas; and in like manner, as the amount of oxygen in the inspired air diminishes, it exhibits less and less tendency to diffuse through the cell membrane into the blood. Watery vapor, too, which is excreted both by the lungs and skin, evaporates sluggishly if the air is loaded with moisture, so that the moment the normal constitution of the air is disturbed, there arises a tendency in the air itself to augment the evil. Not only is there an excess of carbonic acid in the air, which is injurious to the system, but it operates to prevent the escape of what is constantly produced. Not only is there a deficiency of oxygen in the inhaled air, but what there is, enters the body, as it were, with reluctance.

608. *Want of Ventilation in Schools and Churches.*—

What experiment proves that air once breathed will not sustain combustion?
What is the effect of vitiated air upon the excretion of the lungs and the inhalation of oxygen?

The stupefying, depressing effect of the black venous blood poured through the brain is, unhappily, most apparent where there is expected to be the highest degree of mental activity. Churches, public assembly-rooms, and schools are but rarely provided with due means of ventilation, by which a constant supply of pure air may be maintained; and the inattention, languor, dulness, and sleepiness of both auditors and pupils are but the natural and inevitable consequences of taking into the system a vitiated and poisonous atmosphere. It would be wise for preachers who are annoyed with drowsy congregations, and teachers who are afflicted with pupils of dull and stupid intellect, to inquire how far the stimulus of pure air might be advantageously substituted for scolding in the one case, and flogging in the other.

609. *Other Reasons for preferring Pure Air.*—To those inducements to thorough ventilation which spring from its relation to health, ought to be added an abhorrence of the *very idea* of drinking into our systems, over and over again, the foul and disgusting emanations of putrescence and disease, which often load the air in crowded rooms. To a mind really refined, there is little pleasure in the reflection, that each breath inhaled has made the tour of a large assembly, forming an acquaintance with every rotten tooth and ulcerated lung that it contains. "We instinctively shun the approach of the dirty, the squalid, and the diseased, and use no garment that may have been worn by another. We open sewers for matters that offend the sight or the smell and

To what is the languor and drowsiness of schools and churches attributed? What remedy is proposed?

What other reasons are given for preferring pure air? What is said to be opposed to real refinement of mind? How is the inconsistency of our habits shown?

contaminate the air; we carefully remove impurities from what we eat and drink, filter turbid water, and fastidiously avoid drinking from a cup that may have been pressed to the lips of a friend. On the other hand, we resort to places of assembly, and draw into our mouths air loaded with effluvia from the lungs, skin, and clothing of every individual in the promiscuous crowd—exhalations offensive, to a certain extent, from the most healthy individuals; but when arising from a living mass of skin and lungs in all stages of evaporation, disease, and putridity—prevented by the walls and ceiling from escaping—they are, when thus concentrated, in the highest degree deleterious and loathsome."—(*Birnan.*)

ACTION OF POISONS UPON THE LIVING SYSTEM.

610. The substances introduced into the animal organism are generally of three kinds. The first are those whose properties are of such a nature that they yield to the vital action of the system, and are changed or *digested* by it: these are nutrient substances or foods. The second are those which do not yield in this manner, but possess an action of their own *upon* the system, in a limited way, resisting the vital force so as for a time to turn its action into new channels: these substances are known as *medicines.* A third class of bodies are of a nature to overcome the vital force and destroy the organism: these are termed *poisons.*

611. *Effect of Malignant Poisons.*—The most common action of poisons is that in which they unite directly with the membranes and tissues of the organization, forming new chemical compounds, in which the functions may be impaired, or the part perhaps killed. We have constantly

---

How are the substances introduced into the animal system divided? What are nutrient substances? What are medicines? What are poisons?

What is the nature of the action of malignant poisons? How is it shown?

seen that decay, mutation, tendency to change, is the essential condition of life. Now, the malignant poisons act by combining with parts of the living structure, and forming compounds that are fixed—that do not decay, and thus produce death. This is shown by the fact that the parts upon which the poison acts do not undergo change after death, when the remainder of the body passes gradually into decomposition.

612. *Examples.*—Thus corrosive sublimate and common arsenic, for example, are both in extensive use in the arts as antiseptics—that is, to preserve organic substances by forming with them chemical compounds of a very stable nature. In the animal body their behavior is the same; they unite with the tissues, and thus destroy them. Antidotes, to be effective against these substances, must be administered with sufficient promptness to neutralize them before they shall have taken full effect upon the organization; in such case the poisonous action being confined to the surface of an organ, the part destroyed is thrown off. The poisonous action of miasms (135), by which ague, influenza, cholera, &c., are engendered, is supposed to affect the blood upon the principle of the action of ferments (379).

PHYSIOLOGICAL ACTION OF ALCOHOL.

613. *Its Substitution for Water.*—The essential and all-important office performed by WATER in the living organism has been repeatedly noticed (106, 495). Indeed, so completely is its action interwoven with all the processes of organic life, that the nature and functions of living beings must

---

For what are corrosive sublimate and arsenic used in the arts? What is said about administering antidotes? How are miasms which engender ague, &c., supposed to act?

What is said of the importance of water to the animal? Can any other liquid be substituted for it? Does alcohol resemble water in its action?

be looked upon as in all respects adapted and conformed to its properties. The body consists of three-fourths water and but one-fourth solid matter ; and all the rapid changes which incessantly transpire within it are carried on by the agency of the aqueous medium. The attempt to substitute any other liquid with different properties for water, in conducting the natural and healthy operations of the living organism, must hence be looked upon as a doubtful, if not indeed a perilous experiment. The action of alcohol within the system is in no respect analogous to that of water; it is a disturber of the healthy functions, a disorganizer of the structure, and must therefore be ranked among *medicines* and *poisons*.

614. *Effect of Alcohol upon the Tissues.*—The chemical composition of alcohol (380) is such as to forbid the idea of its ever being transformed into the animal tissues. There is no evidence whatever that, under any circumstances, it is capable of serving for animal nutrition. Nevertheless, it has a specific and peculiar action upon the tissues which is due to its powerful affinity for water (381). " If animal membranes, a mass of flesh or coagulated fibrine, be placed in alcohol, in a fresh state (in which they are thoroughly charged with water), there are formed at all points where water and alcohol meet, mixtures of the two; and as the animal texture absorbs much less of an *alcoholic mixture* than of pure water, a larger amount of water is of course expelled than of alcohol taken up, and the first result is a shrinking of the animal substance."* Experiments made by Liebig show that for one volume of alcohol taken up by a membrane, rather more than three volumes of water have

---

* Dr. Carpenter on the Use and Abuse of Alcoholic Liquors.

been expelled from it. That the tissues are acted upon within the body the same as without it, is proved by the experiments of Dr. Percy, who found that when animals are poisoned by alcohol introduced into the stomach, the coats of that organ become so thoroughly imbued with it throughout their whole thickness that no washing can remove it. He also found that the tissues remote from the stomach are impregnated in the same way when alcohol is introduced into the current of the circulation. The shrinking of the tissues and alteration of their chemical relations which thus takes place, must obviously disturb the natural series of operations upon which nutrition depends.

615. *How Alcohol affects the Blood.*—The effects of alcohol upon the blood are of a very marked and important character. It possesses the power of preventing the coagulation of fibrine. When an animal has been killed by the injection of alcohol into its blood-vessels, the blood often remains fluid after death, or coagulates but very imperfectly. The presence of alcohol in the blood is therefore an obstacle to nutrition, or to that vital process by which the solid substances of the fabric are organized or elaborated from the blood. Accordingly, we have the testimony of physicians and surgeons that the nutritive and reparative powers of those who drink largely of spirituous liquors, in cases of wounds, ulcers, &c., are low. The healing process in such is, as a general rule, less certain and active than in others.

616. *It disturbs the Natural Process of Oxidation.*— Again, when alcohol is mingled with fresh arterial blood, the red corpuscles, as may be seen with the microscope, shrink,

What is the effect of alcohol upon the blood? What was the condition of the animal killed by injecting it into its veins? What is the action of alcohol in regard to nutrition? How does it affect the healing process in cases of wounds ulcers, &c

and a portion of their contents is mingled with the liqu *a*
sanguinis, while at the same time the fluid darkens in color,
so as to give it more or less of the venous aspect; and Bou-
chardat found that when alcohol is introduced into the system
in excess, precisely the same change takes place in the arteries—their contents become of a venous appearance.   The
cause of this change is the fact that the alcohol is more combustible than the ordinary constituents of the blood, and consequently rapidly attracts its oxygen and is burned to carbonic
acid and water.   By combustion, therefore, alcohol may become a source of heat in the body, but it is by *arresting the
natural processes of oxidation,* upon which the vigor of the
animal powers depends.   Liebig observes, that "by the use
of alcohol a limit must rapidly be put to the change of matter in certain parts of the body.   The oxygen of the arterial
blood, which in the absence of alcohol would have combined
with the matter of the tissues, or with that formed by the
metamorphosis of the tissues, now combines with the elements of alcohol.   The arterial blood becomes venous, without
the substance of the muscles having taken any share in the
transformation."

617. *It disturbs the Excretion of Carbonic Acid.*—Dr.
Prout discovered that alcoholic liquors possess, in a remarkable degree, the power of *diminishing* the amount of carbonic
acid in the expired air, and that no sooner have their effects
passed off than the proportion of carbonic acid exhaled *rises
much above* the natural standard.   The accumulation of carbonic acid which thus takes place in the blood, and from

How does alcohol affect the red corpuscles of the blood?   What is the cause of
this change?   How may alcohol become a source of heat?   How is the oxygen of
the arterial blood diverted from its true office?
How does alcohol affect the formation and exhalation of carbonic acid?   What
is the effect of its accumulation?

which the system cannot get relief, is probably a partial cause of that prostration, both of physical and mental power, which attends the advanced stages of intoxication.

618. *Effects of Alcohol upon the Nervous System.*—But that part of the body which is attacked most powerfully by alcohol is the *nervous system.* It has a stronger affinity for the nervous substance than for any other tissue, seeking it out, as it were, and combining with it in preference to any other substances. In this case, to the shrinking or corrugating influence of alcohol upon the tissues must be added a *hardening* effect, due to its power of coagulating albumen, of which nervous matter is largely composed. This selective power of alcohol, by which it fastens upon nervous matter, is at once proved by the fact that it has been found diluted in considerable quantity in the substance of the brain of habitual inebriates. That so total a change as is thus produced in the nervous texture by this fiery compound should cause great derangement in its functions is what we might naturally expect, and what is abundantly shown by experience.

619. *It is a Stimulant.*—The action of alcohol upon the nerves is that of a *stimulant;* that is, it arouses or excites them to an unnatural degree of activity. This heightened action is communicated to the heart, which contracts with more force and rapidity, quickening the circulation, and thus exalting the functions of the body generally. As the influence of the alcohol passes off the powers of the body sink into an opposite state, the appetite and digestive powers are lowered in activity, the secretions are diminished, the spirits depressed, and the power of mental exertion for a time impaired.

What change does alcohol produce upon the nerves? How is it shown? What is its general effect? When its influence passes off, what is the condition of the body?

620. *Its Effect upon the Mind.*—The alcoholic stimulus operates powerfully upon the brain, the organ of the mind. In very small quantities its effect is that of a moderate excitant; there is an unusual rapidity of thought and vividness of ideas. In larger quantities the effect is different. It is not a *uniform exaltation* of the mental powers, but in some degree a *perversion* of them; for that voluntary control over the current of thought which is the distinguishing character of the sane mind of man, is considerably weakened, so that the heightened imagination and enlivened fancy have more unrestricted exercise; and whilst ideas and images succeed each other in the mind with marvellous readiness, no single train of thought can be carried out with the same continuity as in a state of perfect sobriety. This weakening of the voluntary control over the mental operations must be regarded, then, as an incipient stage of insanity. When a still larger quantity of alcoholic liquor is taken, the voluntary control over the direction of the thoughts is completely lost, and the excitement has more the character of delirium, or the office of the brain may be completely suspended in profound sleep or a condition of torpor.

621. *It affects different Parts of the Brain unequally.*— As alcohol seizes upon the nervous system in preference to the other tissues, so also it appears to act with unequal intensity upon different parts of that system, making choice of certain regions of the brain, which are more affected by its stimulation than others. This is manifested by the unequal excitement produced upon different faculties of the mind. The imagination, those powers which give rise to poetic creations, to artistic combinations, and to sallies of wit and humor, are aroused to a preternatural activity by the use of

What effect does alcohol in small quantities produce upon the brain? In larger quantities? In still larger quantities?

alcohol, while no such effect is observed upon the reasoning or reflecting powers. Indeed, that spontaneous mental activity which it is the tendency of alcohol to excite is unfavorable to the exercise of the observing and purely reasoning faculties, or to the steady concentration of thought upon subjects of difficult or profound investigation, and accordingly we find that the greatest part of that intellectual labor which has most extended the domain of human knowledge has been performed by men of remarkable sobriety of habit, many of them having been constant water-drinkers.

622. *Influence upon Life and Sanity.*—The general consequences which follow from plying the brain and nervous system with this formidable stimulant, by which the equable course of nature is broken into a succession of alternate paroxysms and prostrations, cannot but be of the most disastrous character. Men of a high order of genius, who are habitually addicted to the use of alcoholic liquors, frequently die at a very early age, from a premature exhaustion of nervous energy. Burns, Byron, and Mozart are striking examples of this result. The relation between intemperance and insanity has been made a matter of inquiry in a large number of lunatic asylums in Great Britain, where it has been established that from 15 to 50 per cent. of all the cases of insanity may be clearly traced to this cause. In a report on *idiocy* made to the Massachusetts Legislature, Dr. Howe states, "that the habits of the parents of 300 of the idiots were learned; and 145, or nearly one-half, are reported as known to be habitual drunkards."

623. *Spontaneous Combustion.*—The human body, in its

What faculties of mind are most excited by alcohol? To what faculties is it unfavorable? How does experience accord with this?

What is said to be the general effect of an habitual use of this substance? Give examples. How is the connection between insanity and intemperance shown?

natural state, is incombustible; that is, it requires the addition of a considerable amount of fuel to reduce it to ashes. Instances are, however, on record of its having taken fire, and been more or less completely consumed *of itself*. This phenomenon is improperly termed *spontaneous combustion*, as there is no complete evidence of its having taken place without the application of external flame. They are more properly cases of *unnatural combustibility* of the body. Nearly all the instances that have occurred were those of spirit-drinkers, and most of them old persons who were fat. The cause of the phenomenon is probably connected with the undue accumulation of phosphorus in the tissues, together with the presence of a large quantity of alcohol. The excessive accumulation of phosphorus in the body may be owing to the effect of alcohol in preventing its oxidation (616) in the nervous matter. The fire, in these cases, is often communicated by inflammable vapors contained in the breath.

RELATION BETWEEN ANIMALS AND PLANTS.

624. The act of respiration in animals completes that wonderful circle of organic life, in which mineral matter is taken up by plants, organized and transferred to animals, by which its organization is destroyed, and its elements returned again to the inorganic world. From the simplest materials—two gases (carbonic acid and ammonia), and one liquid (water), containing dissolved a few salts—that arch-chemist, the sun, through the agency of light and heat, creates the vast world of organization. Green vegetables constitute the laboratory in which this combining and constructive process is driven

---

What is meant by spontaneous combustion? How is it caused? What may cause this accumulation of phosphorus? How is the fire communicated?

From what, and by what, are the worlds of organization created? What is said to be the laboratory where this work is performed?

forward; and the substances produced, although simple in composition, exhibit the infinite resources of nature in the endless variety of their properties.

625. *Antagonism of Plants and Animals.*—The plant having fulfilled its grand office, in a series of formative changes which result in organization, the animal, which is formed entirely from matter thus organized, exhibits a series of completely inverse phenomena. By the all-destroying activity of oxygen, operating through the respiratory mechanism, the work of the plant is undone, the great function of the animal being performed through the breaking up of vital affinities, and the reduction of organized compounds to that condition of simplicity in which they are fitted again to serve for the nutrition of plants. In all their peculiar actions and effects, plants and animals have a relation of distinct antagonism. Their movements take place in contrary directions, and by different and hostile forces. The French chemists contrast the opposing actions, in a very clear and pleasing way, as follows:

THE VEGETABLE	THE ANIMAL
PRODUCES the neutral nitrogenized substances, fatty substances, sugar, starch, and gum.	CONSUMES the neutral nitrogenized substances, fatty substances, sugar, starch, and gum.
DECOMPOSES carbonic acid, water, and ammoniacal salts.	PRODUCES carbonic acid, water, and ammoniacal salts.
DISENGAGES oxygen.	ABSORBS oxygen.
ABSORBS heat and electricity.	PRODUCES heat and electricity.
Is an apparatus of deoxidation.	Is an apparatus of oxidation.
Is stationary.	Is locomotive.

626. *Circle of Organic Life.*—The relations of the several departments of organic nature to each other, and to the in-

What is the office of the animal? What is the relation of plants and animals? How is this shown in the table?

What does the diagram illustrate? What is said of the inorganic world? What

organic world, may perhaps be made clear by the aid of a diagram. The direction of the arrows indicates the course of matter. From the inorganic world, directly or indirectly, all living things originate, and to it they all return. From the mineral world, matter can pass only to the vegetable kingdom. A part of this returns by natural decay to the inorganic world, while another portion is consumed by herbivorous animals, and forms the fabric of their bodies. Some of the herbivorous animals die, are decomposed, and fall back into inorganic nature, while others are devoured by

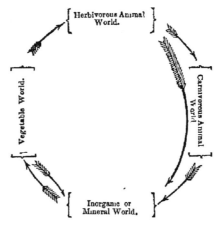

carnivorous animals, and converted into their structure. The carnivora in their turn perish, rot, and are dissolved, like the rest, into gases and earthy elements. Such is the mysterious round of organization of which this globe is the scene. It consists of an eternal cycle — an ever-recurring series of changes, in which destruction is co-ordinate with creation, and the contest between life and death is a drawn-battle.

627. *Relation of Plants and Animals to the Ancient Atmosphere.*—It has been inferred, from geological considerations, that the present harmonious adjustment between the two great orders of organized beings has not existed from the period of their first advent upon the globe. At the time of the deposit of the coal, there is no evidence of the existence of land, or air-breathing animals, upon the earth: their remains are not to be found, either in this or any of the preceding geological formations But vegetation at this time had made great progress, as the existence of the coal-beds proves (357). It is supposed that the excessive growth of vegetation which then took place, and the total absence of air-breathing animals, are to be accounted for by the same fact—namely, a vastly larger proportion of carbonic acid in the atmosphere than exists in it now. If such were the case, the higher animals certainly could not live, while the condition must have been favorable for a luxuriant development of plants.

628. *Stability of the Atmosphere.*—But when the atmosphere was partially purged of its poisonous element, by the withdrawal of that portion of its carbon which was deposited in the earth as coal, the cold-blooded *reptiles* made their appearance upon the earth; which, from their sluggish circulation and imperfect respiration (564), may live without inconvenience in an atmosphere highly charged with impurities. As the growth of vegetation continued, which is shown by later deposits of brown coal (lignite), the atmosphere gradually became more pure, and was at length fitted for the reception of the higher warm-blooded animals. But

Has the present order of things always existed? What was the condition of things at the time of the coal deposit? How is it accounted for?

How was the atmosphere gradually purified and prepared for the presence of the higher animals? Is it now subject to mutation? Upon what does its permanence depend?

to whatever extent the earth's atmosphere may have been subject to mutation in the earlier epochs of its history, we have the clearest evidence that, in relation to plants and animals, its constitution is now of the most stable nature. Its permanence depends upon a great principle of self-adjustment, which springs from the relations of the two worlds of organization; so that no fatal disturbance can occur, unless the present order of things is subverted by a direct intervention of the Almighty Will.

GENERAL INDEX.

29

TESTIMONIALS.

———— • ◆ • ————

OF THE CLASS-BOOK OF CHEMISTRY.

From the N. Y. Commercial Advertiser

Either for schools or for general reading we know of no elementary work on Chemistry which in every respect pleases us so much as this.

From the Albion.

A remarkably interesting and thoroughly popular work on Chemistry, recommended to the general reader by the clearness of its style, and its freedom from technicalities.

From the Boston Common School Journal.

We consider this Chart a great simplification of a somewhat confused subject, and we welcome it as another successful attempt, not only to simplify truth, but to fix it in the mind by the assistance of the eye. If we were called to teach the elements of chemistry in a school-room, we should be very unwilling to lose the valuable assistance of this ingenious chart.

From the National Intelligencer.

Besides the fulness with which this work treats of the chemistry of agriculture and the arts, we regard it as chiefly valuable for the clear account it gives of the action of chemical agents upon the greatly varied functions of life. It is very elementary and practical; and whether for the use of schools or of private libraries, it is an appropriate because an instructive and entertaining book.

From the Scientific American.

Such a book in the present state of chemical science was demanded, but to present the subject in such a clear, comprehensive manner, in a work of the size before us, is more than we expected. The author has happily succeeded in clothing his ideas in plain language—true eloquence—so as to render the subject both interesting and easily comprehended. The number of men who can write on science, and write clearly, is small; but our author is among that number.

From the Farmer and Mechanic.

A Class-Book of Chemistry for the use of beginners and young students, which should be divested as much as possible of its tedious technicalities and dry repulsiveness, so often attending their first efforts in this important study, has long been a desideratum. To supply this need, the present volume is fully adequate. It is designed as a popular introduction to the study of this beautiful science, and presents it in such a manner as to win the attention and engage the interest.

————

OF THE CHEMICAL CHART.

From HORACE MANN, *President of Antioch College.*

I have been highly delighted by inspecting a Chart, shown to me by Mr. E. L. Youmans, of New York, the object of which is to represent the ratios in which chemical atoms are combined to form compound bodies. The different atoms are represented by square diagrams of different colors; and then the compounds exhibit the exact number or numbers of the respective atoms that unite to form them, each atom retaining its original color. Thus the eye of the learner aids his memory; and as the eye, in regard to all objects having form and color, can learn a hundred things by inspection, while the ear is learning one by description, so, when material objects, too minute to be seen, or too intimately combined to be distinguished, can be represented by form and color, the same great advantage is obtained. The power of the learner is multiplied, simply by an exhibition of the object, or its representative, to a superior sense

I think Mr. Youmans is entitled to great credit for the preparation of his Chart, because its use will not only facilitate acquisition, but, what is of far greater importance, will increase the exactness and precision of the student's elementary ideas.

From Dr. John W. Draper, Professor of Chemistry in the University of New York.

Mr. Youmans' Chart seems to me well adapted to communicate to beginners a knowledge of the definite combinations of chemical substances, and as preliminary to the use of symbols, to aid them very much in recollecting the examples it contains. It deserves to be introduced into the schools.

From James B Rogers, Professor of Chemistry in the University of Pennsylvania.

We cordially subscribe to the opinion of Professor Draper concerning the value to beginners of Mr. Youman's Chemical Chart.

JOHN TORREY,
Professor of Chemistry in the College of Physicians and Surgeons, New York.
WILLIAM H. ELLET,
Late Professor of Chemistry in Columbia College, S C
JAMES B RODGERS.
Professor of Chemistry in the University of Pennsylvania.

From Alonzo Potter, LL.D , Philadelphia

The conception embodied in Mr. Youman's Chemical Chart strikes me as a very happy and useful one, and the execution is evidently the fruit of much care and skill I should think its introduction into schools, in connection with the study of the first principles of Chemistry, was much to be desired

From Dr. Robert Hare

I concur in thinking favorably of Mr Youmans' Chemical Chart. The design is excellent, and as far as I have had time to examine the execution, I entertain the impression that it is well done

From Benjamin Silliman, LL.D , Prof. of Chemistry at Yale College.

I have hastily examined Mr. Youmans' new Chemical Diagrams, or Chart of chemical combinations by the union of the elements in atomic proportions. The design appears to be an excellent one

From W F. Hopkins, Professor of Natural and Experimental Philosophy in the U. S. Naval Academy, Annapolis, Md.

Mr Youmans' Chemical Chart is admirably adapted to assist the teacher in communicating, and the learner in receiving, correct notions of the laws of chemical combination I commend it to the patronage of schools and academies where chemistry is taught, and shall immediately introduce it into the institution with which I am connected

From Prof. Gray, Author of Text-Books on Natural Philosophy, Chemistry and Geology.

Mr Youmans' Chart presents to the eye a clearer view of the manner in which the atoms of chemical compounds are united, than could be gained by the most labored description * * * *

It would be especially useful to institutions not furnished with chemical apparatus.

From JOSEPH MCKEEN, *Superintendent of Common Schools in New York.*

I have been greatly pleased with an examination of a Chart of elementary Chemistry, by Mr. Youmans. It seems to me that it so simplifies the subject, that pupils in the best classes in our common schools may acquire from a few lessons, with its aid, more knowledge of the laws and principles of this science, than from months of study without such means of illustration. I know of no other chart like this; and as by its means Chemistry may now be taught with the same facility as geography or astronomy, I would earnestly commend it to the attention of school committees, teachers, and learners.

From JAS. R. CHILTON, M.D., *Chemist.*

I have examined the Chemical Chart of Mr E. L. Youmans, and am much pleased to say that it is a valuable means of readily imparting a correct knowledge of the nature of chemical combinations. A variety of compounds are dissected, so as to show at a glance their ultimate atomic constitution, in such a way as to impress it more forcibly upon the mind than could be effected by any other method with which I am acquainted. To those who are studying to obtain a knowledge of elementary and agricultural chemistry, as well as to all learners of chemical science, Mr. Youmans' Chart will render easily understood what might otherwise appear very difficult.

From Dr THOMAS ANTISELL, *Prof. of Chemistry in the Vermont Medical College.*

Mr Youmans' Chart is got up in a style which renders it a neat appendage to the lecture-room, and wherever Chemistry is taught in schools and public institutions, it will be found an invaluable assistant to both teacher and pupil.

OF THE ATLAS OF CHEMISTRY.

Every one who has studied Chemistry, will remember the many perplexing hours spent in trying to fix in the memory the component parts of various compounds. To us, it was a most irksome and disagreeable task. Had Mr. Youmans' book been placed in our hands, we are certain that we could have mastered our lessons with much less than one fourth of the labor we were obliged to bestow. We call this in all respects a model book.—*Cleveland Plaindealer*

Here we have science in pictures—chemistry in diagrams—eye-dissections of all the common forms of matter around us, the chemical composition and properties of all familiar objects illustrated to the most impressible of our senses by the aid of colors. This is a beautiful book, and as useful as it is beautiful. Mr. Youmans has hit upon a happy method of simplifying and bringing out the profoundest abstractions of science, so that they fall within the clear comprehension of children.—*Home Journal.*

The author was lead to the construction of his plan by noticing the defects of the abstract method by which the science is usually taught in books. Laboring under the disability of blindness, while pursuing his own studies, he became deeply impressed with the importance of visual demonstration in obtaining a knowledge of physical phenomena. We do not hesitate to say that no method has come under our notice, by which the beginner in Chemistry can be so effectually and so agreeably initiated into the rudiments of the science as by the process made use of in this volume.—*Harpers' Magazine.*

An excellent idea, well carried out. The style is lucid and happy, the definitions concise and clear, and the illustrations felicitous and appropriate. —*Utica Morning Herald.*

We have devoted some little time in looking over this Atlas, and comparing its relative merits with similar treatises heretofore published, and feel bound to accord to it the highest degree of approbation and favor.—*Lawrence Sentinel*

This method of using the eye in education, though not the royal road to knowledge, is really the people's railroad—a means of saving both time and labor This work is worth for actual instruction in common schools far more than a set of apparatus, which the teacher might not be able to use, while every one can teach from the Atlas We pronounce it, without exception, the best popular work on Chemistry in the English language.—*Life Illustrated.*

Mr. Youmans is not a mere routine teacher of his favorite science; he has hit upon novel and effective methods for the illustration of its principles In his writings, as well as his lectures, he is distinguished for the comprehensive order of his statements, his symmetrical arrangement of scientific facts, and the happy manner in which he addresses the intellect through the medium of ocular demonstration. In this last respect, his method is both original and singularly ingenious.—*N. Y. Tribune.*

With this plan a vast amount of information is attainable by mere inspection In a manufacturing community like ours, chemistry should be studied by young and old, and in the works of Mr. Youmans the science is presented in its most attractive and useful form.—*Newark Daily Advertiser.*

Mr. Youmans handles his subject in a simple, yet masterly style, and we consider his Atlas unequalled in its simplicity and adaptation to the wants of both teacher and pupil.—*N Y. Sun*

If we were asked by a young lover of science what work we would recommend as an introduction to the interesting science of Chemistry, we would most confidently name this of Mr Youmans. Among all the works upon this part of natural science which have of late years been published, we do not know of one which presents its principles so briefly and yet so clearly It is also a happy idea to apply to Chemistry the method of diagrams, which has succeeded so well in the cognate sciences, and it is a wonder that some of our great ones did not sooner think of it We are not at all surprised that so many professors and principals of academies should have spoken so favorably of it, for were we a professor, we would discard every other class-book on the subject in order to adopt this without delay. * * If there be any thing, however, that should please us as religious reviewers more than all the rest, we could easily find in it the spirit that continually, without any effort, raises the author's mind "from Nature up to Nature's God." It is exceedingly gratifying to see this manifested by one who is certainly no ignoramus, and the contrast it affords to the conduct of so many of our scientific men who are beginning to ape the skepticism and philosophism of Europe, is an honor to Mr. Youmans, of which he may be prouder than even his great chemical knowledge.—*Metropolitan Magazine, (Baltimore.)*

Printed in Great Britain
by Amazon.co.uk, Ltd.,
Marston Gate.